# Scuba Diving

## THIRD EDITION

## Dennis K. Graver, EMT, SEI

Human Kinetics

**Library of Congress Cataloging-in-Publication Data**

Graver, Dennis
    Scuba diving / Dennis K. Graver.-- 3rd ed.
        p. cm.
Includes bibliographical references and index.
    ISBN: 0-7360-4539-2 (softcover)
    1.   Scuba diving.   I.  Title.
    GV838.672  .G74 2003
    797.2'3--dc21
ISBN: 0-7360-4539-2

2002152325

The Web addresses cited in this text were current as of October 14, 2002, unless otherwise noted.

Managing Editor: Anne Cole
Copyeditor: Karen L. Bojda
Proofreader: Julie Marx Goodreau
Indexer: Nancy Ball
Graphic Designer: Andrew Tietz
Graphic Artist: Tara Welsch
Cover Designer: Jack W. Davis
Photo Manager: Dan Wendt
Photographer (cover): Dennis K. Graver
Photographer (interior): Figure 1.3 by Dan Wendt; Figure 3.7 © YMCA of the USA; Figures 2.32, 3.15, and 3.39c © Big Picture Chicago; all other photos by Dennis K. Graver
Art Manager: Dan Wendt
Illustrator: Figure 2.22 by Mic Greenberg; Figures 2.3, 2.5, 2.8, 2.20, 2.24, 2.26, 2.27, 2.30, 2.34, 4.5, 4.7, 4.12, 5.1, 5.4, 6.9, 7.10, 7.16, and table 5.2 by Argosy; YMCA Sport Diving Tables in chapter 6 by Brian McElwain; all other illustrations by Thomas • Bradley Illustration and Design

Printed in China          10   9   8   7   6   5   4   3   2   1

**Human Kinetics**
Web site: www.HumanKinetics.com

*United States:* Human Kinetics
P.O. Box 5076, Champaign, IL 61825-5076
800-747-4457
e-mail: humank@hkusa.com

*Canada:* Human Kinetics
475 Devonshire Road Unit 100, Windsor, ON N8Y 2L5
800-465-7301 (in Canada only)
e-mail: orders@hkcanada.com

*Europe:* Human Kinetics
107 Bradford Road, Stanningley, Leeds LS28 6AT, United Kingdom
+44 (0) 113 255 5665
e-mail: hk@hkeurope.com

*Australia:* Human Kinetics
57A Price Avenue, Lower Mitcham, South Australia 5062
08 8277 1555
e-mail: liahka@senet.com.au

*New Zealand:* Human Kinetics
P.O. Box 105-231, Auckland Central
09-523-3462
e-mail: hkp@ihug.co.nz

# Scuba
# Diving

## THIRD EDITION

# Contents

Preface       ix
Acknowledgments       xi

## CHAPTER 1: DIVING INTO SCUBA      1

The Joys of Diving .................................................... 2
How Diving Evolved ................................................. 3
The YMCA Scuba Program ....................................... 4
The Diving Community ............................................. 5
Diver Training ........................................................ 6
Diving Prerequisites ................................................ 6
Diving Risks .......................................................... 7
Selecting a Dive Course ........................................... 8
Diving Responsibilities ............................................. 9
Summary ............................................................. 9

## CHAPTER 2: DIVING EQUIPMENT      11

Basic Equipment for All Divers .................................. 12
Exposure Suits ...................................................... 17
Weighting Systems ................................................. 24
Buoyancy Compensators .......................................... 25
Scuba Cylinders .................................................... 27
Cylinder Valves ..................................................... 31
Scuba Regulators ................................................... 34
Alternate Air Sources ............................................. 39
Instrumentation ..................................................... 40
Dive Knives and Accessories .................................... 44
Specialized Equipment ............................................ 48
Summary ............................................................. 49

# CHAPTER 3: DIVING SKILLS

Preparing to Skin Dive ................................. 52
Skin Diving Skills ..................................... 55
Preparing to Scuba Dive .............................. 62
Basic Scuba Diving Skills ............................. 65
Proficiency Testing ................................... 81
Managing Physiological Problems ..................... 81
Managing Physical Problems .......................... 84
Managing Emergencies ............................... 90
Summary ............................................ 93

# CHAPTER 4: DIVING SCIENCE

Anatomy for the Diver ............................... 96
Respiration and Circulation .......................... 98
Contrasts in Air and Water Environments ............ 102
Gas Laws ........................................... 106
Air Consumption .................................... 110
Heat, Humidity, Light, and Sound .................... 111
Summary ........................................... 114

# CHAPTER 5: DIVING ADAPTATIONS

Thermal Adaptations ................................ 118
Buoyancy Adaptations .............................. 120
Pressure Equalization ............................... 122
Breathing Adaptations .............................. 124
Heart and Lungs .................................... 128
Equilibrium Adaptations and Seasickness ............ 129
Visual Adaptations .................................. 130
Ingassing and Outgassing Adaptations .............. 130
Dehydration Prevention ............................. 134
Mobility Adaptations ................................ 135
Summary ........................................... 137

# CHAPTER 6: DIVE PLANNING
139

Dive-Planning Factors and Phases ........................... 140
Area Orientations ................................................ 143
Dive Profile Planning ........................................... 144
Dive Tables ...................................................... 145
Dive Calculators and Dive Computers ..................... 157
Postdive Review ................................................. 158
Summary .......................................................... 159

# CHAPTER 7: DIVING ENVIRONMENT
161

Aquatic Biology ................................................. 162
Potentially Dangerous Aquatic Animals ................... 164
Conservation and Preservation .............................. 167
Aquatic Conditions ............................................. 171
Boat Diving ...................................................... 182
Summary .......................................................... 185

# CHAPTER 8: DIVING OPPORTUNITIES
187

Continuing Education .......................................... 188
Local Opportunities ............................................ 189
Dive Travel ...................................................... 190
Career Opportunities .......................................... 194
Leadership Opportunities ..................................... 195
Summary .......................................................... 195

Appendix: Lists and Checklists    197    Glossary of Scuba Diving Terms    199
   Diver Training Organizations    197    Bibliography    203
   Environmental Organizations    197    Index    204
   Scuba Periodicals    198
   Diving Equipment Checklist    198    About the Author    209

# Preface

My goals in writing this book were to create the most complete, up-to-date text available for entry-level scuba instruction and to improve diving safety through education. Toward these ends, I have written *Scuba Diving* for beginners who want to learn to scuba dive and for certified divers who want to refresh their memories and update their knowledge. I have presented the information so that the book will be easy for diving instructors to use with their classes.

In recent years, the trend has been to simplify diving instruction. Simultaneously, advances in diving medicine and diving equipment have complicated the task of educating the beginning diver. This book provides more information than many scuba texts now available and addresses current topics and issues. Specifically, *Scuba Diving* has several unique features:

- Full-color illustrations and photographs
- Explanations of diving science that the average person can understand
- Emphasis on the practical skills of diving
- Modern environmental concerns
- A detailed explanation of equipment for diving in warm and cold water
- New, easy-to-understand YMCA dive-planning tables
- A thorough, yet not frightening, explanation of the risks and hazards of diving

Two items that require a bit of explanation are the "Dive In and Discover" sections in each chapter and new terms. The "Dive In and Discover" sections list specific topics that you will learn about in each chapter. Also, many new terms used in scuba diving and by scuba divers appear in the text in color; their definitions are in the glossary at the back of the book or in the margins of the text. Be sure you are familiar with the terms in a chapter before you proceed to the next chapter.

The eight chapters of this book introduce you to the scuba diving community, the diving environment, diving science, equipment, skills, planning, and opportunities. Everything today's entry-level diver needs to know to enjoy scuba diving in comfort and safety is in *Scuba Diving*. However, you cannot learn everything you need to know in a single course. My focus is on teaching you to dive in average water conditions. You will learn about specialty diving, such as ice diving, night diving, or wreck diving, when you complete intermediate and advanced scuba diving courses. Do not attempt to teach yourself to scuba dive. Do not have a friend who scuba dives teach you. If you want to become a scuba diver, you must complete a sanctioned course of instruction taught by a certified professional scuba instructor.

If you are unsure whether scuba is something that you would enjoy, many YMCAs and businesses offer introductory lessons. You can try scuba diving in shallow water to see whether you would like to learn more. Contact your local YMCA or a local diving professional and ask about an introductory scuba experience, which requires only a few hours and may be free of charge. This experience will introduce you to one of the most exciting and enjoyable leisure activities available. Diving evokes feelings of peace and joy that you can experience as soon as you qualify as a scuba diver. Sign up for a course today and start reading!

# Acknowledgments

I am grateful to many individuals and organizations for their assistance with this book. My first thanks go to Rainer Martens, publisher at Human Kinetics, for his persistence in persuading me to write *Scuba Diving*. It also was a pleasure to work with the rest of the Human Kinetics staff—they are extremely professional.

I offer special thanks to the following members of the YMCA Scuba Textbook Task Force for their assistance with updating the third edition:

Tec Clark, associate director, YMCA of the USA Scuba Program

Tom Leaird, chairman, YMCA of the USA Scuba Program

Ted Maney, American Academy of Underwater Sciences

Dan Marelli, Florida State University Academic Diving Program

Pierre Morell, University of North Carolina at Chapel Hill

Carol Reed, Ball State University

Cheryl Thacker, University of Florida Academic Diving Program

Many people contributed to the photos in *Scuba Diving*. I wish to thank Bill Oliver of SeaQuest, who provided diving equipment for the models, and Harry Truitt of Lighthouse Diving Center and Dick Long of DUI, who both loaned equipment for photos. I am especially grateful to Skip Commagere, owner of Force E, who provided diving support and photographic models. Cliff Newell of the NOAA in Seattle allowed me to photograph the recompression chambers at the NOAA facility. My longtime friend and diving buddy, Fred Humphrey, provided surf entry and exit shots. While many divers appear throughout the book, I want to thank these in particular: Michelle Anderson, Bill Black, Skip Commagere, Beth Farley, Barbara Graver, Scott Harrison, and Tom McCrudden.

The reviewers have my sincere appreciation, but my deepest gratitude is for the members of the diving community who have taught me for the past 34 years and who continue to teach me now. It is a pleasure to be able to pass on to others some of what I have learned.

Finally, I would like to say a special thank you to my loving wife, Barbara, for all the support she gave me while I completed *Scuba Diving*.

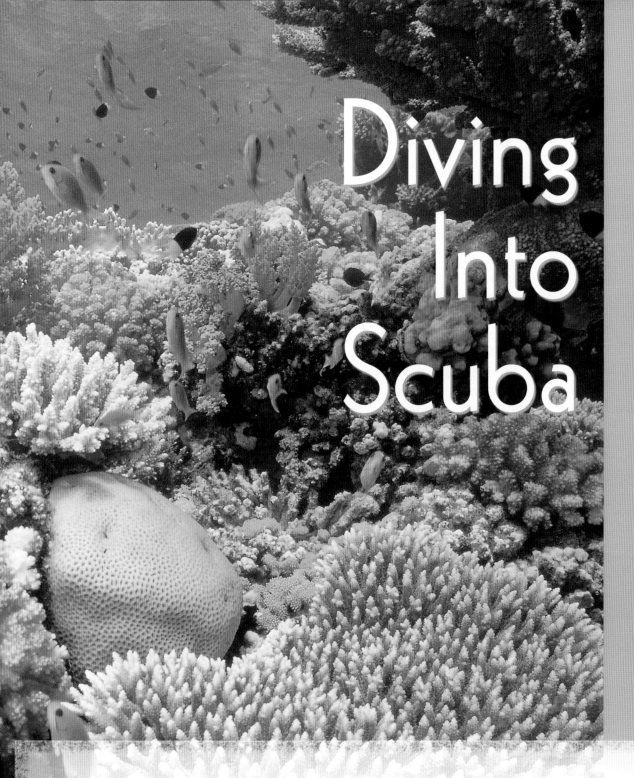

# Diving Into Scuba

# 1

## Dive In and Discover

By the end of this chapter, you will be able to do the following:

- Describe the joys of diving.
- Define the terms *closed-circuit, open-curcuit, scuba, semi-closed curcuit,* and *C-card.*
- Explain the training requirements for participation in scuba diving activities.
- List two medical conditions that disqualify an individual from scuba diving.

- Describe three risks associated with scuba diving.
- List several questions to ask when selecting an entry-level scuba diver training course.
- Explain several responsibilities that you assume when you become a certified scuba diver.

When you descend beneath the surface of the water, you enter an entirely new and beautiful world. You have opportunities to see incredible life forms that only a few ever see. Imagine swimming in a giant aquarium to get a glimpse of what you can expect to experience in the underwater world.

## THE JOYS OF DIVING

As a diver you are weightless and can move in all directions. You approach the freedom of a bird as you move in three dimensions in a fluid environment. Diving weightless in clear water in a forest of underwater plants with sunlight streaming down is only one of many unforgettable experiences awaiting you.

Just as there are mountains, plains, and differing environments above water, there are differing environments for you to experience underwater. Coral reefs, kelp forests, incredible rock formations, and other natural wonders await divers in various geographical regions. Add to this piers, jetties, quarries, mysterious shipwrecks, and other artificial structures—the variety of underwater sights is limitless. There is more to view underwater than anyone could possibly see in an entire lifetime. A wide range of activities, such as photography, hunting, and collecting, make diving challenging and rewarding. There is an activity to interest everyone.

Divers are friendly and easy to get to know. The camaraderie of divers is well known. You will meet fine people and develop lasting friendships. Diving is a sharing activity, and there is much to share. If you enjoy traveling, you will probably love diving. Dive travel is the number one business of recreational diving. Reasonably priced dive vacations to exotic islands abound. Most divers plan one or more diving vacations each year.

▶ Panoramic view of a kelp bed.

▶ Wreck dive.

The feelings and sensations of diving are fantastic but are difficult to explain. Words are inadequate to describe the peaceful solitude of "inner space." Diving contributes to good health, can help reduce work-related stress, can increase self-esteem, and can make you feel great. You will soon experience the emotions and sensations for yourself. You then will begin to know the joys of diving.

## HOW DIVING EVOLVED

Interest in the underwater world has always existed. Driven by curiosity and the need for food, people have ventured beneath the surface of Earth's seas for thousands of years. There are records of sponge divers, oyster pearl divers, military divers, and even salvage regulations dating back to 3000 B.C. The two means of diving employed in ancient times were breath holding and the use of a large, heavy, inverted, air-filled bell. The hand-operated air compressor, invented in 1770, allowed fresh air to be pumped into a submerged diving bell. In 1772, Sieur Freminet of France invented a helmet-hose system that permitted divers to work without a bell. John Lethbridge, another Frenchman, developed an oak cylinder diving engine in 1774. The greatest early advancement of underwater equipment occurred in 1837, when Augustus Siebe, a German living in England, invented the first closed diving dress, which became known as the "Hard Hat" system. Siebe's system was so effective that it dominated underwater work for 100 years and is still in use today.

People were able to eliminate the air hose that restricted them when two Englishmen, Henry Fleuss and Robert Davis, developed a **closed-circuit** oxygen rebreather system in 1878. The unit had great military application because bubbles were not exhausted into the water. Oxygen rebreathers were used extensively by Italian and British frogmen during World War II. The use of oxygen rebreather systems is limited to a maximum depth of 25 feet (about 7.6 meters) because breathing pure oxygen at greater pressures causes convulsions, which can be fatal during submersion.

**closed-circuit**—A scuba system that eliminates carbon dioxide from exhaled breath and resupplies oxygen without allowing gases to escape from the system.

**open-circuit**—A scuba system that permits a diver to breathe compressed air from a pressurized cylinder and exhausts the used gases into the water. Open-circuit systems are the safest and most popular form of scuba system.

**scuba**—Self-contained underwater breathing apparatus.

**semi-closed-circuit**—A scuba system that combines the benefits of closed-circuit and open-circuit systems. Small amounts of used gases are released periodically.

The genesis of recreational diving actually occurred in 1825 when William James, an Englishman, invented the first **open-circuit** self-contained underwater breathing apparatus **(scuba)** system. While not practical, it did solve the problems of the air hose tether and oxygen-poisoning depth restrictions. Benoit Rouquayrol, a French mining engineer, and Auguste Denayrouze, a French naval officer, invented the aerophore in 1865. Their creation is considered the source of modern scuba equipment. Yves LePrieur from France developed a manually controlled, open-circuit scuba system in 1924, but modern scuba diving was launched with the development of a demand scuba system that was perfected by Frenchmen Emile Gagnan and Jacques Cousteau in 1943. A diver could demand compressed air from a steel cylinder by simply inhaling from a pressure regulator held in the mouth. Scuba was introduced into the United States in 1950 and has been popular ever since.

The military has continued to improve underwater breathing systems that have found their way into use by recreational divers. The latest scuba systems are **semi-closed-circuit** rebreathers, which use sophisticated electronics to control the oxygen mixture that a diver breathes and periodically release only a small amount of bubbles. High levels of training, frequent use, and dedicated maintenance are required for the safe use of these expensive rebreathers.

## THE YMCA SCUBA PROGRAM

The YMCA has the proud distinction of organizing and implementing the first national scuba diving course in the United States in 1959, after work with other organizations that began in 1954 to develop a scuba training course outline. The scuba program grew, creating a need for a national scuba headquarters, which was established in Atlanta, Georgia, in 1970. In early 1980, YMCA scuba certification was granted equivalency by the World Underwater Federation/Confédération Mondiale des Activités Subaquatiques (CMAS), making the YMCA part of a worldwide diving organization composed of 12,000 dive clubs, 65 national federations, and 3.5 million divers. Delegates from 15 national underwater federations founded CMAS at Monaco in 1959. An equivalent diving certification from CMAS is recognized in more than 60 countries worldwide. In 1985, the YMCA Scuba Program became part of the Recreational Scuba Training Council (RSTC)—a national scuba standards committee—and works with the council to develop instructional standards for scuba certification.

The YMCA Scuba Program has always relied on strong volunteer support. Hundreds of professional scuba volunteers have contributed countless hours to the cause of safe scuba diving. A current example is the 2000 *YMCA Scuba Standards and Procedures Manual* produced by an appointed volunteer committee. As they are for all YMCA programs, the YMCA's mission, vision, and values are the driving force behind scuba and skin diving training. The YMCA Scuba Program builds healthy spirit, mind, and body—which is *what* the program is about; it offers a place to belong, people who care, and fun—which is *how* the program functions; and it provides effective solutions to social problems—which is *why* the program exists.

Thousands of scuba instructors who are dedicated to scuba diving safety offer skin and scuba diving training at more that 1,500 YMCAs nationwide. No other organization has as many recreational facilities with the wholesome, family atmosphere and traditional values that are available at your local YMCA.

# THE DIVING COMMUNITY

The recreational diving community consists of equipment manufacturers, diving retailers, diving educators, diver training organizations, dive resorts, diving supervisors, dive guides, dive boats, dive clubs and associations, publishing companies, and certified divers. Commercial, scientific, highly technical, and professional diving are not considered recreational pursuits; separate communities are involved in these types of diving.

There are few laws pertaining to recreational scuba diving. The laws that exist do not govern who may dive. The diving industry is self-regulating. The diving community realizes that it is dangerous when people who have not completed a sanctioned course of instruction attempt scuba diving. Dive businesses require proof of completion of training before allowing people to have scuba tanks filled or to participate in diving activities. Many dive operations also require proof of recent experience documented in a diving logbook. If you have not been diving for a year or more, you may be required to do at least one dive under the supervision of a diving professional. The supervised dive requirement helps increase the safety of divers whose skills may need to be refreshed.

When you complete your training requirements as a scuba diver, you receive a certification card, called a **C-card.** Most C-cards do not require renewal, but the recreational diving community universally recommends the completion of refresher training following periods of inactivity in excess of six months.

Certified divers may dive without supervision or may employ the services of a diving guide. Just because there is a divemaster or diving supervisor aboard a dive boat, you should not assume that this person is a guide who will dive with you. Guide services are not necessarily included with diving trips. If you want a guide to lead you about underwater and show you the sights, arrange for guide services in advance.

You will learn more about the community as your diving experience increases. There are many opportunities for adventure and enjoyment. Get actively involved in the community when you complete your training and officially qualify as a scuba diver.

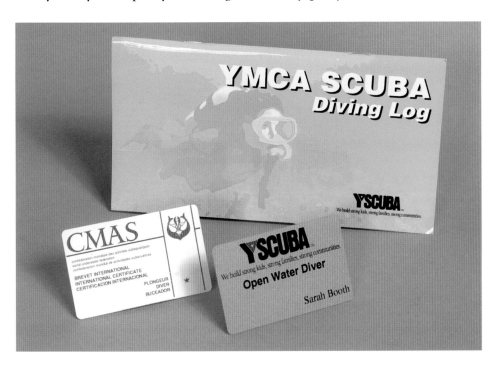

▶ Logbook and certification cards.

# DIVER TRAINING

A national diver training organization must sanction your training. The training organization establishes standards of training that you must meet before the organization will issue a certification card. The appendix includes a list of national diver training organizations. Your instructor should have credentials identifying him or her as a qualified instructor. The instructor's membership in the training organization must be current to qualify him or her to teach and certify divers. Confirm your instructor's qualifications.

Your entry-level training course consists of a series of academic sessions, pool or confined-water (pool-like conditions in open water) sessions, and open-water training (in actual diving locations). You will learn theory in the classroom, learn skills in controlled conditions, and then apply your skills in an actual diving environment. This logical progression is common for all approved diver training courses.

There are minimum requirements for your training. You should have four or more academic sessions, four or more pool sessions, and at least four scuba dives in open water. A skin dive in open water also may be part of your training.

The time involved in your initial training should total 30 to 40 hours of instruction. It is best if the instruction occurs over a period of several weeks instead of a few days. The time between class sessions allows you to reflect on your training and helps you absorb and retain the knowledge and skills better than a concentrated training schedule.

# DIVING PREREQUISITES

Diving can be undertaken by anyone over 12 years of age in normal health with a reasonable degree of physical fitness. You need swimming ability, but you do not need to be a competitive swimmer. At the beginning of the course you need to be able to swim 200 yards (183 meters) nonstop at the surface using any combination of strokes. There is no time requirement for the swim. Being comfortable in the water is more important than being able to swim fast. You also need to be able to swim 25 feet (7.6 meters) underwater with no push-off. By the end of the course you need to be able to swim 300 yards (274 meters) nonstop at the surface using any combination of strokes and 50 feet (15.2 meters) underwater with no push-off. The goal is to increase your aquatic proficiency during the course.

## Scuba Wise

*I nearly drowned at 4 years of age and became terrified of water. When I was 8 years old, I spent a summer with my uncle in Ohio. He would take me to Lake Erie and give me pennies if I would wade into water deep enough to cover my navel. I learned to swim as a Boy Scout at age 11. Although I completed a lifesaving class at age 16, I still was apprehensive. When I learned skin and scuba diving and discovered that I could actually relax in water, it became my ally. For the first time in my life, I enjoyed water and rid myself of my childhood fears. Just because a person feels anxiety about water does not mean that the individual cannot enjoy scuba diving. If you can swim 200 yards, you can learn to dive and to love being in and under the water.*

Normal health means your heart, lungs, and circulation are normal and that you do not have any serious diseases. Any medical conditions—even if controllable under normal conditions—that might incapacitate you in the water could cause you to drown while scuba diving. Some individuals with asthma or diabetes may be able to dive with special medical approval. People with physical disabilities also may dive if they have medical approval from a physician. The air spaces in your body—sinuses, ears, and lungs—must be normal because changes in pressure affect them. Other medical conditions, such as seizure disorders, absolutely preclude diving; a seizure while diving can be fatal. Women who are pregnant should not scuba dive. Increased pressure can adversely affect an unborn child. Pregnant women may participate in snorkeling. Many women ask whether they may dive during menstruation. Menstruation does not preclude a woman from diving if her health permits participation in other sports during that time of her cycle.

You need to be emotionally fit as well as physically fit for diving. If you are terrified of water or of feeling confined, diving probably is an activity you should avoid. Normal concerns are to be expected, but stark terror is unacceptable.

It is a good idea to have a physical examination before you begin your training, especially if it has been more than a year since your last exam. It is best if a diving physician recommended by your instructor does the exam. Physicians who do not understand the physiology of scuba diving sometimes inappropriately grant approval to scuba dive to individuals who have medical conditions that place them at great risk in and under water. Your instructor can recommend a physician who understands scuba medical issues.

# DIVING RISKS

All activities present some risk. There is risk involved in walking across the street or driving a car. To avoid injury while participating in an activity, we take precautions for our safety. There are precautions for scuba diving just as there are for any other pursuit. The risk of diving is similar to that of flying. Both are low-risk activities when done with well-maintained equipment according to established rules and in good environmental conditions. Unfortunately, both are unforgiving if you ignore the rules and recommendations designed to minimize the risks.

The following information and much of this book make you aware of injuries that scuba divers can incur. This information makes you aware of potential hazards and, more important, helps you learn to avoid injury. If you do what you are taught to do as a diver, your risk will be minimal and all of your diving experiences are likely to be pleasant ones.

Pressure changes with depth. Changes in pressure can severely injure bodily air spaces if you are not in good health or if you fail to equalize the pressure in the bodily air spaces with the surrounding pressure. You will learn equalizing techniques as part of your training. Gases are normally dissolved in the fluids and tissues of your body. Increased pressure increases the amount of gas dissolved in your body. If you ascend too rapidly from a dive, the gases in your system can

▶ Being comfortable in the water is important to your enjoyment and safety.

form bubbles and produce a serious illness known as **decompression sickness**. By regulating your depth, the duration of your dive, and your rate of ascent, you can avoid decompression sickness. Failure to heed depth and time schedules and ascent rates can result in serious, permanent injuries.

Diving can be strenuous at times. You need sufficient physical fitness and stamina to handle long swims, currents, and other situations that may arise. If you become winded from climbing a flight of stairs, you may need to improve your level of fitness before learning to scuba dive. Exhaustion in and under the water is hazardous.

Diving takes place in water, an alien environment. You use life-support equipment to dive, but you cannot depend entirely on the equipment for your well-being. Aquatic skills are essential in and around water. People with very weak aquatic ability can drown in the event of minor equipment problems that could be handled easily by a person with good water skills. You must be comfortable in the water to be a scuba diver.

You should not be overly concerned with the potential risks of diving because the possible injuries are preventable. Learning how to dive as safely as possible is the purpose of your training. You will learn to minimize the risk of injury and maximize your enjoyment of the underwater world.

## SELECTING A DIVE COURSE

There are many diver training organizations and thousands of professional diving educators. Your phone book might list diving businesses offering sanctioned courses. Many universities, community colleges, YMCAs, and recreational departments also offer scuba courses. Ask about the qualifications, experience, and reputation of several diving instructors in your area to select the course that can provide you with the best possible training. These are some questions to ask:

▶ You should purchase a mask, snorkel, fins, boots, and gloves for use during your scuba diving training.

- Is this training sanctioned by a diver training agency?
- How long has the instructor been teaching scuba diving?
- Which levels of training is the instructor qualified to teach?
- May I speak with the graduates of a recent class?
- Why is the course offered better than others in the area?
- Are assisting and rescue techniques taught in the course?
- How many instructor-supervised open-water dives are included?

The tuition for diving instruction usually is between $200 and $300. The lowest-priced course may not necessarily be a bargain. Find out what is included with the course fee and, more important, what the total cost will be for you to become certified as a scuba diver. You do not have to purchase all the equipment needed to scuba dive, but you need to have a mask, snorkel, fins, and usually boots and gloves for your training. Use of the additional required equipment typically is part of the course tuition.

Find out whether the price of the course includes the costs of educational materials and certification. There may be additional costs for travel, lodging, parking, boat fees, and equipment rental for open-water training. Determine the complete cost before enrolling in a course.

When you have selected the best program for you and have enrolled in a course, you should receive a reading assignment for your first session. If you are not given an assignment, ask about it; you can learn much better by reading in advance about the topics to be presented in class. Good diving instructors provide a handout with reading assignments.

# DIVING RESPONSIBILITIES

When you qualify as a scuba diver, you assume many responsibilities. You are responsible for your safety, for the safety of those with whom you dive, for the image of scuba divers, and for the preservation of the diving environment. The diving community encourages divers to accept responsibility for their actions. To be part of the diving community, you need to be a responsible diver. Learn what you should do, then do what you learn.

# SUMMARY

Diving can be a source of great joy. There are many exciting experiences awaiting the trained diver. You need dive credentials to participate in diving activities. You must complete diver training to obtain your C-card and logbook. But diving is not for everyone. You must have normal health, good swimming skills, and reasonable physical fitness. Diving poses risks that a well-trained, wise, and fit diver can minimize. Compare training programs and choose the best education, which may not be the quickest or the least expensive. Remember that you accept a great deal of responsibility when you become a diver. Do not assume that you can transfer the responsibility for a dive accident to someone else. Ultimately you control your actions underwater. Become a competent, self-reliant diver who adheres to recommended safety practices and you will discover the joy of diving.

## Character Development

### Responsible Diver Code

I will dive within the limits of my training and ability.

I will evaluate the conditions before every dive and make sure they fit my personal capabilities.

I will be familiar with and check my equipment before and during every dive.

I will respect the buddy system and its advantages.

I will accept responsibility for my own safety on every dive.

I will be environmentally conscious on every dive.

I will be responsible to myself, the people with whom I dive, and the environment.

# Diving Equipment 2

## Dive In and Discover

By the end of this chapter, you will be able to do the following:

- Describe the purpose, types, features, selection criteria, and care and maintenance of skin and scuba diving equipment.
- Contrast steel and aluminum scuba cylinders, wet and dry suits, integrated and nonintegrated weighting systems, and reserve and nonreserve valves.

- Define the terms *buoyancy, compensator, defogging, shorty, jumpsuit, Farmer Johns, K-valve, J-valve, DIN valve, valve seat, burst disk, O-ring, port, stage, octopus, capillary gauge, Bourdon tube, Boyle's law, outgassing, bezel, submersible pressure gauge (SPG), blowout plug, alternate air source (AAS), pony tank, Spare Air unit, lubber line, console,* and *ceiling.*

Scuba Diving

Equipment helps people adapt to the underwater environment. It allows them to see, breathe, move, and rest. Diving is an equipment-intensive activity. In this chapter you will learn what equipment you need, how to select the best equipment for your needs, and how to care for your equipment. You will become familiar with the following equipment:

- Masks
- Snorkels
- Fins
- Skin diving vests
- Exposure suits
- Weighting systems
- Buoyancy compensators
- Scuba cylinders
- Cylinder valves
- Scuba regulators
- Alternate air sources
- Instrumentation
- Dive knives, accessories, and specialized equipment

▶ Figure 2.1 Fully equipped cold-water (left) and warm-water (right) divers.

You need to be equipped properly to dive in open water. A snorkeler (a diver who remains at the surface) should wear a mask, a snorkel, fins, and a skin diving vest. A skin diver (a breath-holding diver who dives beneath the surface) uses snorkeling equipment and may wear an exposure suit and a weight belt (if the suit requires weights). Scuba equipment includes, at a minimum, a mask, snorkel, fins, an exposure suit, a weighting system (if needed), a **buoyancy compensator** (BC), a scuba unit (cylinder, valve, regulator, **alternate air source**), instrumentation, and a dive knife. For cold water, a diver also needs a hood, boots, and gloves. Figure 2.1 shows fully equipped divers.

## BASIC EQUIPMENT FOR ALL DIVERS

The mask, snorkel, fins, and some flotation device are basic equipment for all types of recreational diving: snorkeling, skin diving, and scuba diving.

### Masks

The eyes require an air space in front of them to focus sharply. Your mask provides an air space and a window to another world. There are many styles of masks, but only two basic recreational types: purge and nonpurge. A purge is a one-way valve through which you can expel water that enters the mask. As you will learn in the next chapter, you can remove water from a mask without a valve, so many masks do not feature a purge valve. A third type of mask, a full-face mask, is for commercial and specialty applications only. Figure 2.2 shows the most common types of masks.

The type of mask you choose is not nearly as important as the fit of the mask on your face. The mask must fit your facial contours perfectly so it will remain comfortable and watertight throughout a dive. Fit and comfort are the most important features to consider when you select a mask. To test the fit of a mask,

remove the strap or position it on the front of the mask. Tilt your head back and lay the mask (do not push it) on your face. Make sure your hair is not under the sealing edge of the mask; then inhale gently. If the mask pulls onto your face snugly from the partial vacuum created by your inhalation, the mask fits. If you have to push the mask to get it to seal on your face, the mask probably will leak when you use it underwater.

The style, type of material, and type of sealing edge of a mask affect its fit and comfort. The best masks are made from silicone, which is soft, pliable, and nonallergenic and resists deterioration better than rubber compounds (see figure 2.3). The buoyancy of smaller masks poses no problems, but the tug of buoyancy of a larger-volume mask can affect the seal. Low-volume masks are easier to clear of water and provide excellent visibility. A wide, double-edged seal does a better job of keeping out water than a single-edge seal.

▶ Figure 2.2 Many different masks are available for divers, including purge (center) and nonpurge types.

▶ Figure 2.3 Mask features.

A film of oil from production is on the surface of the glass lenses of new masks. You must remove the film completely—a process called **defogging**—or the mask will fog continuously underwater. Clean your mask thoroughly with scouring powder. The glass, which is tempered, is too hard to be scratched by the abrasive, so do not be timid when cleaning your mask. Commercial defogging solutions help keep your mask clear while you dive. If a clean mask fogs slightly during use, you can allow a small amount of water into the mask and wash it across the fogged area to resolve the problem.

Several options are available for visual correction if you need it. Hard contact lenses cannot be used, because gases that are released from the body during ascent can be trapped between the lens and the surface of the eye and can injure the eye. If you wear soft contact lenses, you can use them for diving after

**Mask features**

Soft, wide sealing edge

Nondeteriorating material

Low volume

Corrective lenses

Nose pocket for equalization access

Purge valve (optional)

Easily adjustable, securely locking strap buckles

you complete your training, but you should not use them during training because you may lose them when you are learning how to clear water from your mask. Some contact lens wearers prefer a mask with a small purge valve because they can expel water from the mask with little risk of losing a contact lens. Several companies prepare and bond corrective lenses into any diving mask. Interchangeable corrective lenses are available for some masks. If you require only a simple correction, you may be able to obtain corrective lenses for your mask when you purchase it.

Store your mask in a mask box when you are not using it. The box helps keep the mask from getting damaged and helps prevent discoloration of the silicone mask skirt.

## Snorkels

A human head weighs about as much as a bowling ball. If you had to swim while holding a bowling ball out of water, you would become exhausted quickly. If you swim while holding your head above water, you will tire rapidly. But if you allow buoyancy to support your head in the water, you can relax and swim for hours. A snorkel allows you to breathe while water supports your head—allowing you to conserve energy and enjoy continuous underwater viewing.

In its simplest form, a snorkel is nothing more than a breathing tube that extends from a diver's mouth to a point above the waterline. A basic diving snorkel is a J-shaped tube with a mouthpiece on one end. Just as with masks, there are two types of snorkels: purge and nonpurge (see figure 2.4). A purge snorkel has a one-way valve through which you can expel water that enters the tube. As you will learn in chapter 3, you can clear water from a snorkel that lacks a purge valve, so some snorkels do not have a valve. Some types of purge snorkels are self-draining; gravity drains water from the tube automatically when you are at the surface of the water.

Additional snorkel options include a swivel mouthpiece and a flexible hose for the lower half of the tube so that the lower part that usually is curved hangs straight down when you are not using your snorkel (see figure 2.5). The flex-hose snorkel reduces interference between the snorkel and your scuba regulator. There are special mouthpieces to maximize comfort and devices to prevent water from entering the top end of the snorkel, although water exclusion devices are not essential.

The fit of your snorkel is the most important consideration, much more important than the type. The mouthpiece must not irritate your mouth, gums, or jaw when in place for extended periods of time. The angle of the mouthpiece in your mouth should not require you to bite hard to hold the mouthpiece in place. A snorkel that fits poorly may cause sore gums or jaws. A snorkel tube should have an inside diameter of approximately 3/4 inch (1.9 centimeters) so that resistance to airflow through the tube does not make breathing difficult.

Attach the snorkel to your mask strap on the left side using a snorkel keeper. There are several types of keepers. Popular keepers are the simple ones depicted in figure 2.6. The adjustment is correct if the snorkel mouthpiece remains in your mouth when you open your mouth wide.

▶ Figure 2.4 The two common types of snorkels are nonpurge (left) and purge (center and right).

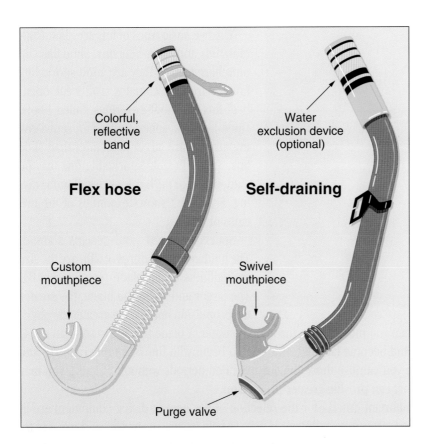

▶ Figure 2.5   Snorkel features.

Colorful, reflective band

Water exclusion device (optional)

**Flex hose**

**Self-draining**

Custom mouthpiece

Swivel mouthpiece

Purge valve

▶ Figure 2.6   Two types of snorkel keepers.

# Fins

Diving would be much less enjoyable without fins. They increase your ability to move in the water and free your hands for other activities. You move in water by pushing against the water. Fins increase your ability to move by presenting a larger surface area than your hands or feet alone. The muscles of your legs are much larger and stronger than your arm muscles. Your arms would tire quickly if fins were attached to your hands, but your legs are strong enough to handle the load. Fins also help stabilize you in water by providing a large surface to resist movement. The resistance provides leverage for counter-movement and directional control.

The two basic types of fins are shoe (full-foot) fins and open-heel fins. Shoe fins slip onto bare feet, so they are good snorkeling fins for tropical climates. You wear open-heel fins with foot coverings called boots. Open-heel fins, generally used for scuba diving, usually are larger and stiffer than shoe fins. Small, flexible snorkeling fins may be inadequate for the harder work of scuba diving. Figure 2.7 shows examples of the two types of fins.

Special materials and designs abound. The fundamental features of a fin are the size and stiffness of the blade (see figure 2.8). The larger and stiffer the blade, the greater the propulsion but also the greater the physical demand when you move the fin through the water. A blade that is too stiff can cause you to cramp and become fatigued. It is best to begin with fins of a moderate size and stiffness. When you can use those fins for extended periods without difficulty, you may consider fins that can provide greater propulsion.

▶ Figure 2.7 Open-heel fins (left) and shoe fins (right) provide alternatives for different diving needs.

The most important criteria for the selection of any item of diving equipment are fit and comfort, and this is especially true of fins. To help ensure proper fit, sit down and try on a fin. Wear a boot if trying an open-heel fin. Hold your foot in the air and wiggle it up and down and from side to side. The fin and your foot should move as a single unit. If your foot moves inside the foot pocket, the fin is too large. Diving equipment should fit snugly but not tightly. A fin that is too tight can cause your foot to cramp. The foot pocket of the fin should fit snugly but not exert pressure on your foot. Select your fins using fit, comfort, and blade size and stiffness as your primary criteria. Features, fashion, and cost should be secondary considerations.

▶ Figure 2.8 Features of dive fins.

Elongated foot pocket

High-tech material

Blade size and stiffness

Easily adjustable, securely locking straps

## Skin Diving Vests

When you blow air into a skin diving vest, you can achieve positive buoyancy (floating), which is invaluable when you want to rest at the surface or carry items you have collected while diving. Wear a buoyancy vest whenever you dive. You can achieve negative buoyancy (sinking) by venting air from the skin diving vest.

Divers use one basic type of skin diving vest, which fits around the neck and secures at the waist (see figure 2.9). A standard feature of a skin diving vest is an oral inflation tube, which comes in various sizes. It is easier to use larger tubes with mouthpieces than smaller tubes without mouthpieces. Some vests feature a $CO_2$ detonator. You must tend to the mechanism at the end of every day of diving or it will not function reliably.

## Care and Maintenance of Skin Diving Equipment

Your skin diving equipment will provide years of service if you take care of it properly. Rinse the equipment with clean, fresh water after use; dry it in the shade; and store it in a cool, dark, smog-free location. Prolonged sunlight, smog, salt crystals, and swimming pool chlorine harm your equipment. Fill a skin diving vest partially with fresh water after use, and swish the water inside. Drain the vest completely, and then inflate it for drying and for storage. If the vest has a $CO_2$ detonator, remove the $CO_2$ cartridge, rinse the cartridge and assembly thoroughly, and lubricate the cartridge threads. Screw the cartridge back into the assembly only after the vest has dried thoroughly. Periodically inspect the straps on your mask and fins for drying and cracking, and replace straps when they begin to deteriorate. After your mask has dried, rub a drop of defogging solution on the lens to help keep the lens clean during storage.

▶ Figure 2.9   Skin diving vests.

# EXPOSURE SUITS

Wear some type of exposure protection regardless of the water temperature when diving. An exposure suit provides protection against scrapes and stings as well as insulation.

The two basic types of exposure suits are wet suits and dry suits. Generally speaking, the colder the water, the thicker your suit should be and the more of your body should be covered by the suit. There are many suit configurations, but most are one piece or a combination of a jacket and pants. Vests are accessories that help conserve heat in vital organs. Hoods, boots, and gloves help reduce heat loss from the head, feet, and hands, respectively.

## Wet Suits

A wet suit is a good exposure suit for water temperatures ranging from 60 to 85 °F (15.6 to 29.4 °C). A wet suit allows water inside, but any water that enters also can exit and carry heat with it. The better the fit of the suit, the less water inside and the warmer the suit. Table 2.1 provides a comparison of wet-suit types. The following descriptions provide some additional information.

Spandex suits are thin, stretchy, attractive, full-body garments that are popular for diving in tropical waters. Spandex garments provide 45 percent more insulation than bare skin and provide protection against stings, scrapes, and sunshine. Spandex suits are light and compact for travel. They also are useful as undergarments for thicker neoprene wet suits, to add an extra layer of insulation and allow you to slip into the heavier suit

### Table 2.1 Wet Suits

| Type | Warmth | Features | Temperature range |
|---|---|---|---|
| Spandex | 45% more than bare skin | Light, compact; useful as under-garments for thicker suits | 78 °F (25.6 °C) + |
| Thermoplastic | 30% warmer than spandex | Neutrally buoyant; no weights required; wicks perspiration; windproof | 75 °F (23.9 °C) + |
| Plush-lined thermoplastic | 10% warmer than unlined | Same as thermoplastic | 72 °F (22.2 °C) + |
| Foam neoprene<br>• ⅛ in. (2-3 mm)<br>• 3/16 in. (4 mm)<br>• ¼ in. (5-6.5 mm) | 20-100% warmer than plush-lined thermoplastic | Buoyant; weights required; long drying time; evaporation chills wearer; minor repairs easy to do | Down to 60 °F (15.6 °C) |
| Hoods, vests, boots, and gloves or mitts | 16-66% more warmth | Reduces water circulation; layering allows flexibility for various temperatures | Down to 60 °F (15.6 °C) |

more easily. If you live in a temperate climate, you can use a spandex body suit beneath a neoprene wet suit for local diving and use the spandex suit by itself for vacation diving in the tropics (see figure 2.10).

Thermoplastic—sandwiched between two layers of spandex—is another type of wet-suit material. A suit made from this three-ply material is about 30 percent warmer than a spandex suit. Thermoplastic suits are thin (1.2 to 1.4 millimeters) and designed for use in tropical waters (75 to 85 °F, or 24 to 29 °C). Some suits feature soft, plush lining for extra warmth. The plush lining increases the warmth of the suit by about 10 percent. You can wear a thermoplastic suit beneath a neoprene wet suit for extra warmth in colder water.

▶ Figure 2.10 Common styles of warm-water wet suits: foam neoprene (left and center) and nylon (right). The style of the suit on the left is a jumpsuit. The suit in the center is a shorty.

Thermoplastic material offers several advantages: The balance between the weight and volume of this unique material makes it neutrally buoyant, so you may not need a weight belt. The stretchy fabric allows you to move freely. The material draws perspiration away from your body but is windproof.

A third type of wet-suit material is foam neoprene, as in the suits shown in figure 2.11. The foam contains tiny bubbles of inert gas, which provide insulation. The thicker the wet-suit material, the greater the insulation quality of the suit. A 1/8-inch (about 3-millimeter) neoprene wet suit is about 20 percent warmer than a plush thermoplastic suit.

The thickness of wet-suit foam neoprene ranges from 1/8 inch (about 3 millimeters) for warm-water diving to 3/8 inch (about 9 millimeters) for extreme cold-water diving. The most common wet-suit thicknesses are 1/8 inch (about 3 millimeters), 3/16 inch (about 4 millimeters), and 1/4 inch (about 6 millimeters). You can layer wet-suit material on critical areas of your body to reduce heat loss, but the thicker the insulation you wear, the more difficult it is for you to control buoyancy. Choose the thickness of wet-suit material used by experienced divers in the area where you plan to dive.

Nylon usually covers both sides of the neoprene used for wet suits. The nylon increases the strength and durability of the suit, which is glued and sewed together. You can make minor repairs with wet-suit cement, but you should have a wet-suit manufacturer do extensive repairs.

▶ Figure 2.11  Common styles of cold-water wet suits. Jackets on left (with or without an attached hood) are worn over Farmer John bottoms (right) to form layers.

Neoprene wet suits require weights to achieve neutral buoyancy. The suit provides immediate buoyancy when you release the weights, but the buoyancy of the suit can be either a benefit or a hazard. Neoprene is not windproof, and the evaporation of water from the suit between dives can chill you. You can wear a wet-suit overgarment to retain warmth between dives in colder climates. Neoprene suits take longer to dry than other types of exposure suits. Mobility is good with thin neoprene wet suits but decreases as the thickness of the material increases.

There are numerous wet-suit designs, including the **shorty**, the one-piece **jumpsuit**, and **Farmer Johns** (see figures 2.10 and 2.11). You must consider several features when selecting a wet-suit design. The more zippers a suit has, the more water circulates inside the suit and the greater the loss of heat. You can get zipperless suits for cold-water diving. Good wet suits feature a spine pad to minimize water circulation along the channel formed by your spine, and some suits for cold-water diving have attached hoods to minimize water circulation at the neck. You may spend time kneeling around and in the water, so kneepads are a desirable feature.

Heat packs are available for wet suits. These packs contain a nontoxic, reusable chemical that heats to about 130 °F (54 °C) for half an hour or more, depending on conditions. The packs fit into special pockets that are an optional suit feature.

You can buy wet suits in standard sizes, or you can have a suit tailored for a custom fit. The fit of a wet suit is its most important feature. The suit must fit snugly all over but must not fit so tightly that it hampers your breathing and circulation. A suit that fits well may feel slightly restrictive out of the water. The true test of the fit of a suit is to dive with it. You may be able to rent a wet suit identical to one you would like to purchase.

## Wet-Suit Accessories

Scuba divers usually wear foot protection. There are several types of footwear, called boots or booties, for various needs. Boots, usually made from neoprene, may cover only the foot or both the foot and the ankle (see figure 2.12). Boots range from inexpensive neoprene socks to sturdy footwear with durable, molded soles. They may or may not

▶ Figure 2.12   Boots are available with or without zippers.

▶ Figure 2.13   Gloves and mitts provide protection for divers' hands.

▶ Figure 2.14   Hoods conserve warmth.

have zippers. Zippered boots are easier to don and remove, but boots without zippers are warmer.

You should wear hand coverings when the water temperature is less than 70 °F (21 °C). Some divers wear gloves for protection, such as when catching lobsters. Types of hand coverings include gloves, mitts, and gauntlets (see figure 2.13). Wear mitts in cold water because they are thicker and have less surface area for heat dissipation than gloves have. Wear gauntlets (neoprene mitts with long cuffs) when the water is extremely cold. Thin neoprene gloves provide sufficient insulation in temperate water. Do not wear gloves in tropical areas. You are more likely to touch things when wearing gloves, and grabbing delicate coral reefs and marine animals while wearing gloves harms the animals.

A hood is an important warmth accessory that can reduce your heat loss from 20 to 50 percent, depending on the temperature of the water. Two basic types of hoods, attached hoods and separate hoods, are available for wet suits (see figure 2.14). Cold-water divers like attached hoods because they restrict water circulation in a suit more than separate hoods do. Some separate hoods have skirts that end at the base of the neck; other cold-water hoods with large bibs cover the neck and shoulder area. There are thin hoods for protection in warm water and thicker hoods for insulation and protection in cold water.

You can increase the warmth of your wet suit by as much as 16 percent by wearing a vest. Wet-suit vests come in all types of material and provide an additional layer of insulation (see figure 2.15). Layering is an effective technique that reduces water circulation while increasing insulation. Some vests have attached hoods.

## Wet-Suit Care and Maintenance

With proper care, wet suits can provide years of service. Soak your wet suit in clean, fresh, warm water after each use. If you can't soak your suit, rinse it. Hang your suit on a wet-suit hanger, which is wider than a typical clothes hanger; dry the suit in the shade; and store it on the hanger in a cool, dark, smog-free location. A garage is a poor environment for storing equipment. Do not fold your wet suit for storage because folds can form permanent creases, which insulate poorly. Inspect your suit regularly for seam integrity and tears. Make repairs or have them made as needed.

# Dry Suits

When the water temperature is less than 60 °F (15.6 °C), consider using a dry suit, an exposure suit that keeps out water. Dry suits are much warmer than wet suits for three reasons:

▶ Figure 2.15   The addition of a vest can increase the warmth of your wet suit by as much as 16 percent.

1. Air is in contact with your skin instead of water. Since air conducts less heat than water, you lose less heat via conduction.

2. You wear undergarments beneath a dry suit. The undergarments trap a layer of air, which is a good insulator.

3. Suit compression affects two of the three types of dry suits only slightly, so the insulating ability of those types of dry suits remains nearly constant regardless of depth.

Dry suits are identified by the material from which they are made. Table 2.2 compares the three most common types of dry suits. The foam neoprene dry suit is made of the same material as a wet suit, but the dry suit has seals at the wrists and neck, attached dry boots, and a waterproof zipper (see figure 2.16).

A dry suit can cost two to five times as much as a wet suit, but with proper care and maintenance, a good dry suit will last many times longer than a wet suit. If you dive primarily in cold water, a dry suit is a good investment.

A dry suit creates a closed air space that is subject to squeezing. A low-pressure inflator valve, a standard feature, allows you to add air to the suit during descent to prevent suit squeeze. Since air expands during ascent, an exhaust valve is another standard feature. Get a dry suit that has a constant-volume exhaust valve that automatically maintains a constant state of buoyancy during ascent.

| Table 2.2   Dry Suits | | |
| --- | --- | --- |
| Type | Advantages | Disadvantages |
| Foam neoprene | Form fitting and streamlined | Long drying time; hard to locate and repair leaks; buoyancy control difficult |
| Crushed neoprene | Durable; easy to repair; long lasting; less buoyant than foam neoprene | Less insulation than foam neoprene; expensive; somewhat bulky |
| Shell (two kinds)<br>• Coated nylon<br>• Rubberized fabric | Fast drying; easy to repair; nylon suits inexpensive; rubberized suits long lasting | Easily punctured; bulky; nylon suits do not last long; rubberized suits expensive |

▶ Figure 2.16 Dry suits can be made from foam neoprene (left), crushed neoprene (center), or nylon (right).

▶ Figure 2.17 Dry-suit boots and gloves help keep divers warm.

Diving is a diuretic activity: It increases the amount of urine you produce. Urination in a wet suit is a regular practice by divers in open water, but the problem is more complex when you wear a dry suit. An optional feature for a dry suit is a relief zipper, which is useful only when you are out of the water. Dry-suit divers have to exit the water to urinate, and those without a relief zipper must disrobe.

There are several types of undergarments for dry suits. Some are inexpensive but compress with depth and lose insulating ability when wet. More expensive undergarments are highly resistant to compression and retain most of their insulating quality even if wet. Many dry-suit divers prefer to wear two layers of undergarments: a thin garment against the skin to carry perspiration away from the body and a thicker overgarment for the bulk of the insulation. Moisture conducts heat, so you are warmer when perspiration is wicked away from your body.

Dry suits have several drawbacks. Controlling buoyancy is more difficult with a dry suit than with a wet suit. Rapid, uncontrolled ascents can occur unless you control the suit. Training is essential before attempting to dive in a dry suit. Dry suits are bulkier than wet suits. It is easier to don and remove a dry suit than a wet suit, but the bulkiness of a dry suit makes surface swimming difficult, and a dry suit restricts your mobility more than a wet suit does. The inconveniences of a dry suit are of little consequence, however, when warmth is your primary concern.

## Dry-Suit Accessories

Most dry suits have attached boots, a desirable feature. Thin latex booties are found on less expensive suits, with hard-soled boots on more expensive suits. You should wear heavy socks for insulation with latex booties, and you must wear wet-suit boots over the latex booties to protect them. The end result is that dry-suit divers usually need fins with large foot pockets.

You can wear neoprene gloves or mitts with a dry suit. If the water is extremely cold, you can get dry gloves with insulating liners that attach to some dry suits. An attached latex dry hood is an option for some models, but most dry-suit divers use a separate neoprene dry-suit hood. Figure 2.17 shows examples of dry-suit accessories.

## Dry-Suit Care and Maintenance

Dry suits require more care than wet suits. The zipper is expensive to replace, as are the control valves, so do not allow salt crystals to form in the zipper or in the valves. Soak and rinse the zipper and valves in clean, fresh water as soon as possible following a saltwater dive. Wash the neck and wrist seals with soapy water, and then rinse them. Coat latex seals with pure talc after they dry. The talc helps protect the rubber from the elements. Fold dry suits in half over a wide hanger for drying. Lubricate the suit zipper according to the manufacturer's instructions, then store the suit with the zipper open. If the suit needs to be repaired, have an authorized dealer make the repairs.

## Exposure-Suit Selection

There are many factors to consider when you select an exposure suit and accessories: your physical characteristics, where you intend to dive, how you intend to dive, how much diving you intend to do, and what you intend to do while diving. The amount of money you invest also is a factor, but keep in mind that buying an inexpensive suit may be false economy. If the suit does not meet your needs, you will have to spend more money for another suit.

The amount of diving you intend to do is an important factor. If you plan to make only one dive per day, your insulation requirements are not as great as if you plan to dive several times per day. The more time you plan to spend in the water, the warmer the suit you should have.

If you are a thin person who gets chilled easily, you need more insulation than the average person for a given water temperature. People with more-than-average body fat may not require as much insulation as those with average body fat; fat is a good, natural insulator. Thermal comfort is essential for diving safety and enjoyment.

If you intend to do most of your diving in one area, the most popular type of suit in the area probably is the best type for you. If the local waters are cold, you have to choose between a wet suit and a dry suit. If you choose to get a wet suit as your first exposure suit for cold-water diving, a layered design with Farmer John pants, a vest, and a step-in jacket with an attached hood retains more warmth than high-waisted pants, a regular jacket, and a separate hood. A custom fit retains more warmth than a suit of a standard size.

Dry suits are not desirable for long surface swims because you can overheat, and the drag caused by the bulkiness of some dry suits may cause you to tire or cramp. On the other hand, dry suits retain much more warmth at depth than wet suits. If most of your diving will be deeper than 40 feet (12 meters), if the water is 60 °F (15.6 °C) or colder, and if you can avoid long surface swims, a dry suit is a good choice, as long as you obtain training before using the suit.

If you plan to dive in a variety of climates, a spandex or thermoplastic suit combined with a neoprene wet suit may be a good option. You can wear different parts of the suits to meet different warmth requirements. Your diving activity affects your needs. An underwater hunter looking for game generates more body heat than an underwater photographer whose movements are minimal. The less active you are while diving, the more insulation you need. Your desires, needs, and budget determine the features you select for your exposure suit. Features that are popular with local experienced divers and diving leaders are desirable features to consider for your suit.

The accessories you select for your suit depend on the type of suit you choose, the temperature of the water, the activity you intend to pursue, and your budget. A hood may be thin and short for warmer water, thick with a long skirt for colder water, or a dry-suit

▶ Figure 2.18 Weighting systems.

type. Foot coverings may be low-cut, ankle-high, or attached to the suit. The soles may be soft or hard. Hand coverings range from nothing to thick mitts, gauntlets, or dry gloves.

Local diving professionals can help with your selection of an exposure suit and accessories. No matter what type of exposure suit you choose, keep in mind that it is an investment in your enjoyment of diving. Diving is not fun if you get cold.

# WEIGHTING SYSTEMS

Exposure suits increase your buoyancy. You need weights for ballast to achieve neutral buoyancy. One type of weighting system is a weight belt; another type integrates the weights into the scuba unit. Figure 2.18 shows examples of weighting systems.

Weights can be attached to or inserted into a belt that you wear around your waist. The belt is heavy nylon webbing two inches (five centimeters) wide. You can thread the belt through lead weights, wrap pouches of lead shot around the belt, or put weights or pouches of lead shot into pockets on pocket-type belts. A hollow fabric belt that you can fill with lead shot is more comfortable on your hips than hard weights. Lead shot, which comes in different sizes, causes less damage than hard lead weights if you drop the belt accidentally. Smaller-diameter shot weighs more per volume than larger shot, so the more weight you need, the smaller the shot you should use.

Because exposure suits compress with depth, a weight belt around your waist loosens unless it has a means of compensating for the suit compression. An elastic compensator is a desirable feature for a weight belt; you can select from a variety of designs.

Secure the weights on your weight belt so that they will not shift position. Pocket-type belts are good in this respect. When you thread separate weights onto a belt, secure the first and last weights with retainers, which are available as accessories.

The most important feature of any weighting system is the quick release. In the event of an emergency, you must discard weights quickly to establish positive buoyancy. No matter what type of system you choose, a reliable, easily located, and easily operated quick release is essential.

There are several types of weights. Large, curved hip weights help offset the buoyancy of cold-water exposure suits. Smaller, rectangular weights find widespread use because they are economical. Coated weights are attractive and practical. Manufacturers mold weights into various shapes and offer a heavy vinyl coating as an option. The coating reduces pollution from lead, improves appearance, makes the weights easier to see in the water, and reduces suit abrasion. Fabric mesh packets filled with lead shot are popular. You can get bulk lead shot for hollow fabric belts. Coated lead shot, although slightly more expensive, is better than uncoated shot. There are shot-filled tubular ankle weights, although some diving experts believe ankle weights are unnecessary.

An integrated weighting system eliminates the need for a weight belt by holding lead weight in the **backpack** that holds the scuba cylinder or in the buoyancy compensator. An integrated weighting system makes the scuba unit heavier, but it also allows better distribution of weight than a separate system can provide. Some divers consider an integrated weighting system advantageous because weights are less likely to shift, there is no need for a suit-compression compensator, and having the weight above your waist improves your trim in the water and reduces strain on your lower back. However, when you raise your center of gravity, you are more likely to lose your balance and fall when you are out of the water. You need strength, good balance, and caution to use an integrated weighting system. Integrated systems usually use lead shot, either in bulk or in pouches.

## Weighting System Care and Maintenance

Weighting systems do not require as much care and maintenance as other items of diving equipment. Do not soak or rinse raw lead after use because lead in the runoff pollutes the environment. If gray water seeps from your weight system, replace the lead with new, coated lead. (You can recycle old lead, so do not throw it away.) Pocket-type weighting systems allow you to remove the weights and rinse the remainder of the system.

Regularly inspect the functional aspects, such as the quick release and the compensator. If you use a belt, inspect the weight retainers to make sure they are not broken, and make sure the end of the belt is clean and neat for easy insertion into the buckle. If the end of your belt is frayed, trim and singe it. When you fix a frayed end, be careful that you do not cut or burn yourself.

## Weighting-System Selection

When selecting a weighting system, consider your physical characteristics, the amount of weight you need, and how frequently you will need to change the amount of weight you use.

If you have a large build, your waist is larger than your hips, and your exposure suit is thick, a weight belt may not work well—especially if you need more than 30 pounds (13.6 kilograms) of weight. In chapter 3 you will learn how to test your buoyancy to determine the amount of weight that you need. Consult with divers whose physical characteristics are similar to yours for advice about weighting systems. If you require more than 30 pounds (13.6 kilograms) of weight, you may need weights on a weight belt plus an integrated system. If you require only a small amount of weight, nearly any type of weight system is acceptable.

If the type of diving you do varies, the amount of weight you need also varies. If you dive in fresh water and in salt water, you need to adjust your weights. When you vary your exposure suit configuration, you also need to vary the amount of weight you wear. The more you need to change weights, the more you need a weighting system that allows changes to be made easily.

# BUOYANCY COMPENSATORS

A buoyancy compensator (BC) helps you control buoyancy. You can inflate your BC at the surface to increase buoyancy, deflate it to reduce buoyancy for descent, and add air to it to achieve neutral buoyancy underwater. Most BCs also contain a backpack to hold your scuba cylinder.

The three types of BCs are jacket-style, back-mounted, and front-mounted. Figure 2.19 shows examples of the types, and table 2.3 compares them. Most BCs used in diving today have a wraparound jacket design, which provides front and rear buoyancy. There

▶ Figure 2.19 Buoyancy compensators come in front-mounted (left), jacket (center), and back-mounted (right) styles.

are two basic jacket designs: One style has inflation tubes over the shoulders; a newer style has straps over the shoulders. The straps have convenient, adjustable releases.

Back-mounted BCs place buoyancy chambers behind you. These systems are useful for underwater modeling and for specialty diving activities. Models look better without bulky BCs covering them, and back-mounted units do not interfere with dry-suit valve operation as much as other types of BCs.

Front-mounted BCs fit around your neck and cover your chest area. This was the first type of BC, but few divers use front-mounted BCs today. Most divers today feel that BC jackets are superior to front-mounted ones. You can use a front-mounted BC for both skin diving and scuba diving. Jacket-style and back-mounted BCs are not suitable for skin diving.

In its simplest form, a BC is a bladder with attachments (see figure 2.20). The bladder may be coated material that constitutes the BC itself, or a separate bladder may be inside a fabric shell. The seams of a BC bladder are glued or electronically welded, depending on the type of material.

## Buoyancy Compensator Selection

When selecting a BC, consider your physical characteristics, where you plan to dive, and the type of diving you plan to do. Some BCs provide more buoyancy than others. A cold-water wet-suit diver needs more lift than a warm-water diver wearing a thin exposure suit, although a large amount of lift is not necessarily desirable.

### Table 2.3  Buoyancy Compensators

| Type | Location of buoyancy chamber | Advantages | Disadvantages |
|---|---|---|---|
| Jacket-style | Front and rear | Even lift; diver can remain upright | Not suitable for skin diving |
| Back-mounted | Rear | Does not interfere with dry-suit valve operation | Pushes diver forward; difficult for diver to remain upright |
| Front-mounted | Front | Suitable for skin diving; allows diver to remain upright | Need separate backpack for cylinders; requires disconnection of inflator hose before removal; does not provide as much lift as jacket |

If you are a large, strong individual, the size and bulk of a BC may not be of much concern, but if you are small, you may be wise to choose a small, compact BC. The length of the BC is important. A BC that extends downward too far makes donning and removing your weight belt difficult. If you are short-waisted, consider an integrated weighting system. The fit is important because a BC needs to support you in the water. The BC should fit snugly and not ride up on your body. Models that allow adjustment for a custom fit are desirable.

Another desirable feature is a single-bladder construction, which is less expensive and requires less maintenance than a separate bladder. Renting and using different types of BCs will aid you in making a selection. Talk to experienced divers and diving professionals, and observe BC preferences in the area where you dive.

Some BCs are equipped with a $CO_2$ detonator, an optional feature many diving professionals consider neither necessary nor desirable. The detonators can be unreliable, especially when used in salt water—they are troublesome to maintain and rust from the cartridges can damage your BC. If you choose to equip your BC with this option, take care of the mechanism and know how to operate it.

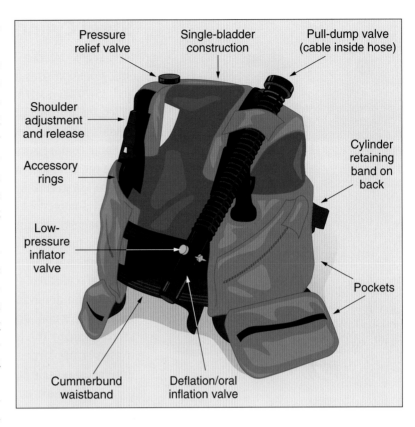

▶ Figure 2.20  Desirable BC features.

## Buoyancy Compensator Care and Maintenance

Your investment in a BC is large. But, like most diving equipment, your BC will provide years of service if you take care of it. You need to rinse your BC inside and out after use, especially after use in a swimming pool or in the ocean. Chlorine in pool water and salt crystals from seawater are harmful to your BC. Drain the water from your BC after use, fill it about a third full with fresh water, swish the water around, and then drain the bladder. Rinse the inflator assembly thoroughly, and leave the BC fully inflated until it dries. Inflation tests the airtight integrity of the bladder and valves. If the BC does not remain firm for at least an hour, take it to a professional repair facility. Anytime your BC fails to function properly, have it professionally repaired. It is hazardous to attempt BC repairs without special training, tools, and parts.

# SCUBA CYLINDERS

A scuba cylinder stores compressed air at high pressure. The container must be strong and free of corrosion. Scuba cylinders (also called tanks) are made of either aluminum or steel. Each type has advantages and disadvantages. Figure 2.21 shows examples of various steel and aluminum tanks.

▶ Figure 2.21 Scuba cylinders are made from steel or aluminum.

## Steel Cylinders

Steel scuba cylinders come in various sizes with various pressure ratings. Common sizes are 50, 71.2, and 94.6 cubic feet (1,416, 2,016, and 2,679 liters). The pressure to which the cylinders can be filled, called the working pressure, ranges from 1,800 to more than 4,000 pounds per square inch (psi), or 122 to 272 standard atmospheres.

Some compressors pump air only to 2,500 psi (170 atmospheres). When you cannot get air at a pressure higher than 2,500 psi (170 atmospheres), a steel tank may be more desirable than an aluminum tank. A steel 71.2-cubic-foot (2,016 liters) scuba tank filled to 2,250 psi (153 atmospheres) contains about 5 cubic feet (142 liters) more air than an 80-cubic-foot (2,265 liters) aluminum tank filled to the same pressure. The aluminum tank must be filled to 3,000 psi (204 atmospheres) to obtain 80 cubic feet (2,265 liters).

The main disadvantage of a steel cylinder is that it can rust, which can render a tank unsafe and unusable. Do not allow water inside a scuba cylinder. The high-pressure atmosphere has a large amount of oxygen to fuel corrosion. You can keep the inside of a steel scuba tank dry, but the outside is exposed to moisture. Galvanizing inhibits rust on the outside of steel tanks, but the inside may not be galvanized because galvanization affects air purity. Painting a galvanized surface may improve the appearance of a cylinder, but paint alone is an inadequate finish because cracks or chips in the paint allow moisture to reach the steel. The tank will begin to rust unless there is a galvanized coating beneath the paint.

Another disadvantage of a steel scuba tank is that it has a rounded bottom because of the manufacturing process. The tank cannot stand by itself unless you place a rubber or plastic boot, called a tank boot, on the end of the cylinder. The boot makes the base of the tank flat so it will stand. Some boots have flat sides to help keep a tank from rolling when you lay the cylinder on its side. Moisture and salt trapped between the tank boot and the cylinder can cause corrosion. Boots with internal ridges—the preferred type of boot—are self-draining.

## Aluminum Cylinders

Aluminum alloy cylinders also come in various sizes with various pressure ratings. Common sizes are 50, 63, and 80 cubic feet (1,416, 1,784, and 2,265 liters). The working pressure for aluminum cylinders is 3,000 psi (204 atmospheres).

Aluminum corrodes, but the oxide that forms arrests the corrosive process—a significant advantage over the corrosive process of rust in steel tanks. Rust is an accelerating process, but corrosion in an aluminum cylinder is a self-arresting process.

The bottom of an aluminum cylinder is flat. You do not need a tank boot on the cylinder to allow it to stand by itself, but many divers put boots on aluminum tanks to protect the tank and objects struck by the bottoms of the cylinders.

Aluminum cylinders also have drawbacks. Aluminum is softer than steel, so aluminum tanks can be dented and gouged more easily than steel tanks. Brass cylinder valves control the flow of air, and electrolytic action between the dissimilar metals of the cylinder and the valve can cause the valve to seize in the aluminum cylinder threads unless the valve is removed periodically and coated with a special compound. Valve seizing seldom is a problem with steel cylinders.

Aluminum cylinders do not need to be galvanized. You can paint them to improve appearance, but do not bake the paint finish. Temperatures hotter than 180 °F (82.2 °C) reduce the strength of an aluminum cylinder and can cause it to explode when filled. If you would like your cylinder painted, have it done by a professional tank-painting service.

## Cylinder Markings

Several rows of markings on the neck of a scuba cylinder provide useful information about the cylinder. You should be able to determine the meaning of several of the marks. Figure 2.22 shows an example of cylinder neck markings.

The first row of marks on U.S.-manufactured tanks discloses the government agency that sanctioned the manufacture of the tank, the type of metal from which the tank was made, and the working pressure. The first letters in the row identify the government agency, such as DOT (U.S. Department of Transportation), CTC/DOT (Canadian Transportation Commission and the U.S. Department of Transportation), or ICC (the former U.S. Interstate Commerce Commission). The next characters in the first row identify the type of metal from which the tank was made. The marks 3A and 3AA are designations for steel cylinders. The marks 3AL, E 6498, and SP6498 are designations for aluminum cylinders. The final figures in the first row—the important ones for you to remember—are numbers indicating the working pressure of the cylinder in pounds per square inch.

The second row of markings includes the serial number of the tank (which you should record for identification purposes) and letters or numbers identifying the manufacturer of the cylinder. The month and year of the tank's first pressure test is located somewhere below the second row. U.S. regulations require compressed gas cylinders to be pressure-tested before being put into service and every five years thereafter. Subsequent test dates can be stamped anywhere on the neck of the tank. A registered symbol between the month and year of a pressure test identifies the facility that did the testing.

When you take your scuba tank to an air station to have it filled, the facility examines the tank markings to determine whether the cylinder test date is current and the pressure to which the tank can be filled.

## Cylinder Selection

The main criteria for the selection of diving equipment—fit and comfort—apply to scuba tanks as well. A small person should use a small tank. Larger divers may require larger tanks because they have larger lungs and use more air.

The material from which a tank is made affects its capacity, size, and working pressure. Although steel is heavier than aluminum, aluminum tanks are larger and heavier than steel tanks with similar capacities. Because aluminum is not as strong as steel, the walls of an aluminum tank are thicker than the walls of a steel tank of approximately the same capacity. The higher the pressure rating, the greater the capacity of a tank of a given size. Modern high-pressure

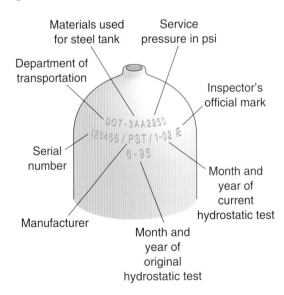

▶ Figure 2.22  Cylinder neck markings provide useful information.

steel scuba tanks are high-capacity cylinders, but they are quite heavy. Good sizes for small divers to consider for an initial scuba tank are 50 and 63 cubic feet (1,416 and 1,784 liters). Popular sizes for divers of average size are 71.2 and 80 cubic feet (2,016 and 2,265 liters).

Another important factor to consider when selecting a scuba tank is the buoyancy of the cylinder, which is determined by the volume and weight of the tank. Aluminum tanks are more buoyant than steel tanks. High-capacity tanks have a greater change in buoyancy than smaller cylinders as you use air from them. The change in buoyancy between a full and an empty tank can vary by more than eight pounds (3.6 kilograms; see table 2.4). Some tanks are negatively buoyant whether full or empty, but most tanks sink when full and float when empty. Buoyancy for tanks varies so much that you should select the tank most often used for diving in your area or try diving with several different tanks to determine which is easiest to manage.

Multiple-tank scuba units are for specialty applications. As a beginning diver, you do not need double or triple scuba tanks. A single tank is adequate for most diving activities.

## Cylinder Accessories

Fabric or plastic sleeves can help protect the exterior of your scuba cylinder. Some sleeves have places to attach items within easy reach. Tank bands vary. Some allow you to attach a small, backup scuba cylinder to your main cylinder. There are additional accessories to help you carry or transport your scuba cylinders. Tank boots are a desirable cylinder accessory.

## Cylinder Care and Maintenance

Scuba tanks are high-pressure vessels. They are strong, but you should handle them with care. Exterior damage can render your scuba tank useless. Avoid throwing scuba tanks or allowing them to roll about on the deck of a boat or in the trunk of your car. Secure

### Table 2.4 Cylinder Size, Working Pressure, and Buoyancy

| Capacity (ft³/L) | Working pressure (psi) | Buoyancy (lb) from full to empty |
|---|---|---|
| Aluminum 50/1,416 | 3,000 | −2.7 to +1.3 |
| Aluminum 63/1,784 | 3,000 | −2.3 to +2.7 |
| Steel 71.2/2,016 | 2,250 | −2.0 to +3.6 |
| Aluminum 80/2,265 | 3,000 | −2.0 to +4.4 |
| Steel 76/2,152 | 2,400 | −6.5 to −0.1 |
| Steel 80/2,265 | 3,500 | −7.4 to −1.0 |
| Steel 102/2,888 | 3,500 | −7.6 to +0.5 |

cylinders for transportation or storage. Unless you are holding a scuba cylinder, do not leave it standing in an upright position, especially at a dive site. But do store your scuba tanks in an upright position so that any moisture inside will settle to the bottom where inspectors can detect it with relative ease. Rinse the outside of your cylinder with clean, fresh water after use, and pay special attention to the tank-boot area of steel tanks.

Corrosion can ruin a cylinder rapidly, and pieces of corrosion can damage a tank valve or scuba regulator. One way to prevent moisture from entering a tank is to keep air in the tank. Water can get into an empty scuba cylinder while diving, so avoid using all the air in your tank. Moisture can enter an empty tank if you store it with the valve open. Store your scuba cylinder with a few hundred pounds (about 20 atmospheres) of pressure inside. A low pressure keeps moisture out but provides little oxygen to aid corrosion if there is moisture in the tank.

The filling process can force water into the tank. A water trap in an air compressor is supposed to remove moisture from air, but if the moisture-removal system does not function properly, water can be pumped into your tank along with air. The filling hose attachments for scuba tanks can get wet, and water inside the filling attachments can be forced into your cylinder. Using a high-quality air station is important.

The diving industry requires an annual visual inspection of scuba cylinders. The examination consists of an external inspection, the removal of the valve from a cylinder, an internal inspection using a special light, special electrical testing for aluminum cylinders, the replacement of the valve, and the attachment of a decal indicating the inspection date. Most air stations require a current visual-inspection sticker on a tank before they will fill it. When you handle your scuba tank, listen for sounds of anything moving inside the cylinder. If you hear anything, have the tank visually inspected.

U.S. government regulations specify that compressed gas cylinders must be pressure-tested every five years. Some countries require pressure testing every year or two. The test is hydrostatic because it takes place in water. An inspector fills a scuba tank with water and submerges it in a closed container that is completely filled with water. The inspector applies pressure to the scuba tank hydraulically, and the tank expands slightly from the pressure. The expansion displaces water from the container holding the scuba tank. The inspector measures the expansion and then releases the pressure. The tank must return to within 10 percent of its original volume within a specified period of time. If the tank is too brittle to expand and contract correctly, the inspector condemns it.

You may transport a scuba tank on an airplane only if the tank is completely empty and the valve is open—a situation that is not good for scuba tanks. Do not transport your cylinder by air. Diving destinations have tanks readily available, so there is no need to take a tank on a dive trip.

## CYLINDER VALVES

Cylinder valves control the flow of a liquid or gas. Four types of valves are available for scuba tanks: the simple valve, the reserve valve, the high-pressure valve, and the multiple-cylinder valve. Since multiple tanks are for advanced specialty diving activities, this section addresses only the simple, reserve, and high-pressure valves. Figure 2.23 shows examples of valves.

▶ Figure 2.23  K-valves (left) and J-valves (center) control the flow of air from the cylinder. DIN valves (right) withstand greater pressure than other types of valves.

**K-valve**—Simple type of cylinder valve that operates like a faucet.

**J-valve**—A reserve valve that restricts the flow of air at a specified tank pressure.

## The Simple Valve

A simple valve is an on-off valve that operates like a faucet. You turn the valve handle counter-clockwise to open it and clockwise to close it. The first catalog of diving equipment listed this type of valve as item K, and the valve has been identified as a **K-valve** ever since.

The **valve seat** is a soft-sealing surface. It is the portion of the valve that closes and stops the flow of air. You can damage the seat with excessive closing pressure.

Valves for scuba tanks have several features, one of which is a snorkel tube that extends from the bottom of the valve into the scuba cylinder. The valve snorkel prevents moisture or particles from entering the valve when you invert the tank. Another standard feature of tank valves is a thin, metal disk called a **burst disk.** If a tank is overfilled or the heat from a fire causes the tank pressure to increase to a hazardous level, the disk will burst and vent the tank to prevent an explosion. The disks corrode over time, and occasionally a burst disk ruptures. The failure makes a loud noise and the tank hisses loudly, but the situation is not dangerous, even if it occurs while diving, which is unlikely. If the burst disk in your tank valve ruptures, you need to have the valve serviced professionally. Manufacturers rate burst disks for various pressures, and the correct disk must be used. Keep the burst-disk pressure rating in mind if you want to change a valve from one scuba tank to another. A valve with a low-pressure burst disk will rupture if you use it on a tank with a higher pressure rating.

There are two types of outlets for scuba tank valves. The traditional outlet is nearly flush with the surface of the valve and surrounded by a soft, circular ring called an **O-ring.** The ring forms the high-pressure seal between the valve and the scuba regulator, so the ring must be clean and free of nicks or cuts. A newer type of threaded outlet with a recessed O-ring seal is a **DIN valve,** which withstands higher pressures than a traditional O-ring valve. Tank pressures in excess of 3,000 psi (204 atmospheres) require a DIN fitting.

## The Reserve Valve

A **J-valve** (the valve was listed as item J in the first equipment catalog) maintains a reserve of air to permit a normal ascent. A reserve valve was much more necessary years ago than it is today. Until the introduction of **submersible pressure gauges** (SPGs) for scuba tanks, it was difficult to estimate how much air remained in a cylinder. Divers ran out of air at depth unless they used a J-valve. All divers today use SPGs to monitor the amount of air in their tanks.

A J-valve is a spring-loaded reserve valve. Pressure in the tank holds the spring-loaded valve open so that air can flow through the valve until the tank pressure is insufficient to overcome the force of the reserve valve spring. At this point, a pressure of 300 to 600 psi (20 to 41 atmospheres), the spring begins to close the reserve valve and restricts the flow of air. The diver senses the increased breathing resistance and must open the spring-

loaded valve manually by turning the reserve lever on the valve. Activation of the lever removes the restriction on airflow (see figure 2.24).

The reserve lever on a J-valve creates problems. If the lever is in the incorrect position (down), the valve will not maintain a reserve. If you fail to put the reserve lever in the up position before a dive or if the lever is bumped during your dive, you might rely on a reserve of air that will not be available. During the filling process, the reserve lever of a J-valve must be in the reserve position (down). If the lever is in the up position when the operator applies high-pressure air to the tank valve, the seat of the reserve valve will be damaged. Because J-valves cost more than K-valves to purchase and service and because of the problems just mentioned, the J-valve's popularity has declined steadily over the years.

## Valve Care and Maintenance

Cylinder valves are made of soft metal and have thin areas, so physical abuse can ruin them. A protective cap is a desirable accessory for a tank valve. The cap helps prevent loss of the O-ring, helps keep dirt out of the valve, and helps prevent physical damage to the high-pressure sealing surface around the valve opening. Protection of the valve is one reason that you should secure scuba tanks when you store them and should not leave

▶ Figure 2.24   Tank valves.

them standing unattended. A tank's rolling about or falling over can damage the valve and render it inoperable.

When you open a tank valve, turn it slowly, open it all the way, and then close it one half turn. If something strikes the handle, a valve seat that is fully open will be damaged more than if it were closed slightly. When you close the valve, avoid excessive force, which shortens the life of the valve seat.

It is good to rinse your tank valve after use, but soaking the valve by inverting your scuba tank in a container of warm water is better than rinsing. Water remains in the valve opening after rinsing or soaking. Open the valve momentarily to blow the water from the opening. If you leave the water in the opening and have the tank filled before the water evaporates, moisture will be forced into the tank.

Have your tank valve serviced annually by a professional. Also have your valve professionally serviced anytime it fails to operate easily or when the burst disk needs to be replaced. Valves receive partial servicing (lubrication) during the annual visual inspection of your scuba tank. The large O-ring that seals the valve to the scuba tank can be replaced at the time of the visual inspection. But partial servicing of your valve during a tank inspection is not the annual servicing of the valve. In a complete valve servicing, a qualified repair technician completely disassembles the valve, cleans the parts, replaces various parts, reassembles the valve, and then tests the unit.

▶ Figure 2.25 Scuba regulator nomenclature: 1—first stage, 2—dust cover, 3—low-pressure hose, 4—low-pressure inflator hose, 5—console, 6—high-pressure hose, 7—primary second stage, 8—extra second stage.

# SCUBA REGULATORS

The function of a regulator is to reduce high-pressure air to a breathable level. Most scuba regulators use two **stages** of pressure reduction. The first stage of a regulator attaches to the valve of a scuba cylinder and reduces the high pressure to an intermediate pressure of about 140 psi (9.5 atmospheres). The first stage of the regulator connects via a hose to the second stage, which contains the mouthpiece. The second stage reduces the pressure from the intermediate level to the surrounding pressure. A scuba regulator is a demand system; it delivers air only when you demand it by inhaling, unlike a constant-delivery, free-flow system, which commercial divers use. Scuba regulators are highly reliable and have a fail-safe design that turns the demand system into a free-flow system in the event of a component failure. Figure 2.25 provides more information about scuba regulator terms.

## First Stages

The first stages for scuba regulators are either balanced or unbalanced. Changes in tank pressure affect the performance of a balanced first stage only slightly. With an unbalanced first stage, the performance of the regulator changes as tank pressure changes, so a balanced first stage is desirable.

The two main types of regulator first-stage valves are diaphragm and piston (see figure 2.26). A diaphragm first stage has a diaphragm that keeps water and dirt from the working parts inside. A bias spring combined with water pressure pushes the valve open. Tank pressure closes the valve when the first-stage pressure equals intermediate pressure plus water pressure. A diaphragm valve has more parts than a piston first stage, so it is more expensive to manufacture and service. The diaphragm valve's exclusion of water and dirt from the mechanics allows high performance for longer periods of time than a piston valve.

Piston first stages have an open, simple design with few moving parts. Water pressure in direct contact with the piston combines with the force of a bias spring to open the piston valve. Tank pressure causes the piston to move and the valve to close when the first-stage pressure equals intermediate pressure plus water pressure. Piston first stages are easier and less expensive to service than diaphragm first stages. But dirt, salt crystals, and mineral deposits that accumulate inside a piston regulator can affect its performance. Each type of first stage has advantages and disadvantages, so either type is acceptable. A diaphragm-piston regulator combines the diaphragm and piston concepts. The diaphragm excludes water and dirt and transfers pressure to a piston.

A first stage must have a means of attachment to the tank valve. A typical regulator has a yoke that surrounds the valve and mates the regulator to the tank valve. The regulator inlet, which has an inlet filter, secures to a tank with a yoke screw. Scuba regulators that operate at above-average pressures use a DIN fitting instead of a yoke screw. A DIN fitting screws directly into a DIN valve and does not have a yoke.

There are multiple openings, called **ports,** in first stages. One of the ports is for high-pressure air measurement with an SPG. The remaining ports are for low-pressure air. A regulator should have several low-pressure ports to supply air to the primary second stage, an alternate second stage, a BC inflator, and possibly a dry-suit inflator. The sizes of ports vary. The high-pressure port usually is larger than the low-pressure openings to prevent connection errors; a low-pressure hose inadvertently connected to the high-pressure port would rupture.

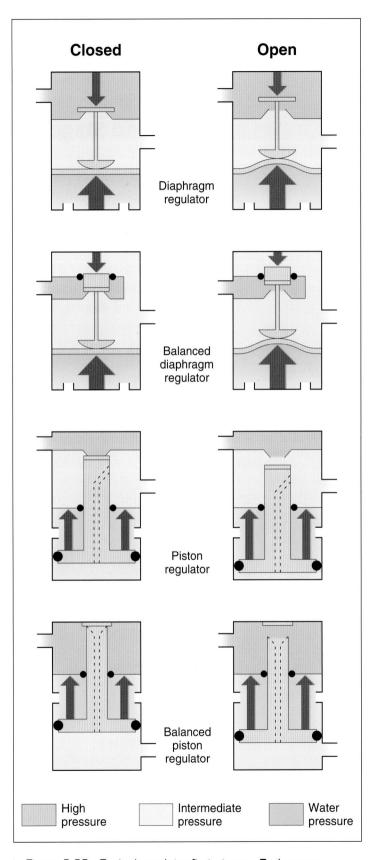

▶ Figure 2.26 Typical regulator first stages. Red arrows represent spring pressure. Black dots represent O-rings.

Some regulators feature environmental shielding by sealing special fluid inside a flexible chamber attached to the first stage. The sealed, flexible chamber transmits water pressure to the regulator, but no water, salt, or dirt can enter the first stage. Extremely cold water can cause an unshielded regulator to freeze, but the fluid in an environmental chamber does not freeze.

## Second Stages

The most common second stage is shaped like a cup lying on one side (see figure 2.27). Imagine a pliable diaphragm across the top of the cup, a mouthpiece attached to the bottom of the cup, and an exhaust valve attached to the lower side. A lever that activates a valve inside the container is in contact with a static diaphragm. An inhalation through the mouthpiece creates a partial vacuum inside the second stage. The pressure reduction pulls in the diaphragm, which moves the lever and opens the valve, allowing air to flow from the first stage of the regulator into the second stage. When you stop inhaling, the buildup of pressure returns the diaphragm and lever to their normal positions, closing the valve and stopping the flow of air. When you begin to exhale, increased pressure inside the second stage opens the exhaust valve, allowing air to escape.

The two types of scuba-regulator second-stage valves are the downstream valve and the pilot valve. In a downstream-valve regulator, a small bias spring holds a valve closed. Inhalation moves the diaphragm, which moves a lever. The lever movement overcomes the resistance of the bias spring and opens a valve, allowing intermediate-pressure air to enter the second stage. After inhalation, air flows until the diaphragm moves outward, allowing the bias spring to close the valve. Downstream second-stage valves are simple, inexpensive, and tolerate more sand and dirt than pilot valves do.

▶ Figure 2.27 Regulator operation.

| Static | Diver inhales | Diver exhales |

**Do not depress purge button when rinsing a regulator.**

**Have regulator serviced professionally every year.**

In a pilot-valve regulator, the movement of the diaphragm in the second stage opens a small valve that in turn opens a larger valve. When you stop inhaling from the regulator, the diaphragm returns to its normal position, and the valves close. A pilot valve delivers air up to four times more easily than a downstream valve. But pilot valves are more expensive to manufacture and service than downstream valves, and in shallow water you may experience the effect of shuddering air movement with a pilot-valve regulator.

All regulators have a purge button or area on the regulator that you depress to manually open the second-stage valve. Use the purge to test the regulator, expel water and debris from inside the second stage, and relieve the pressure in the regulator after you close the tank valve.

The location of the exhaust varies. The exhaust valve may be at the bottom, side, or front of the second stage. The position of the exhaust affects the bubble pattern and the clearing of the regulator when it has water inside and the mouthpiece is in your mouth. Some regulators direct exhaust bubbles by means of an exhaust tee. You will learn more about regulator positioning for clearing in chapter 3.

A regulator is either right-handed, left-handed, or bidirectional, referring to the direction from which the regulator hose must come when the regulator is in your mouth. For example, the hose must come from the right side when you are using a right-handed regulator. The hose may come from either side when using a bidirectional regulator. The directional configuration is important only for knowing how to orient the regulator when you place it in your mouth. Figure 2.28 shows the possible directional configurations.

Some second-stage casings feature strong, light, durable materials that do not bend or corrode as metal does. Several types and styles of mouthpieces are available. Use a soft, comfortable mouthpiece that does not cause jaw fatigue. A repair technician can replace mouthpieces quickly and easily.

## Regulator Accessories

A regulator hose is flexible but has rigid metal connectors crimped onto the ends. The points where the hose and the metal meet are stress points because the hose fibers strain against an unyielding surface. To prevent the breakdown of the hose fibers at the stress points, use hose protector sleeves. At a minimum, equip all regulator hoses with hose protectors at the first-stage end of each hose.

Padded regulator bags help protect your regulator during transportation or storage. The bag should be large enough to accommodate the regulator and all hoses without bending the hoses sharply.

Adapters allow you to use DIN-fitting regulators on standard cylinder valves. Use protective covers for the threads on DIN fittings.

Purge depressors are a built-in feature on some regulators and an accessory for regulators that do not have them. A purge depressor partially depresses the purge button to remove bias spring pressure from the second-stage valve when you are not using the regulator, thus extending the life of the valve seat.

▶ Figure 2.28  Scuba regulators have different configurations.

Colored second-stage covers allow you to color-coordinate your regulator with your other equipment. Other accessories include various mouthpieces and hose adapters, as previously mentioned.

# Regulator Selection

It takes effort to inhale and to exhale through a scuba regulator. Effort is needed to overcome resistance; good regulators have minimal breathing resistance. Compare the performance data for various regulators, and select one that lets you breathe easily over a wide range of tank pressures, which implies a balanced first stage.

Choose a widely used and easily serviced regulator. You should get a regulator that can be serviced by facilities anywhere you happen to be and that uses readily available parts.

The type of diving you do should affect your selection. If you plan to do most of your diving from shore, you should avoid a pilot-valve second stage, which is adversely affected by sand and dirt. Diaphragm first stages are a better choice if most of your diving is from shore.

If you do not have a scuba tank, consider purchasing the tank and regulator at the same time so that you can match the fittings of the regulator and the cylinder valve. If you will be diving in water that is near freezing, you should select an environmentally shielded regulator.

# Regulator Care and Maintenance

Your regulator is a precision instrument; it requires care and maintenance to ensure the best possible performance. Keep sand and dirt out of your regulator. Do not allow salt crystals to form inside. Soak your regulator in clean, fresh, warm water as soon as possible after diving in the ocean. You need to remove salt before it dries. If you cannot soak your regulator, at least rinse it. A combination of soaking and rinsing is best. Follow these rules when rinsing or soaking a regulator:

- *Keep the inside of the first stage dry.* The purpose of the dust cover on the first stage is to keep out water and dust. Develop the habit of replacing the dust cover and securing it in place with the yoke screw anytime you do not have the regulator attached to a tank. Make certain the dust cover is in place before you rinse or soak a regulator.

- *Allow low-pressure water to flow gently through the second stage and also into the openings on the first stage.* High-pressure water can force dirt and grit into crevices, where it causes damage. Gentle pressure washes the dirt away.

- *Do not press the purge button when you rinse the second stage unless the regulator is pressurized.* If you do not pressurize the regulator and you press the purge button while water is inside the second stage, you open the second-stage valve and allow water to flow through the hose into the first stage.

When the regulator has dried thoroughly, lay it flat for storage. For prolonged storage, place the regulator in a plastic bag to help protect it against the harmful effects of smog. Do not bend the hoses sharply because bending damages hose fibers. Replace hoses that are cut, bulging, or leaking.

You can avoid most problems with your regulator by having it serviced annually. Have your regulator serviced even if it seems to be functioning properly. Failure to invest in regular service can affect your safety and shorten the life of your regulator.

# ALTERNATE AIR SOURCES

Several equipment options can help if you run out of air underwater (although running out of air is due only to sheer negligence). Your best option is an alternate air source (AAS), which is a source of compressed air other than your primary scuba regulator. An AAS is valuable if your primary source of air begins free-flowing or leaking during a dive; you can switch to the AAS and make a normal ascent. The two primary types of AAS are extra second stages and backup scuba units. An extra second stage allows two divers to share air without passing a single mouthpiece back and forth. Backup scuba units are fully redundant scuba systems that provide an independent source of air in an emergency. You are not dependent on a buddy to provide air when you are equipped with a backup system. Extra second stages are less expensive than backup scuba units but do not provide the benefits of an independent scuba system.

## Extra Second Stages

There are two types of extra second stages: an extra second stage for your regulator and a BC low-pressure inflator that has an integrated regulator second stage (see figure 2.29). An extra second stage, or **octopus,** should meet the following criteria:

- The first stage of the regulator should be capable of meeting the airflow demands of two second stages.
- The hose on the extra second stage should be several inches longer than the primary second stage hose.
- The extra second stage should attach to your chest area in such a way that your buddy can remove it quickly and easily. Do not allow the extra second stage to dangle.
- The attachment device should cover the mouthpiece opening of the extra second stage to prevent the regulator from free-flowing and to keep dirt and debris from getting inside.
- The extra second stage should be brightly colored for easy identification.

There are two ways to integrate a regulator second stage into a BC low-pressure inflator. It can be built-in, or quick-release hose fittings on the regulator second stage can allow it to be connected in series in the low-pressure hose leading to the inflator assembly. Both types of extra second stages have advantages and disadvantages. An integrated second

▶ Figure 2.29  A primary second stage (top), an extra second stage (center), and an integrated second stage (bottom).

Pony tank

Spare Air unit

▶ Figure 2.30 A pony tank and a Spare Air unit.

stage requires one less hose on your regulator because a single hose provides air for both the extra second stage and the BC inflator. When you must share air and you have an integrated second stage, you must breathe from the integrated second stage because the hose is too short for your buddy to use. With an extra second stage, you or your buddy can use either air source. Extra second stages integrated into the BC inflator may leak air. To stop a leak, you must disconnect the low-pressure air, thereby losing the functions of the low-pressure inflator and the extra second stage.

## Backup Scuba Units

There are two types of backup scuba units: a **pony tank** is a small (about 13- to 20-cubic-foot, or 368- to 566-liter) scuba cylinder with a separate, standard regulator. You clamp a pony tank to the side of your main scuba cylinder. A **Spare Air™ unit** is a smaller (2- to 4-cubic-foot or 57- to 113-liter) scuba cylinder with a special regulator integrated directly into the valve. A pony tank provides an adequate supply of air for many situations, but a Spare Air unit provides only enough air to permit an ascent from shallow depths. On the other hand, a Spare Air unit is small and light, whereas a pony tank is bulky and heavy (see figure 2.30).

## Alternate Air Source Care and Maintenance

AAS equipment should receive the same care and maintenance as your primary scuba equipment. Some divers attempt to save money by having only their primary scuba equipment serviced annually. This is false economy. AAS equipment needs servicing just as much as primary scuba equipment does.

# INSTRUMENTATION

You move in three dimensions in water the way a pilot does in air. Instruments are important safety requirements for flying. A pilot needs information about altitude, direction, time, and amount of fuel remaining. Similarly, you need information about depth, direction, time, and amount of air remaining. The minimum instrumentation you need is a depth gauge, an underwater timer, a submersible pressure gauge (SPG), and a compass. You may also find it helpful to have a dive computer.

## Depth Gauges

To tell how deep you have descended, you can use one of four types of depth gauges: a **capillary gauge, Bourdon tube,** diaphragm gauge, or electronic gauge. Manufacturers calibrate depth gauges in seawater. The gauges do not indicate the correct depth in fresh water, but they indicate the equivalent seawater depth if you use them starting at sea level in fresh water or if they adjust for altitude pressure changes. The reading of gauges

### Caution:

*Do not attempt to lubricate or service scuba equipment. Improper servicing can cause equipment failure.*

in fresh water is acceptable because tables for time limits at various depths are based on sea-level depths. Table 2.5 compares the four types of depth gauges.

A capillary depth gauge is a simple instrument. It is a hollow, air-filled, transparent plastic tube sealed at one end and placed around a circular dial. The open end of the tube aligns with zero on the gauge dial. A capillary gauge uses the principle of **Boyle's law.** Water pressure compresses the air inside the tube during descent. The position of the air-water interface inside the tube relative to markings on the dial indicates the depth. At two atmospheres of pressure, the air column in the tube compresses to one half its original length.

A Bourdon tube is a thin metal tube formed into a spiral. The tube may be open to the water or closed and placed inside a housing filled with oil. Oil-filled Bourdon gauges are more popular than open-tube gauges. Pressure on an open-tube gauge begins to straighten the tube and increases the coil diameter. The straightening produces a spiral movement of the tube, which is linked mechanically to a needle to indicate the depth. Water pressure causes the coil of a closed-tube gauge to decrease in diameter. The coil movement, linked mechanically to a needle, indicates the amount of pressure exerted on the gauge.

The accurate but expensive diaphragm gauge uses elaborate mechanics to connect a thin, movable diaphragm to an indicating needle. Electronic depth gauges, also accurate and expensive, use a pressure sensor (transducer), electrical circuitry, a display, and a battery to indicate depth.

A maximum-depth indicator is a desirable feature for all depth gauges. As you will learn in chapter 6, you must know the depth of a dive for planning purposes. A digital depth gauge retains the maximum depth you attain. The instrument displays the information until the next dive or for 12 or more hours following a dive, then resets automatically. Many modern depth gauges with needle displays have a thin indicating wire that the gauge needle pushes along the dial face. When the needle retreats, the wire remains at the highest point reached on the dial. You can reset the indicating wire by turning a screw on the dial face. You must remember to reset the maximum-depth indicator before each dive when you use a needle-display gauge.

## Table 2.5   Depth Gauges

| Type | Accuracy | Advantages | Disadvantages |
|---|---|---|---|
| Capillary | Accurate only to depth of about 40 ft (12 m) | Rugged, inexpensive | Can clog with debris or air bubbles |
| Bourdon tube | Reading accurate within 1% to 2% | Accurate | Can be damaged by reduced pressure at altitude |
| Diaphragm | Very accurate | Can adjust zero setting for pressure changes at altitude | Expensive |
| Electronic | Reading accurate within 6 in. (15 cm) | Gauge may zero itself to compensate for changes in atmospheric pressure | Must have sufficient battery power; expensive |

## Underwater Timers

You can use either an automatic or a manual underwater timer to keep track of time during a dive. Either type may indicate time with hands on a dial or with a digital display. Pressure activates automatic timers, which start timing at a depth of about three to five feet (1 to 1.5 meters) and stop timing when the depth is less than that. Automatic timers are better than watches because you do not have to remember to start or stop the timing of your dive, although you have to reset some watch-type automatic timers before a dive. Waterproof watches that you can use as underwater timers usually feature a rotating **bezel,** a movable ring that you can set to indicate elapsed time. Digital watches are accurate, but their small buttons can make them difficult to operate. The best timers are electronic automatic timers, which can keep track of how long you dive, how long you are at the surface between dives, and how many dives you make. You do not have to remember to reset or activate anything when you use an automatic electronic timer.

## Dive Compasses

Rarely can you see more than 100 feet (30 meters) underwater, so a navigational aid can be valuable. If you dive without a directional reference, you can end a dive a long distance from your planned exit point. A dive compass can help you avoid long surface swims or swims through thick surface canopies of water plants. You can use a compass to navigate beneath the canopies, where there are passages through the plants. A compass also is useful for relocating a precise area underwater and as a surface navigation device if fog arises.

Two types of compasses are card types and needle types. Both are mechanical. Magnetic deposits in the earth near the North Pole attract either a magnetized disk or a magnetized needle to provide a directional reference. The compass card or needle can deviate from its correct alignment if it is in close proximity to ferrous metal or a source of magnetic forces such as a magnet or electrical motor.

**lubber line**—A reference line on a compass that indicates the direction of travel.

Diving compasses have liquid inside to dampen the swinging of the needle or disk. To be useful for diving, a compass needs a reference line, called a **lubber line,** to indicate the direction of travel relative to the needle reference. A rotating bezel with bracketing index marks that allows you to mark the needle position for a specific direction is also desirable.

You view some compasses from the top and some from the side. Side-reading compasses display the course in a window on the side of the instrument. You look across a top-reading compass. You will learn how to read and use a compass in chapter 3.

## Submersible Pressure Gauges

An SPG (shown with the console in figure 2.31) is analogous to the gas gauge of a car and is just as essential. It measures scuba cylinder pressure. You can use either a mechanical or an electronic SPG. A mechanical SPG is a high-pressure Bourdon tube. High-pressure air from the cylinder passes through the regulator first stage, through a high-pressure hose, and into a Bourdon tube inside a housing at the end of the high-pressure hose. The pressure tries to straighten the spiral tube, which moves a needle on a dial to indicate the tank pressure. Physical shock can damage a mechanical SPG.

An electronic SPG has a pressure sensor (transducer), circuitry, a battery, and a display. It is a form of a high-pressure depth gauge. The display may be digital or graphic.

Either a symbol or numbers (in pounds per square inch or atmospheres) indicate the amount of air in your tank. If the electronics get wet or if the battery dies, an electronic SPG will not function.

You should retain at least 300 to 500 psi (20 to 34 atmospheres) in your tank at the end of a dive. Mechanical SPGs typically have a red area on the dial for the last 500 psi (34 atmospheres). When you dive, you should monitor your air supply and make sure that you surface before the needle gets into the red area. Electronic depth gauges usually warn of a low supply of air by blinking the display.

An SPG has a **blowout plug** to relieve pressure in the housing in the event of a high-pressure leak. Identify the blowout plug on your SPG, and do not place anything over the plug that will prevent it from functioning. If the plug cannot come out to release high pressure inside the SPG housing, the face of the instrument can explode.

▶ Figure 2.31 This console includes an SPG, a dive computer, and a compass. The SPG is always the first instrument located at the end of the hose.

## Instrument Consoles

You can purchase diving instruments individually or in combination. It is convenient to combine several gauges into a display unit called a **console.** An instrument console attaches to the high-pressure hose coming from your regulator first stage. When your instruments are in a console, your arms are free of gauges and dive preparations are quicker.

The two types of instrument consoles are mechanical and electronic. A mechanical console contains an SPG and a depth gauge. Some also contain an underwater timer, a compass, and a thermometer. The instruments usually feature luminous displays, which are easy to read in low light.

With an electronic console, all instrument information except direction is in a single display. (There is only one electronic underwater compass, and it is a separate instrument.) If one gauge fails in a mechanical console, the remainder can still function; but when an electronic console fails, all the information provided by the unit is lost. Electronic displays are difficult to read in the dark unless they feature some type of illumination. Figure 2.31 shows various diving instruments mounted in a console.

▶ Figure 2.32 Dive computer and SPG.

## Dive Computers

A dive computer is an electronic instrument with a pressure sensor, electronic circuitry, a battery, and a display (see figure 2.32). A programmed computer inside the instrument uses pressure and time information to calculate continuously the uptake of nitrogen by various compartments that have different half-times. A half-time is the length of time required for a mathematical model (compartment) to increase or decrease its gas absorption or elimination by one-half. Six half-times completely saturates or desaturates a compartment. When the absorption by any one of a computer's compartments reaches a predetermined level, the device indicates that you are approaching the time limit after which a direct ascent to the surface will no longer be possible. Upon reaching that time limit, the computer indicates a minimum depth—a **ceiling**—that you cannot exceed during ascent. You risk decompression sickness unless you wait until the computer indicates that sufficient **outgassing** has occurred to allow you to continue your ascent. A dive computer provides extremely accurate time and depth information. Other common features are a low-battery warning, a rapid-ascent warning, a dive log mode, a dive-planning mode, and information about flying after diving. Additional information about dive computers is in chapter 6.

**ceiling**—The minimum depth that a diver cannot rise above without the risk of DCS.

## Instrument Care and Maintenance

Physical abuse can damage instruments, so protect your instruments from shock. Secure your console instead of allowing it to swing freely.

Heat or prolonged exposure to hot sunlight can cause oil in a liquid-filled gauge to expand and break the seal on the housing encasing the instrument. If you break the seal, you must have the gauge repaired. Hot water in a whirlpool or a shower can cause an underwater timer to expand, break a seal, and allow water inside. Do not subject diving instruments to high temperatures.

Have air leaks in SPGs repaired at the first opportunity. Have your depth gauge tested for accuracy from time to time by a professional repair facility or compare your gauge with an extremely accurate instrument, such as a digital depth gauge. Follow all the manufacturer's recommendations. Reduced pressure at elevations above sea level can damage some instruments. Unless an instrument is designed for use at altitude, pack it in an airtight container for flying. Soak and rinse instruments with clean, fresh water after use. Give special attention to pressure-sensing areas to prevent them from becoming clogged with dirt or salt crystals.

▶ Figure 2.33   Dive knife and accessories.

# DIVE KNIVES AND ACCESSORIES

This section addresses some additional required and optional equipment. Figure 2.33 shows examples of a dive knife and other dive accessories.

## Dive Knives

Do not consider a knife optional equipment. Lines and cords in water can cause entanglements, so it is important to have a knife to cut yourself or your buddy free if necessary.

The many designs of dive knives include large knives and small knives. A small knife positioned where you can reach it easily is better than a large knife that you cannot reach. The most important feature of a dive knife is an effective cutting edge. Good blades are corrosion resistant and hold a sharp edge; serrated blades cut lines more effectively than straight blades.

Some knives are multipurpose tools designed for prying, digging, pounding, and measuring in addition to cutting. If you have a multipurpose knife as a diving tool, it is a good idea to also have a small, separate dive knife.

A dive knife comes with a sheath, which has some means to lock the knife in place. Make sure the sheath lock is reliable to prevent losing a knife. You can attach a small knife to your leg, your arm, your console, or your BC. Wear a large knife on the inside of your leg and secure it with straps that stretch to compensate for exposure suit compression.

To prevent corrosion, rinse your dive knife after diving. Inspect the edge for sharpness, remove any rust, and coat the blade with grease.

## Accessories

You are likely to need several small, but important, accessory items, including a gear bag, a dive flag and float, dive lights, dive kits, signaling devices, and a diver's first aid kit.

### Gear Bags

You need so much equipment for diving that you also need a means to carry it. Gear bags can be simple or complex. They can feature multiple compartments, padding, novel ways for carrying or moving, sealed fabric edges, and various fabrics. The best type for you depends on your needs and how much you want to invest. Be sure to get a bag with webbing handles that completely surround the bag to provide full, durable support. No matter what your budget, you need a gear bag for your equipment.

### Dive Flags and Floats

In many areas, local law requires use of a dive flag while diving. In the United States, the traditional dive flag is a red flag with a white diagonal stripe (see figure 2.34). The flag usually is vinyl, mounted on a fiberglass staff, and

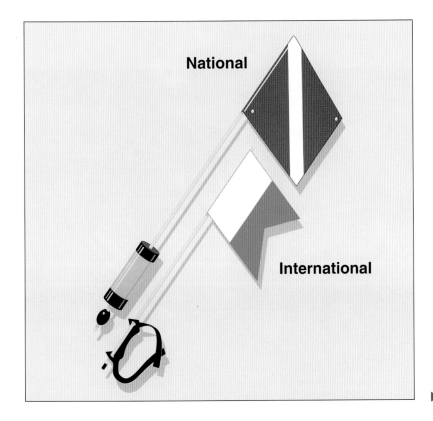

▶ Figure 2.34  Dive flags.

stiffened with a wire so that it stands out from the staff at all times. In addition to the red-and-white flag, use the international Alpha flag, a swallow-tailed blue-and-white flag, when diving from a vessel. The Alpha flag is a general dive flag in countries other than the United States.

Unless you are diving from a boat, you need a float to support your dive flag. Some flagstaffs have a float attached. There are attachments to secure a dive flag to an inner tube and flag-holding canvas coverings for inner tubes.

### Dive Lights

A dive light can increase your diving enjoyment. Light levels are low underwater, and a light restores color to objects at depth and allows you to peer under ledges and into holes. You can see and enjoy much more when you use a dive light.

The many types of dive lights available include large, powerful, rechargeable lights and small lights that use disposable batteries. Consider a small dive light initially. A large light is for night diving, which is an advanced activity. A small light is easy to carry and is useful both for day dives and as a backup light for night diving. Many of today's small dive lights are bright and compact (see figure 2.35). Maintain your dive light according to the manufacturer's instructions.

### Dive Kits

Two equipment kits are recommended: a dive kit and a save-a-dive kit. The dive kit contains items you use frequently for diving. The save-a-dive kit contains items you may need to salvage a dive. The items that you might include in each are listed on page 47. Because the items in your dive kit are small and get wet, you may wish to keep them in a container by themselves so you can find them easily.

Once you get yourself and your equipment to a dive site, you don't want a minor equipment problem to keep you from diving. A broken strap, a missing O-ring, or a torn mouthpiece are examples of problems that can stop you from diving unless you have spare parts. Keep save-a-dive items in a waterproof box. Do not mix wet items from your dive kit with dry items in your save-a-dive kit.

▶ Figure 2.35 A dive light can improve underwater viewing.

# Equipment Kits

## Dive Kit

- ☐ Defogging solution for your mask
- ☐ Wet-suit shampoo
- ☐ Sunscreen
- ☐ Lip balm
- ☐ Seasickness medication

## Save-a-Dive Kit

- ☐ Mask strap
- ☐ Fin strap
- ☐ Snorkel keeper
- ☐ Tank valve O-rings
- ☐ Quick-release buckle
- ☐ Weight keepers
- ☐ Regulator mouthpiece
- ☐ Crescent wrench
- ☐ Screwdrivers
- ☐ Cable ties
- ☐ Twine
- ☐ Duct tape

**Dive Slates**     You need to record and refer to information around and in the water when you dive. Plastic slates are better than paper because water does not affect the slates. You can write on dive slates with a standard lead pencil or a grease pen. Dive slates include checklist slates, reference slates, logbook information transfer slates, and writing slates. All types have value. You probably will have several slates when you become an experienced diver. Initially, you should have an equipment checklist, a dive-planning slate, and an underwater writing slate.

**Signaling Devices**     Long-range signaling devices are invaluable if you become adrift, especially in areas where currents are strong. You should have a whistle readily available. A whistle is more effective than shouting to gain attention. The sound from a whistle does not require much energy to produce, and it travels well over water.

A small diver's air horn, powered by low-pressure air, works with as little as 50 psi (3.4 atmospheres) of tank pressure and produces a sound that can be heard up to a mile away. The device is so loud that you must point the horn away from yourself to avoid hearing damage.

You can get long, bright, thin, inflatable safety tubes that fit easily into your BC pocket. Inflate a safety tube at the surface to make yourself easier to spot in the water.

You can use a signal mirror to flash sunlight long distances over water. Other forms of signaling devices for divers are flashlights, strobe lights, and waterproof flares. The greater the chance of being caught in a current, the greater your need for signaling devices.

**Diver's First Aid Kit**     Diving takes place in remote areas, and because it is a physical activity, someone may be injured. It is a good idea to be prepared for an emergency. You should have a first aid kit at the dive site. The items helpful in a standard first aid kit are listed on page 48. Pack the items in a waterproof container to make a diver's first aid kit. Chapter 3 addresses the use of the first aid items.

## First Aid Kit

- ☐ Rescue breathing mask
- ☐ Seasickness medication
- ☐ Isopropyl alcohol
- ☐ Hydrogen peroxide
- ☐ White vinegar
- ☐ Baking soda
- ☐ Analgesic and antiseptic ointment
- ☐ Hot packs
- ☐ Eyewash
- ☐ Tweezers
- ☐ Bandage scissors
- ☐ Penlight
- ☐ Coins for emergency phone calls
- ☐ Emergency contact information for diving accidents
- ☐ Diving first aid book
- ☐ Space blanket
- ☐ Pen and small notebook

## Scuba Wise

*If you want to avoid diving accidents, use familiar, correctly fitting, well-maintained dive equipment the way that it is intended. As I look back over my 37 years of dive experience, I can recall many instances when divers got into trouble because they did not follow the essential equipment safety procedures summarized in the previous sentence. Diving allows us to explore an alien environment using life-support equipment. Modern scuba equipment is manufactured well, but you must take care of it and have it serviced periodically to keep it functioning properly. Would you even consider going into outer space with life-support equipment that was not carefully maintained and serviced? We go into inner space when we dive. Our life-support equipment is just as vital to us as an astronaut's.*

*Equipment problems while diving do arise, but equipment failure is rarely the cause of an accident. Problems cause anxiety and stress. A diver experiencing stress from environmental factors and fear may panic from the added stress that a minor equipment problem might pose. Learning to manage yourself and your equipment helps you reduce stress, avoid panic, and prevent an accident. One of the most important rules of accident-free diving is to have good, familiar equipment that is in good condition and to use it properly.*

## SPECIALIZED EQUIPMENT

Other specialized equipment for scuba diving includes nitrox (oxygen-enriched air) equipment, mixed-gas equipment, and rebreathers. This equipment permits divers with specialty training to obtain longer dive times. The risks associated with the use of specialized equipment make training and adherence to the rules pertaining to its use absolutely essential.

# SUMMARY

Diving involves a great deal of equipment. You are beginning to understand the equipment you need to have, how to select it, and how to care for it. You will learn more about equipment from your instructor, from retailers, from magazines, and from other divers. Get good equipment, and give it the best care possible. Diving is not enjoyable if you have constant equipment problems.

# Diving Skills 3

## Dive In and Discover

By the end of this chapter, you will be able to do the following:

- Prepare, assemble, don, adjust, inspect, and disassemble your equipment for skin and scuba diving.

- Demonstrate 16 skin and scuba diving hand signals.

- Explain how to test and control buoyancy.

- Explain how to clear water from a mask, a snorkel, and a scuba regulator.

- Explain how to descend, swim with fins, and ascend when skin and scuba diving.

- Explain how to handle, remove, and replace skin and scuba diving equipment.

- Describe various entry and exit techniques for skin and scuba diving.

- Explain how to use dive flags.

- Explain the buddy system and lost buddy procedures.

- Explain how to use a compass for underwater navigation.

- Explain how to prevent and manage seasickness, dizziness, stress and panic, overexertion, coughing, cramps, entanglement, loss of buoyancy control, loss of air supply, and dive emergencies.

- Explain how to rescue a diver who is not breathing and the first aid procedures for an injured scuba diver.

- Define the following terms: *buddy system, flutter kick, scissors kick, modified frog kick, dolphin kick, surf, neutral buoyancy, diver's push-ups, open-valve ascent, reference descent, nonreference descent, buddy line, compass heading, compass course, reciprocal compass course, flaring,* and *buddy breathing.*

Diving requires many skills, and you must repeat them correctly until you can execute them automatically. When you have mastered the skills of diving, your enjoyment can begin because you will be able to devote more attention to things of interest. The basic skills of skin diving and scuba diving are introduced in this chapter.

You will learn most of the diving skills in controlled conditions; when you have developed the basic skills, you will apply them in open water. (Open water is any body of water representative of dive sites in the local area.) When you can demonstrate the skills of diving in open water, you are ready to receive your diving certification.

# PREPARING TO SKIN DIVE

Skin diving is breath-hold diving underwater. This section discusses the skills of skin diving, many of which apply to scuba diving.

## Preparing Equipment

Be ready to start your lesson when you come to your first water session. Prepare your mask, snorkel, and fins in advance. Clean your mask lens thoroughly so it will not fog (a description of the cleaning procedure is in chapter 2). Adjust the mask strap so it is snug but not tight. Attach the snorkel to the mask strap on the left side, and adjust the snorkel so it is comfortable in your mouth. If your fins have heel straps, adjust them so they are snug but not tight. Complete all adjustments before your first water session.

Inspect your skin diving vest or BC by inflating it, making sure it does not leak, and then deflating it. Put it on, reinflate it, and adjust the strap or straps so it will stay in position in the water. You may need to use a strap that runs between your legs and attaches to the front and back of the flotation device to keep it from riding up when you are in the water. Inspect the $CO_2$ cartridge and detonator if the flotation device has them.

Your instructor will suggest an initial amount of weight for your weight belt. Adjust the length of the belt at the buckle end so the excess strap at the opposite end does not exceed six inches (15 centimeters). Allow two inches (five centimeters) for each two-slot weight that you thread onto the belt. Distribute the weight on both sides of the belt so that you will be balanced in the water. Lock the weights in place with weight retainers.

Mark your personal equipment with your initials so that you can identify it. You can use special paint or markers (available at dive stores) or colored tape. Pack your equipment in a gear bag. Place the items you will don last, such as your fins, on the bottom. Place the items you will don first, such as your exposure suit, on the top.

## Donning and Inspecting Equipment

Don your exposure suit pants or legs first, then your boots, and then the top part of your suit. Donning a snug-fitting wet suit is easier if you wet the inside of your suit with water to which you have added some mild shampoo or if you wear a spandex suit as an undergarment. Place the ends of the legs of your wet suit over the tops of your boots so that water can drain from your suit when you exit from a dive. If the boots are outside the legs of your wet suit, water from the suit will balloon your boots when you get out of the water. If you become warm while donning the exposure suit, cool yourself before proceeding with your preparations. For open-water diving, don a cold-water hood before donning your wet-suit jacket so that the skirt of the hood is underneath your jacket. Figures 3.1 through 3.5 illustrate the process of putting on equipment.

▶ Figure 3.1 Getting into your exposure suit.

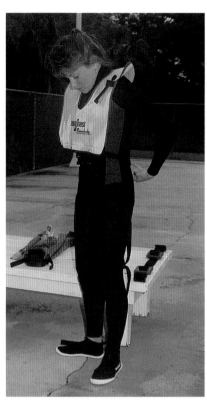

▶ Figure 3.2 Strapping on your skin diving vest.

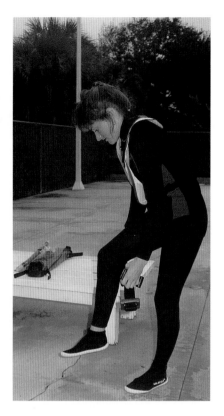

▶ Figure 3.3 Donning your weights.

▶ Figure 3.4 Putting on your fins.

▶ Figure 3.5 Adjusting your mask.

After you put on your exposure suit, it is a good idea to clean and defog your dive mask and set it aside until you are ready to don it (see description of cleaning procedure in chapter 2). Leave about one-half inch (1.27 centimeters) of water inside the mask so it will not dry before you put it on, and place it where it will not get damaged.

Don your skin diving vest or BC next. Place a skin diving vest over your head, and then secure the straps. Inflate the vest fully to make sure it will not be too tight. The straps should be as snug as possible without being uncomfortable or interfering with breathing.

Don your weight belt after the skin diving vest so it will be clear of the vest straps. Grasp the free end of the weight belt (the end without the buckle) in your right hand and the buckle end in your left hand. Pick up the belt, step through it, pull it into position across your back, bend forward so that gravity supports the weight of the belt, then tighten the belt and secure the quick release. Always wear the weight belt with a right-hand release, even if you are left-handed, so that a rescuer will know how to release your belt in an emergency. If you always hold the free end of the belt in your right hand when donning it, you always will have a right-hand quick release.

Don the remainder of your skin diving equipment—mask, snorkel, and fins—at the water's edge or, if it is calm, in the water. Place the mask on your forehead and pull the mask strap over the back of your head using both hands to position the strap. Position the mask on your face, clearing any hair from beneath the sealing edge of the mask. Reposition the mask strap so it lies flat. If the mask has a split strap, position the split above and below the crown of your head. Don your snorkel when you don your mask. Check the adjustment of the snorkel when your mask is in place.

Stabilize yourself when putting on fins so that you don't lose your balance and fall. Hold onto your buddy (see "The Buddy System" section) or an object for support, or sit at the water's edge. Hold one side of a fin, bend one leg into a figure-four position, push the fin onto your foot, and pull the strap or heel pocket into place. Repeat the process for the other fin. Avoid walking with fins. If you must walk a few steps while wearing fins,

# The Buddy System

A qualified partner is appropriate for activities that involve risk, such as swimming, rock climbing, and skin and scuba diving. Safety is the primary purpose of the buddy system, but increased enjoyment makes having a dive buddy a benefit. The following list describes the duties and responsibilities of a good dive buddy:

- Helps to plan the dive in advance and upon arrival at the dive site
- Reviews signals and emergency procedures
- Assists with the donning of the scuba unit
- Inspects equipment
- Maintains contact while diving and follows reunion procedures if separation occurs
- Provides reminders concerning depth, direction, time, air pressure, and ascent rate
- Points out items of interest
- Identifies problems of which you are unaware, such as an air leak
- Provides reassurance and assistance as needed
- Summons additional assistance as needed
- Provides first aid as needed
- Assists with exits and the removal of the scuba unit

## Character Development

Skin diving and scuba diving are always done with a partner, or buddy. This relationship provides the opportunity for divers to put into practice the four character development values of caring, honesty, respect, and responsibility, which are expressed by the above logo. Buddy divers must rely on each other to check equipment thoroughly prior to diving, watch for dangers during the dive, and help out in case of emergencies. An honest appraisal of the condition of the equipment and your own diving abilities is crucial during these activities. You also need to be responsible for each other during the dive and to care enough to do what's needed to keep each other safe. Finally, you must show respect by protecting each other and the aquatic environment from harm.

shuffle your feet and walk backward. If you try to walk forward, you can lose your balance or damage your fins.

After you have donned your equipment, inspect it for completeness, correct positioning, and adjustment. When you are satisfied with your equipment, inspect your buddy's while he or she inspects yours. Inspect from head to toe. You may be able to see something that your buddy could not see, or vice versa. Develop the habit of inspecting each other's equipment before every dive.

# SKIN DIVING SKILLS

There are three categories of diving skills: skin diving skills, scuba diving skills, and problem management skills. This section introduces skin diving skills.

## Skin Diving Hand Signals

You cannot talk with a snorkel in your mouth and your face in the water, so you use hand signals as a primary means of communication. You need to learn and use the standard hand signals shown in figure 3.6. You will learn additional hand signals for scuba diving. Display hand signals clearly and deliberately when you send them, and acknowledge all hand signals you receive.

## Using a Skin Diving Vest

You inflated and deflated your skin diving vest as part of your diving preparations. You also need to learn how to deflate and inflate the vest in the water. To deflate the vest, position your body so the exhaust port is the highest point. Hold the deflation valve open while you sink lower in the water. The water pressure helps force the air from the vest. You may have to hold the collar of the vest down with one hand to remove the air from that area. When you have vented all the air from the vest, close the valve. Get your buddy to confirm that all the air is out of your vest.

1. Descend      2. Ascend      3. Stop

4. Okay a.      4. Okay b.      4. Okay c.

5. Something's not right      6. Emergency

▶ Figure 3.6   Skin diving hand signals.

It is easier to inflate the vest in the water with your head underwater instead of above water. Take a breath of air, duck your face beneath the surface, insert the oral inflator into your mouth, open the valve, exhale into the vest, and close the valve. Repeat this process until you have the desired buoyancy.

If your vest has a $CO_2$ detonator and you choose to use it to quickly inflate the vest, grasp the activation cord and pull it downward firmly, and then pull it from side to side. If your vest has $CO_2$ inside, avoid inhaling the gas, which is harmful to your lungs in strong concentrations. If you use a $CO_2$ cartridge to inflate your vest, remove and replace the cartridge at the first opportunity. It is unwise to leave an expended cartridge in the vest because rust particles inside the cartridge can damage your vest.

## Testing Buoyancy

Your buoyancy should be neutral at the surface. If you are too buoyant, you will have to struggle to descend and remain underwater. If you are not buoyant enough, you will tire quickly at the surface and sink while swimming underwater. It is important to adjust your buoyancy correctly.

If you are wearing an exposure suit, you need weights to offset the buoyancy of the suit. With all equipment in place, position yourself in chest-deep water. Exhaust all air from your skin diving vest. Take a full breath, hold it, lift your feet from the bottom, and remain motionless while you slowly count to 10. If you sink, remove some weight and try again. If you exhale half of your fully inflated lungs and still can't submerge, you need to add weight until you can. When your weighting is correct, you remain at the surface while holding a full breath and sink when exhaling. Adjust your weighting until you achieve **neutral buoyancy,** which means that you neither sink nor float when holding an average breath. Have your buddy watch while you make the final test. With your lungs about half full of air, the top of your head should remain even with the surface of the water when you are motionless in a vertical position.

## Clearing the Mask

Above the surface, water inside a mask will run out if you pull the bottom of the mask away from your face. Water inside a mask underwater also flows out the bottom of the mask if you displace the water with air. It is easy to put air inside the mask: Just exhale lightly through your nose. A long, light exhalation is better than a short, forceful one because a strong exhalation blows air past the seal of the mask and does not displace water effectively.

To clear a mask that has a purge valve, seal the mask against your face, tilt your head downward to make the purge the lowest point in the mask, and exhale through your nose until the mask is clear of water. To clear a mask without a purge, hold the top of the mask against your forehead, take a breath, and start exhaling slowly (see figure 3.7). When the level of the water is below your eyes, tilt your head back while continuing to exhale and the remainder of the water will flow out the bottom of the mask. You must be exhaling when you tilt your head back or water will run up your nose. Bubbles from the bottom of the mask indicate when you have cleared all the water from your mask. It may sound as though it takes a long time and a lot of air to clear a mask, but with practice you will be able to flood and clear your mask several times after a single inhalation. Clearing requires only a few seconds.

## Using the Snorkel

Stand in the water and lean forward with the snorkel in your mouth. Place your face in the water and inhale gently. If you inhale forcefully at first, you might inhale water. When you are sure the tube is clear, you may breathe more forcefully through your snorkel. When you descend beneath the surface, the snorkel tube can fill with water. Self-draining snorkels drain nearly all the water from the tube when you surface.

▶ Figure 3.7   Mask clearing.

If your snorkel is not the self-draining type, you have to blast the water from the tube with a strong, sharp exhalation. To do this, blow hard into the snorkel to force the water out. Inhale cautiously after exhaling. If a little water remains in the tube, you can breathe past it if you inhale gently. After you fill your lungs again, expel the remaining water with another forceful exhalation.

If you have a simple snorkel without valves, you can clear the tube while ascending by using the displacement method. Begin by looking up to invert the snorkel; then exhale a small amount of air into the tube. As you ascend, the air expands according to Boyle's law and displaces the water in the tube, which will be clear of water when you reach the surface. The tube is inverted at this point, however, so when you turn it to the upright position, water will flow into the tube unless you exhale while rolling your head forward at the surface. Continuous exhalation prevents water from entering the tube. When you use the displacement method, which is easier than the blast method, you can take a breath the moment you reach the surface. Figure 3.8 shows the displacement method.

Learn to keep the snorkel in your mouth when you are in the water. Avoid the temptation to remove the mouthpiece and shake the water from your snorkel. You do not have to remove the mouthpiece when you can clear your snorkel proficiently. When your hands are occupied, you will not be able to remove and replace the snorkel to clear it.

▶ Figure 3.8  Displacement method of clearing a snorkel.

## Using Fins

Fins provide large surfaces that the strong muscles of your legs can push against the water for propulsion. The blades of the fins need to push the water the way a broom sweeps a floor. A broom cannot sweep if you move it up and down, and your fins will not provide propulsion if you move them lengthwise in the water. You must kick them back and forth in wide, sweeping kicks. Small fins allow short, quick kicks, but larger fins require wider, slower kicks. Moving efficiently, not speedily, is your objective when wearing fins.

The most common fin kick is the **flutter kick,** which is an up-and-down kick that you can do facing down, up, or to the side. Your fins need to be under water to provide propulsion. It is easier to keep your fins submerged at the surface when you are on your back or on your side instead of your stomach. Move your legs up and down from the hip while bending your knees only slightly. Extend your legs almost fully throughout each stroke, and use wide, slow kicks. Keep your hands at your sides or extend them in front. Do not use your hands and arms to swim. Figure 3.9 shows the flutter kick.

The **scissors kick,** shown in figure 3.10, is a resting kick. The scissors kick is similar to a flutter kick, but requires less energy. While lying on your side, slowly extend one leg backward while you extend the other leg forward, and then pull your legs together quickly. Hold a streamlined position with your toes pointed while you glide through the water. When you come to a stop, repeat the stroke. Extend your legs almost fully throughout the stroke.

A **modified frog kick** is useful because it uses different muscles than the flutter and scissors kicks. Changing kicks is helpful if you become tired or develop leg cramps. The modified frog kick is different from a swimmer's frog kick. Assume a facedown position with your fins perpendicular to the bottom, rotate your ankles so that the tips of the fins point outward, slide the fins tip-first in an outward direction, then pull the bottoms of the fins together quickly in a wide, sweeping arc. Extend your legs almost fully throughout the stroke, and then hold the final position with your feet together, your toes pointed, and glide (see figure 3.11). When you come to a stop, repeat the stroke.

The **dolphin kick** is also useful for a change of pace or if you lose a fin. Hold both feet together continuously. Exert force against the water with a wavelike up-and-down motion of your body. To begin, straighten your body, extend your feet together, bend your shoulders forward, and pull your feet slightly backward. Next, lift your shoulders, thrust forward forcefully with your hips, and then pull down with your fins. When you see this kick demonstrated, you will be able to learn it by imitation. If you lose a fin, you can use the dolphin kick to propel yourself. Cross your legs and put the leg without a fin behind the one that has a fin. Figure 3.12 shows the dolphin kick.

## Surface Dives

You need to be able to dive down to see the beautiful world beneath the surface. The initial dive beneath the surface of the water is a surface dive. The principle of a surface dive is simple: You raise part of your body above the water and point yourself straight down; the part of your weight above the water drives you downward. Once you are submerged, you start swimming to continue your descent.

There are three types of surface dives: pike, tuck, and feet-first (see figure 3.13). You do the pike dive while moving forward at the surface. Bend forward at the waist to make your trunk vertical in the water. Next, quickly lift your legs out of the water to a vertical position. The more of your legs you can lift out of the water, the farther your surface dive will push you under the water. For shallow dives, you can do the pike dive by lifting only one leg.

When you have learned the pike dive, you are ready for the tuck dive, which is similar. Do the tuck dive from a stationary position. Begin in an upright position in the water, pull your knees to your chest, and sweep backward with your arms to roll yourself forward in the water. When you are inverted, extend yourself fully into a vertical position. The procedure is a coordinated movement that you must do quickly to get your legs above water. After you extend your legs, the remainder of the dive is the same as the pike dive.

Use a feet-first dive in areas where surface plant growth is dense because you are less likely to get entangled. Begin in a stationary, upright position, and use a strong scissors kick to propel yourself up and out of the water as far as possible. Pull your arms downward to your sides for added lift. When you reach the highest point, point your toes downward, and hold your arms to your sides. The weight of your body will push you below the surface. When your downward momentum ends, do a tuck dive to invert yourself, then continue your descent.

▶ Figure 3.9  Flutter kick.

▶ Figure 3.10  Scissors kick.

▶ Figure 3.11  Modified frog kick.

▶ Figure 3.12  Dolphin kick.

▶ Figure 3.13  Surface dives.

**Pike**

**Tuck**

**Feet-first**

# Descents, Underwater Swimming, and Ascents

To prepare to descend, vent all air from your flotation device. Use an ear clearing maneuver (described in chapter 5) at the surface so that it will be easy to equalize pressure in your ears while you descend. Hyperventilate three times, inhale as fully as possible, and don't exhale until you return to the surface.

Initiate your descent with a good surface dive. Equalize the pressure in your ears and mask every couple of feet during your descent. Use wide, slow, powerful kicks to propel yourself to your desired depth, then relax as much as possible.

Swimming underwater sounds simple, but some people have trouble controlling direction. Your head is your rudder. Pull your head backward while swimming facedown to go up. Bend your head forward to go down. Bend your trunk to the left or right to turn. With practice, you can go in any direction you choose without using your hands.

Follow these four rules for ascents (figure 3.14 shows a skin diver ascending):

1. Reach up; extend one arm over your head for protection.

2. Look up to avoid obstructions and determine when the surface is near.

3. Come up slowly. A slow ascent is better than a rapid ascent because swimming rapidly uses more oxygen.

4. Revolve once or twice during your ascent to check your surroundings.

Alternate breath-hold dives with your buddy. One diver should remain at the surface, watching, while the other diver is underwater. Make sure your buddy knows where you are at all times.

# Handling Equipment

Occasionally you may need to remove, adjust, and replace skin diving equipment while you are in the water. You should be able to handle your equipment easily with training and practice.

To remove, adjust, and replace your mask, begin by inflating your skin diving vest. Because you will make the adjustment above water, use buoyancy to reduce the effort. After you make the adjustment, replace your mask using the procedure for donning the mask described earlier in this chapter.

You may need to adjust a fin strap or remove sand or gravel from your fins while diving. The fins are easier to remove, adjust, and replace than the mask is. You do not need as much buoyancy to work with your fins because you can look into the water and make the adjustment underwater. In fact, too much air in your skin diving vest can be a nuisance. Keep your face in the water, breathe through your snorkel, and work with one fin at a time.

You may need to tighten, adjust, or replace your weight belt. The weights may slip or the belt may fall off. To tighten or replace your weight belt, you need to get the belt across the small of your back while you are in a facedown position breathing through your snorkel. If you try to replace or tighten the belt in an upright position, you will have a constant fight with gravity. When you are in the correct, facedown position, gravity becomes your ally while you secure the buckle. To get the belt into position across your back begin in an upright position, holding the free end of the weight belt against the outside of your right thigh. Lean back into a horizontal, faceup position momentarily, then roll to your left to a facedown position while continuing to hold the free end of the belt against your right thigh. At this point, the belt will be draped across the backs of your thighs. Clear your snorkel so that you can breathe. While holding the free end of the belt in your right hand, reach down with your left hand, grab the buckle end, and pull the belt into position across your back.

▶ Figure 3.14   Extend your arm for protection during a skin diving ascent.

## Removing Equipment

Your equipment helps you adapt to the underwater environment. Develop the habit of keeping it in place while in the water. You may need to defog your mask or make an adjustment, but other than that you should wear your equipment continuously. Avoid the tendency to prop your mask on your forehead when you are at the surface. Mask propping is a sign of distress and a good way to lose your mask and snorkel. If you must remove your mask while in the water, pull it down around your neck where it will be secure.

Bottom conditions at the dive site determine whether you should remove your fins when leaving the water. In some areas you can remove your fins in waist-deep water and wade out of the water. In other areas you need to wear your fins until you are clear of the water. There are several ways to remove fins. When you prepare to climb a boat ladder, hold the ladder continuously while crossing your legs in a figure-four position to remove each fin. If the boat has a platform at the rear, swim onto the swim step and remove your fins in a kneeling position. When you remove fins in waist-deep water or on land, use your buddy for support. On steep beaches you may choose to crawl from the water. Your buddy can remove your fins while you are on your hands and knees. Your buddy then crawls ahead of you, and you remove your buddy's fins. When you stand up, you exchange fins.

Weight belt removal also varies. When you can walk or climb out of the water, wear your belt. When you remove a weight belt, lower it gently instead of dropping it. You can cause damage or injury if you develop the habit of dropping your weight belt. If you must pull yourself onto a dock or into a small boat, remove your belt first and hand it up.

Keep your skin diving vest in place until you are clear of the water. Remove your skin diving vest, then your wet suit. Remove your wet suit by turning it inside out. Be sure to remove your boots before your wet suit pants. You will need assistance from your buddy to remove a pullover jacket or a jumpsuit.

# PREPARING TO SCUBA DIVE

Nearly all of the skills of skin diving are used in scuba diving, but you need to learn many additional skills for scuba diving. This section introduces the preparatory skills of scuba diving; the next section covers basic and post-dive skills. The more familiar you become with the skills by studying them, the better you will be able to perform them. It is important to learn skills correctly from the outset to develop good habits for diving safety.

## Packing Equipment

It is inconvenient to get ready to dive and discover that something is missing or not right. You should take steps to prevent equipment inconveniences. Begin by using a checklist when you pack your diving equipment to be sure you have everything you need (see the diving equipment checklist in the appendix). After taking inventory, inspect your equipment as you pack it. If you have not used your equipment for a while, assemble it and test it first. Make sure everything works properly.

▶ Figure 3.15 The proper way to carry equipment.

Pack your equipment in your gear bag except for your weight belt, tank, and BC. When you have to carry your equipment, put your BC on your tank, carry the tank on your back, your gear bag in one hand, and your weight belt in the other hand (see figure 3.15). Equipment-carrying devices can reduce the work of moving your diving equipment.

## Assembling Equipment

Today's backpacks are part of the BC and have one or more bands to secure the scuba cylinder. Many of the bands are made of webbing, which stretches when wet. Soak a fabric tank band in water for a couple of minutes before securing it around a scuba tank. The soaking softens the webbing and allows it to stretch when you tighten the band. A dry fabric belt may allow the tank to slip when the band gets wet and stretches. A tank that slips from a pack can be a hazard.

Orient your backpack with the opening of the tank valve facing the backpack. Stand the tank up with the valve handle facing to your right. Slide the tank band over the tank with the tank between you and the pack. Tighten the band so the valve opening points directly toward the pack.

---

The height of the tank band on the tank varies with the type of backpack. Generally, the top of the pack is even with the base of the tank valve. After you attach the pack and before you attach the regulator, don the scuba tank and check the height adjustment by slowly tilting your head backward. If your head hits the tank valve, the tank is too high in the pack. Reach over your shoulder for the tank valve. If you cannot touch it, the tank is too low in the pack. Adjust the height as needed. When you become familiar with the correct height adjustment, you will not need to test it before completing the assembly of the scuba unit, but you should check it before entering the water.

Tighten the band as much as possible before securing it, and test the tightness by grasping the tank valve with one hand and the top of the pack with the other hand. Try to move the pack up and down on the tank. If there is movement, the band needs to be tighter.

Attach the regulator assembly to the scuba tank. The tank valve should have a valve protector or a piece of tape over the valve opening. Remove the cover or tape (but do not litter—put the tape in a trash container or in your gear bag). Make sure that the O-ring remains in place and is free of debris. Loosen the regulator yoke screw, and remove the dust cover. If your regulator second stages have purge depressors, release the purges. Expel any water or dirt from the valve by opening the tank valve slightly and momentarily before you attach the regulator to the tank.

Your regulator has several hoses. Orient the hose to your primary second stage toward the same side of the tank as the handle of the tank valve so that the hose will come over your right shoulder. When you orient the hose this way, the other hoses are properly oriented automatically as long as they are untangled and can hang freely.

Carefully seat the inlet opening of the regulator on the tank valve outlet, and then turn the yoke screw or DIN fitting until it is snug but not tight. Tighten the fittings using only your fingers and thumb. See figure 3.16 for an example of regulator attachment.

Attach the various regulator hoses to the scuba unit. It is easier to attach the low-pressure hose to the BC before you pressurize the hose. Attach your instrument console to the BC, but do not attach your extra second stage yet.

Turn on the air. Hold the SPG with the front facing away from you and others so it will not cause an injury if it fails when pressurized. The SPG blowout plug should prevent an explosion from occurring, but holding the gauge is a good precaution. Open the tank valve slowly in a counterclockwise direction. Open the valve all the way; then close it one quarter turn. You should feel the hoses stiffen under pressure. Listen for leaks in the system. If the regulator free-flows, cover the mouthpiece opening with your thumb to stop the flow. If air leaks from the tank valve seal, turn the air off, remove the regulator, and inspect the seal. You may have to replace the O-ring. Solve all air leakage problems before you use the scuba unit.

▶ Figure 3.16 Your regulator and hoses should look like this if attached correctly to the cylinder.

Testing the unit is the final step. Use your SPG to make sure the tank is full. Reset instruments in your console as needed. While looking at the SPG, depress the regulator purges momentarily to test the second stages and clear them of any debris; then breathe deeply through each second stage several times. The tank pressure reading should remain constant while you breathe from the regulator. If the pressure reading drops when you inhale, you have not opened the tank valve sufficiently. Do not open the valve partially to check the pressure of the tank. When you have finished testing the regulators, attach the extra second stage to the BC. Depress the low-pressure inflation valve on the BC for one or two seconds to make sure the valve functions correctly. When you have completed the assembly and testing of the unit, lay it on its side with the regulator and instruments on top.

Equipment assembly procedures are the same for both new and experienced divers. Always assemble and test your scuba equipment before you suit up. Practice will help you recall the assembly procedures.

# Donning and Inspecting Equipment

With skin diving equipment, you don the weight belt after the skin diving vest, but with a jacket-type BC, you should don the weight belt before the scuba unit.

A good way to don a scuba unit out of the water is for your buddy to hold the system and help you into it. Once your arms are through the shoulder straps, bend forward and balance the unit on your back while you secure the waistband. Place the regulator hoses over your shoulders while you fasten the waistband so the hoses are not trapped beneath the waistband. Some dive boats have vertical tank racks on seats to allow you to sit while donning the system. Do not sit on the deck or ground to don a scuba tank, however, because the tanks of other scuba divers can strike you in the head.

Some divers prefer to don the scuba unit in the water—a good practice if you dive from a small boat or have a minor back problem. Put the scuba unit into the water first. To don a jacket BC unit in the water the way you would don a coat, inflate it fully, sit on it, put your arms through the arm holes, and slide off and into the unit. Or you may put your scuba unit on over your head. Maneuver the tank in front of you with the valve facing you and the backpack facing up. Place the regulator in your mouth and keep the primary second stage hose between your arms. (If you place your right arm inside the loop of the hose, it will wrap around your arm when you try to lift the tank over your head.) Place your forearms completely through the armholes just past your elbows, and begin to lift the scuba unit over your head. Rather than lifting the unit, push yourself down in the water and duck beneath the scuba unit. Lower the tank into position on your back. Use your left hand to pull your snorkel clear of your BC as the tank lowers into position. When the tank is in place, lean forward and secure the waistband.

When you have donned your scuba equipment and the remainder of your diving equipment, inspect all your equipment to make sure it is positioned, adjusted, and functioning correctly. Your buddy should do likewise. Then inspect each other's equipment.

Do a head-to-toe buddy check. Specific checks for each equipment item are listed in the "Head-to-Toe Buddy Check" section on page 65.

Equipment inspections are important. Solving problems is easier before you enter the water than afterward. It does not take much time to inspect each other's equipment, but the practice can save a lot of time later. Make predive inspections a habit.

## Head-to-Toe Buddy Check

☐ Mask—In place, flush on face, no hair under skirt, not fogged

☐ Snorkel—Attached to left side of mask

☐ Scuba cylinder—Valve open all but a quarter turn, valve facing user's right side, height OK, snug in pack

☐ SPG—Full pressure, not damaged or leaking

☐ Scuba regulator—Primary and alternate air sources function OK, both buddies know the placement of the alternate air systems, regulator hoses oriented properly and free for use

☐ Buoyancy compensator—Inflates and deflates properly, $CO_2$ detonator (if present) OK

☐ Weighting system—In place, proper amount of weight, right-hand quick release accessible, weights clear to drop, both buddies familiar with weight release system

☐ Exposure suit—Properly positioned and zipped

☐ Dive knife—Attached properly, easy to access, secured

☐ Fins—Securely strapped or worn

☐ Instruments—Start watch, dive timer, or dive computer

*YMCA Character Development*

# BASIC SCUBA DIVING SKILLS

To be a scuba diver and enjoy diving with minimum risk of injury, you need to learn the proper procedures for entering and exiting the water, controlling your buoyancy, descending and ascending, monitoring your instruments, and coordinating with a buddy. This section provides a helpful introduction to these skills, but you must learn them by doing. You will learn the skills in pool-like conditions and then apply them in open water.

## Entry Techniques

The four basic types of water entries for divers are wading, seated, feet-first, and back-roll. You need to learn when to use which type and the procedures for each. The objective of any entry is to get into the water as easily as possible without injuring yourself or losing any equipment. After you enter the water and are under control, switch from your regulator to your snorkel if you are going to swim or remain at the surface.

You can make open-water entries from the shore or from a boat. You can wade in from the shore, or you can enter from an artificial structure such as a dock, pier, or jetty. The conditions vary greatly, and so do the entry techniques. There may be **surf.** Bottom conditions can range from smooth and soft to rough and firm. The bottom may slope gradually or steeply, and there may be holes and drop-offs. There may be plants, animals, and rocks in the entry area. A good entry technique for one location is inappropriate for another. It takes experience and knowledge of the area to determine an effective entry procedure.

Some general techniques are good to keep in mind when making wading entries at an open-water site. A wading entry sounds simple, but keep in mind that diving equipment affects your center of gravity, your mobility, and your peripheral vision. You must walk backward when wearing fins.

If there is little or no surf, you can wade in, don your fins, and begin your dive. Breathe through your regulator and have your BC inflated partially. Shuffle your feet to detect holes and rocks and to chase away bottom-dwelling creatures. When the water reaches your thighs, lie down in the water and start swimming (see figure 3.17). In some areas with muddy bottoms, do not wade because you can sink deeply into the mud and lose a fin when you try to extract your foot. When the bottom is firm and the water is calm, you can wade into the water without your fins and don them in the water. It is helpful to have information about the bottom conditions of a dive site.

In most areas where there is surf, don your fins before you enter the water, and do not remove them until you are clear of the water after the dive. Time your entry to coincide with small waves (see the discussion of waves and surf in chapter 7). Keep all equipment in place, and breathe through your regulator. Deflate your BC because you need to duck beneath breaking waves when they are higher than your waist. If you inflate your BC, you will be unable to duck beneath the waves, and a large wave could lift and toss you. Hold your mask with one hand at all times; spread your fingers and curl them over the top of the mask so you can see. Keep your knees bent and shuffle sideways into the waves to minimize your profile to the moving water. Stop moving just before a wave hits you, allow the wave to pass, and then resume your shuffling until the water is deep enough to swim. Allow incoming waves to pass over you, and move through the surf zone quickly.

From a commercial dive boat, you can enter the water from the side or from a water-level platform at the back of the boat. Have all equipment in place, breathe from your regulator, and hold your mask securely. Have any specialty items, such as a camera, handed to you after you are in the water, or retrieve them from an equipment line. When entering from the side of a boat, note the direction of boat movement. Wind will cause an anchored boat to swing from side to side. If you enter the water on the side of the boat when the boat is moving in that direction, the boat may pass over you after you enter.

You can do a controlled, seated entry from a dock, swimming platform on a boat, or any surface where you can sit close to the water, whether the water is only a few feet deep or too deep for standing. With all equipment in place, turn and place both hands on one side of your body on the surface on which you are seated, lift yourself slightly, move your body out over the water, and lower yourself into the water. A controlled, seated entry is a simple and easy entry (see figure 3.18).

Use feet-first entries when the distance to the water is too high for a seated entry, such as when entering from a commercial charter boat. There are two types of feet-first entries: giant stride and feet-together.

▶ Figure 3.17  Wading in.

Use the giant-stride entry, shown in figure 3.19, when the distance to the water is about three to five feet (1 to 1.5 meters) and you desire to remain at the surface during the entry. Stand at the entry point with your equipment in place and your BC partially inflated. Observe the point of entry and make sure the area is clear. Hold your mask firmly with one hand, spreading your fingers so you can see. Look straight ahead while stepping out with one leg. The entry is a step, not a hop or a jump. If you step out as far as you can, your trailing leg follows automatically. Keep one leg extended forward and the other leg extended backward until you hit the water; then pull your legs together quickly to stop your downward momentum. As soon as you stabilize at the surface, turn and signal that you are OK, and then move away from the entry point so that the next diver can enter.

Use the feet-together entry to avoid discomfort from the impact when the distance to the water is too high for a giant-stride entry. The procedures are the same as for the giant-stride entry, except that after you step out from the entry point, you bring your legs together before you hit the water (see figure 3.20). A feet-together entry submerges you. After you bob back to the surface and stabilize, signal the next diver and clear the entry area.

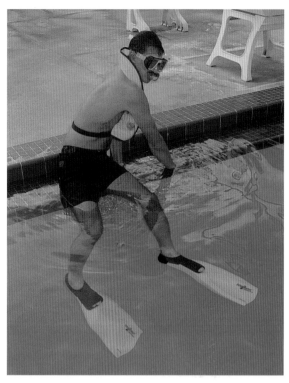

▶ Figure 3.18 Entry from a seated position.

▶ Figure 3.19 Giant-stride entry.

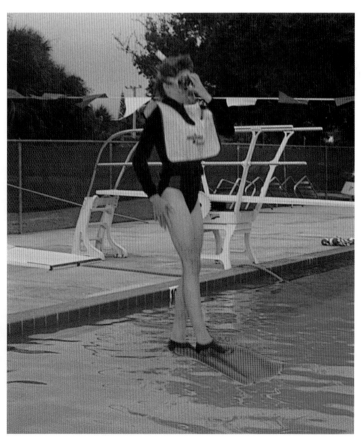

▶ Figure 3.20 Feet-together entry.

A seated back-roll entry can be done from either a seated or squatting position. Use the seated back-roll entry from a low, unstable platform, such as a small boat. Use a back-roll entry when the distance to the water is too high for a seated entry and the platform is too unstable for you to stand. To do a seated back-roll, sit with all equipment in place and your back to the water. Move your bottom to the very edge of the surface on which you are sitting. Have someone make sure the entry area is clear. Hold your mask with one hand and your mask strap with the other hand. If you do not hold the mask strap, the force of the water may wash it up over your head and your mask may fall off. Lean backward to begin the entry. Hold your knees to your chest as you roll backward; if you don't, you may clip your heels on the edge on which you were seated (see figure 3.21). You are likely to do a backward, disorienting somersault in the water with this entry. You can reorient yourself when you bob back to the surface.

A squatting back-roll is used when there is no suitable surface on which to sit. The thin side of a small, rocking boat is a good example of an unsuitable seat. For a squatting back-roll entry, prepare yourself while sitting on an adequate seat immediately adjacent to the entry area. Make sure the entry area is clear, then stand partially, turn your back to the entry area, and literally sit down into the water. Pull your knees to your chest as you enter so that you do not catch your heels (see figure 3.22).

## Surface Snorkeling With Scuba Equipment

You should use your snorkel for surface swimming to conserve the air in your scuba tank. When snorkeling while wearing scuba equipment, inflate your BC partially. Excessive air in your BC combined with the weight of your scuba tank can cause you to roll sideways when swimming facedown. It is better to swim on your back or side; these positions allow wider kicks than swimming facedown, and the tank weight is not a factor.

▶ Figure 3.21   This diver should have held his knees to his chest to avoid clipping his heels as he executed the seated back-roll entry.

▶ Figure 3.22   Squatting back-roll entry.

If you swim on your back, you can breathe without the snorkel. Swim beside—not behind or in front of—your buddy. Move slowly and steadily, pacing yourself. If you feel short of breath after snorkeling, rest before beginning your descent.

## Recovering and Clearing the Regulator

When you are in the water wearing scuba equipment and have removed your regulator second stage from your mouth, such as when snorkeling or talking at the surface, you need to recover it from behind your right shoulder (where it falls naturally). The second stage will have water inside, and you must clear the water before you breathe. If you start with the regulator in your mouth, you need to place the regulator in the water. The task is more difficult than it sounds because if you place the second stage in the water with the mouthpiece facing up, the regulator free-flows. Place the second stage in the water with the mouthpiece facing downward to prevent free-flow.

There are two ways to recover the regulator second stage from behind your shoulder. The most popular technique is the sweep method. Lean to the right side so gravity swings the second stage away from you. Reach back with your right hand until you touch the bottom of your scuba tank, and then extend your arm and sweep it forward in a large arc. The hose will lie across your arm, where you can retrieve the second stage easily.

The second method of recovering the second stage is the over-the-shoulder reach. Reach back toward your regulator first stage with your right hand while lifting the bottom of your scuba tank with your left hand. Grasp the second stage hose where it attaches to the first stage and follow it down to the second-stage end. Some divers find this recovery method difficult or impossible.

Clearing the regulator can be as simple as exhaling into it. As long as the exhaust valve is at the lowest point, the water inside the second stage will be displaced. If the exhaust valve is not at the lowest point when you exhale, only part of the water may be exhausted, and you may inspire some water when you inhale. To avoid choking on inhaled water, find out where the exhaust valve is on your regulator, be sure to make it the lowest point when you clear your regulator, and inhale cautiously after clearing the regulator.

Another method to clear a regulator second stage—the purge method—uses low-pressure air to clear the water from the chamber. If you insert the mouthpiece into your mouth and depress the purge, you may blow water down your throat. There are two ways to prevent this. One way is to depress the purge lightly as you place the bubbling regulator in your mouth, and use back pressure from your lungs to keep water out of your mouth and throat. The other method is to place the regulator into your mouth, block the opening

## The Three Most Important Scuba Diving Rules

1. Equalize pressure in your ears early and often (see page 122).
2. Always breathe; avoid breath-holding (see page 124).
3. If the scuba regulator is out of your mouth, exhale continuously.

with your tongue, and depress the purge momentarily to clear the chamber. Either method is acceptable. If you are purging the regulator while placing it in your mouth, release the purge the moment the regulator is in place to avoid overinflating your lungs. Develop the habit of blowing a continuous stream of tiny bubbles any time the regulator is out of your mouth to avoid holding your breath while breathing compressed air.

## Snorkel–Regulator Exchanges

You need to be able to switch between breathing from your snorkel to breathing from your regulator and vice versa. When you prepare to descend for diving, you exchange your snorkel for your regulator; when you surface after a dive, you exchange your regulator for your snorkel. Do both exchanges with your face in the water. Take a breath, exchange one mouthpiece for the other, and clear the new breathing device.

## BC Inflation and Deflation

You should be familiar with the three ways to inflate a BC and the two ways to deflate it. The easiest and most commonly used means of inflation is the low-pressure inflator, which is used to add air to the BC in short bursts. Inflating the BC for several seconds can cause serious buoyancy control problems if the inflator valve sticks. By adding air a little at a time, you have better control of your buoyancy.

If your low-pressure inflator or your integrated second stage develops a problem while you are diving, you may need to disconnect the low-pressure hose. When you disconnect the hose, the low-pressure inflator no longer functions, so you have to control buoyancy by orally inflating the BC. The mouthpiece of a BC usually is more elaborate than the mouthpiece of a skin diving vest. To help keep water out of a BC, the mouthpiece has a purge so that the water inside can be cleared before you open the valve to the BC. To clear the BC mouthpiece and orally inflate the BC, follow this procedure:

1. Insert the mouthpiece into your mouth.
2. Exhale a small amount of air into the mouthpiece to clear it.
3. Keep the mouthpiece in your mouth.
4. Depress the manual inflator-deflator valve.
5. Exhale into the BC.
6. Release the manual inflator-deflator valve.
7. Repeat the procedure until you achieve the desired amount of buoyancy.

You can use the same bobbing technique at the surface that you learned for the skin diving vest (see previous explanation in this chapter), but oral inflation procedures are different underwater. To inflate a BC orally underwater, follow these steps:

1. Grasp the inflation valve with your left hand and your regulator second stage with your right hand.
2. Take a breath.
3. Insert the BC mouthpiece into your mouth.
4. Clear the mouthpiece.
5. Exhale most of the air in your lungs into the BC.

6. Save enough air to clear the regulator, which fills with water when you remove it from your mouth.

7. Repeat the procedure until you achieve the desired amount of buoyancy.

The third method of BC inflation is with a $CO_2$ detonator, an optional feature many diving professionals consider neither necessary nor desirable.

You can deflate your BC with the manual inflator-deflator valve or with a dump valve. If you do not use a dump valve, you must open the deflator valve at the lower end of the BC hose and hold it higher than the highest point of the BC. It is more convenient to use a dump valve than the deflator valve. Note that you can deflate your BC only when the exhaust port is the highest point. Air cannot escape if you try to deflate a BC in a horizontal or inverted position, so you need to be in an upright position to deflate your BC.

## Testing Buoyancy

There are similarities between buoyancy testing for skin diving and buoyancy testing for scuba diving, but there also are some important differences. Buoyancy varies more when you scuba dive than when you skin dive. The volume of air in your lungs varies more in scuba diving. You dive deeper, so suit compression affects your buoyancy more. As you use air from your scuba tank, your buoyancy changes. You need to sense buoyancy changes quickly to maintain control of your buoyancy.

Your initial buoyancy test for scuba diving can be the same as your buoyancy test for skin diving. Begin by testing your BC at the surface. Inflate it fully and then deflate it. Make sure the low-pressure inflator and all deflation valves function correctly. With your regulator in your mouth and your BC completely deflated, relax and breathe slowly. When your lung volume is high, you should remain at the surface with your eyes just below the surface–water interface. If you sink with your lungs full of air, you need to remove some weight. When you exhale completely, you should sink. If you cannot sink after a complete exhalation, you need additional weight. Test your buoyancy while you are close to your point of entry, and correct any buoyancy problems before you attempt to dive.

As you descend in open water, you may need to add air to your BC to maintain neutral buoyancy. Strive to maintain neutral buoyancy continuously. Add air to your BC in small amounts, and test your buoyancy by stopping all motion and observing what happens. If you are sinking, inhale and add air to your BC. If you are rising in the water, exhale and release air from your BC. With experience you will know when to add air to or vent air from your BC and how much to add or release.

To learn buoyancy control in a swimming pool, assume a rigid, facedown position with your arms at your sides. If your buoyancy is correct, a slow, full inhalation raises your shoulders while your fin tips remain on the bottom, and a slow, complete exhalation causes your shoulders to sink. Some people call this buoyancy evaluation **diver's push-ups** (although you do not use your hands). If you do not rise with a full inhalation, add a small amount of air to your BC and try again. Figure 3.23 illustrates a diver doing diver's push-ups.

As a scuba diver, you need enough weight to get down at the beginning of a dive and enough weight to allow you to remain in control when you ascend at the end of the dive. The precise weight for scuba diving is the amount you need to hover at a depth of 15 feet (4.6 meters) with 300 psi (20 atmospheres) of air in your tank and no air in your BC.

**diver's push-ups**— Buoyancy evaluation where, when weighted properly, a full inhalation will raise the shoulders while the fin tips remain on the bottom and an exhalation will cause the shoulders to sink.

▶ Figure 3.23 Successfully performing diver's push-ups indicates good buoyancy control.

This amount may overweight you slightly at the beginning of a dive. Test your buoyancy at a depth of 15 feet (4.6 meters) at the end of a dive to see if you need to make an adjustment for your next dive.

## Controlling Buoyancy

No skill identifies a scuba diver's ability as much as buoyancy control. The ability to finely control buoyancy is important for safety, for enjoyment, and for the welfare of the environment. When your buoyancy is out of control, a hazard exists for both you and the environment around you.

With your buoyancy adjusted to the point where you can pivot slightly up and down on your fins on the bottom (in a pool) while inhaling and exhaling, push yourself about two feet (0.6 meters) off the bottom and remain motionless. You may or may not remain in a horizontal position, but that is not important. Maintain your depth by controlling your average lung volume, but remember to breathe continuously. If you are sinking, keep more air in your lungs. If you begin rising, reduce the amount of air in your lungs. With practice, you will be able to hover motionless just off the bottom.

To demonstrate mastery of hovering, assume a vertical position in the water. Cross your legs at the ankles, grasp a wrist with the opposite hand, and remain motionless. Find an eye-level reference and develop the ability to hover motionless while upright in the water. Pay attention to the buoyancy effects of breathing. Once you master hovering both horizontally and vertically, you will realize several benefits. Your air will last longer, swimming will not tire you as much, you will need fewer buoyancy adjustments, and you will do less damage to the diving environment. Your buoyancy control continues to improve with practice until you become a highly experienced diver.

**open-valve ascent**—A method for maintaining neutral buoyancy during an ascent by keeping the BC inflator-deflator valve open while holding the valve in a special way.

A useful skill for maintaining neutral buoyancy during ascent is a BC venting technique called an **open-valve ascent**. When you ascend, air in your BC expands and affects your buoyancy. You must release the expanding air to control buoyancy. If you vent the air from time to time, your buoyancy is in a constant state of change: You may not release enough air, or you may release too much. The open-valve ascent is a better alternative. Hold the BC inflator-deflator valve just below the level of your shoulder, point the mouthpiece of the inflator-deflator valve downward, and open the deflator valve. Air cannot escape because the opening is lower than the exhaust port on the BC. While you hold the mouthpiece downward and the deflation valve open, raise the inflator-deflator slowly until air just begins to bubble from the mouthpiece. Bubbling occurs when the mouthpiece and the exhaust port on the BC are at the same level. If you hold the inflator-deflator valve at the bubbling level while ascending, the expanding air inside the BC bubbles out through the open valve and your buoyancy remains constant. If you need to release additional air to control buoyancy, raise the inflator-deflator slightly; if you need to decrease the amount of air you release, lower the assembly slightly.

## Using the Dive Flag

You should display the appropriate dive flag or flags when diving. Authorities in some areas require you to use a flag, but all areas encourage flag use. Follow these conventions when you use a dive flag: Display the flag only when divers are in the water, and surface within 100 feet (30 meters) of your flag—the closer the better. The flag does not guarantee your safety from boaters, who are supposed to give the flag a berth of at least 100 feet (30 meters), but it does serve as a signal to many boaters who recognize that the flag means there are divers in the vicinity. Figure 3.24 shows divers using a dive flag.

If you support your flag with a surface float, you need to tow your float to the area where you wish to dive. In areas lacking underwater plants, you can tow the float while you dive. In areas with plants, you need to anchor the float to keep it from drifting away, and you must navigate back to the flag at the end of your dive. Tow a surface float behind you when entering through surf, and push it ahead of you when exiting through surf.

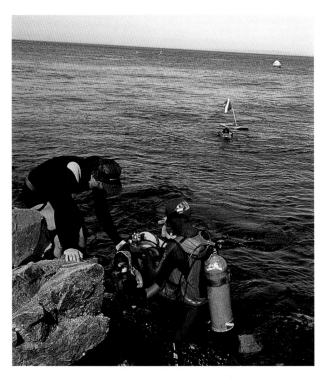

▶ Figure 3.24 Surface as close as possible to your dive flag.

## Descending

Scuba descents are different from skin diving ascents. You usually descend headfirst as a skin diver, but scuba divers descend feet first. A feet-first descent allows better control of buoyancy, provides better orientation, allows buddies to maintain contact during descent, helps prevent the swallowing of air, and allows easier pressure equalization of air spaces.

Descending involves learning several procedures, which seem complex at first but become routine with practice. The process of descending includes preparing to descend, initiating the descent, and completing the descent.

1. Preparing to descend
   - Check your instruments. Orient yourself at the surface and set a reference on your compass. Be sure your underwater timer and depth gauge are zeroed.
   - Confirm that your buddy is ready to begin.
   - Exchange your snorkel for your regulator.
   - Pressurize your ears slightly to begin the equalization process (see chapter 5).
   - Hold your BC deflator valve in your left hand.
   - Give or acknowledge the signal to descend.
2. Initiating the descent
   - Begin the descent by venting your BC. It is better to do this with the dump valve than by holding the deflator valve above your head. Hold the inflator-deflator valve in your left hand throughout the descent so you can add or release air from your BC at any time. Exhale fully to help get started downward.
   - Breathe shallowly for the first 10 feet (3 meters).

- Equalize pressure in your ears about every 2 feet (0.6 meters) for the first 15 feet (4.6 meters). If you experience equalizing problems, ascend a few feet to reduce the pressure, equalize again, and descend again. Exhale some air into your mask to prevent a mask squeeze. (See chapter 5 for a description of pressure equalization.)
- Keep your fins still while you descend so that you do not stir up silt on the bottom.
- Control your rate of descent by the average amount of air you keep in your lungs. When you begin sinking while your lungs are full, add a short burst of air to your BC to regain neutral buoyancy.

3. Completing the descent

- Remain with your buddy throughout the descent.
- Avoid contact with the bottom.
- Hover above the bottom, level off to a swimming position, agree on a direction with your buddy, and begin your exploration.

There are two types of descents in open water: reference descent and nonreference descent. A descent that you control by following a line or the slope of the bottom is a reference descent, which you should do whenever possible. A descent made vertically in water without any external reference is a nonreference descent, which is more difficult to control than a reference descent.

## Clearing the Mask

To clear a mask while scuba diving, you need to develop the skill of breathing through your mouth with your nose exposed to water. With concentration and practice, you can master this skill quickly. Try inhaling through your mouth and exhaling through your nose first, and then try inhaling and exhaling through your mouth. If you feel any water going up your nose, exhale immediately to keep the water out.

To practice clearing a mask, you need to flood it with water. This is not difficult, but a few tips make it easier. If you exhale lightly while tilting the mask forward on your face to break the seal at the top, the mask releases from your face easily, and the air escapes at the highest point. When you reseat your mask to begin clearing it, be sure to hold back any strands of hair with one hand while you reseat the mask with the other. Hair under the mask causes leakage. If you are wearing a hood, make sure that the hood is clear of the mask before attempting to clear water from the mask.

## Buddy Diving

You should always dive with a companion using the buddy system. A buddy provides reminders and assistance and sees things that you might not see. Buddies inspect each other's equipment, provide feedback based on observations, and work as a team. Dive buddies should remain close enough to each other that one can immediately assist the other in the event of an emergency. The more turbid the water and the greater the depth, the closer buddies should remain to each other. During your training you should strive to remain within touching distance of your buddy at all times; learn to keep track of your buddy. Maintaining contact with a dive buddy in open water is not difficult when you follow a few standard procedures.

Agree upon a position relative to one another and maintain that position as much as possible. That way, your buddy will know where to look for you, and you will know where to look for your buddy. The best dive team configuration is side by side; the least desirable is for one diver to be behind the other.

Agree on a direction of movement. Both parties should maintain that direction until both agree to proceed in a different direction. When you follow this practice, there are fewer directions to consider if you and your buddy become separated.

Confirm your buddy's position every few seconds. If you scan the areas ahead from side to side while swimming, you should get a glimpse of your buddy each time you turn your head in your buddy's direction.

When visibility is poor, physical contact can keep you and your buddy together. Holding hands is appropriate. Or you can use a short line—a **buddy line**—to keep in contact with each another. If you become separated from your buddy underwater, look for your buddy for up to one minute. If you are unable to locate your buddy, ascend slightly and turn in a circle while looking for bubbles. The visibility often is better a few feet above the bottom than it is at the bottom. If you do not see your buddy's bubbles, ascend to the surface and wait for your buddy, who should also duplicate this procedure. When you have reunited at the surface, you can descend again and continue your dive. Obviously, it is better to remain together underwater than to surface to reunite.

If you are unable to relocate your buddy underwater and your buddy does not surface promptly, look at your surroundings to mark your position so that you will know the approximate location where your buddy was last seen. If someone is overseeing the diving operations, notify this person that that your buddy is missing so that a search can be initiated. If you are alone, try to locate bubbles that could indicate your buddy's position.

## Underwater Swimming

When you swim along the bottom, your fins can raise a cloud of silt that harms the environment and reduces visibility. Silting is more of a problem when you are overweighted because the excess weight angles your fins toward the bottom when you swim (see figure 3.25). The first step in reducing silt is to weight yourself properly. In areas where the bottom silt is thick, add air to your BC to make yourself slightly buoyant underwater. The buoyancy forces you to swim at a slight downward angle and keeps your fins' thrust directed upward. Another way to reduce silt is to remain far enough from the bottom to keep from disturbing it. Finally, consider changing your kick if you boil up silt with your kick strokes.

▶ Figure 3.25 Overweighting can cause divers to create a cloud of silt.

▶ Figure 3.26  A dive compass.

When you kick something while swimming, you must overcome the tendency to want to get away from whatever you kick. Your kicks are strong and can damage the environment or another diver. As soon as you feel something with a fin, stop kicking, look back to see what you have hit, and maneuver yourself clear before proceeding.

## Navigating

To find your way underwater, you can use natural navigation and compass navigation. You can best determine your relative position with a combination of both types of navigation.

With natural navigation, you use your natural surroundings to determine where you are. Light, shadows, plants, formations, water movement, depth, and other indicators can help you navigate. As you move, note your surroundings. Observe which way you are going relative to the movement of the water, sand ripples on the bottom, the depth contour, and the angle of the sun. By noting natural aids to navigation, you can find your way underwater.

A dive compass increases the accuracy of navigation. Figure 3.26 shows an example of a dive compass. You need to be able to set a direction (called a **compass heading**) and to determine which way you are going relative to the directional reference you have set. Your compass should have a reference line, called a lubber line, that you point in the direction of travel. The north-seeking needle or card of the compass establishes a position relative to the lubber line as long as you hold the compass in a level position. Many dive compasses have index marks on a movable bezel. You set the index marks to indicate the heading.

To go in the direction set on the compass, you must hold the compass so the lubber line is directly in line with the centerline of your body. If the lubber line

▶ Figure 3.27  Compass-lock position.

**square compass course**—A series of headings that allows the diver to travel in a square pattern so that the dive ends where it began.

**reciprocal compass course**—A course where the diver moves in a given heading for a given distance and returns to the origination point by reversing the direction of travel.

points to one side, you will not be on course even though the north reference is at the correct point on the dial. Figure 3.27 shows a compass-lock position.

A **compass course** is a series of headings that leads to a destination. There are many types of compass courses. One frequently used course is the **square compass course.** To navigate a square course, set your initial heading and proceed in that direction for a given distance, which can be measured by time, tank pressure, or fin kicks. Stop and turn 90 degrees to the right while continuing to keep the lubber line aligned with the centerline of your body. Note the relative position of north on the compass, and proceed in the new direction for the same distance as you covered on the first leg of the course. Stop again, and turn another 90 degrees to the right. Note the position of north on the compass, which should be opposite your initial heading. Proceed along the third leg of the course for the same distance as before. Stop once more, turn again 90 degrees to the right, note the relative position of north, and follow the new heading back to your starting point.

Divers also frequently follow a **reciprocal compass course**—an out-and-back course. Set the initial heading on the compass. At the midpoint of the dive, turn 180 degrees until north on the compass is directly opposite the original heading, and follow the reciprocal heading back to your starting point. Advanced scuba diving courses provide additional compass navigation training.

If you do not know precisely where you are when the end of a dive approaches, it may be wise to surface, find a reference for your exit, and set a compass heading that leads directly to the end-of-dive location. Be especially careful if you surface more than 100 feet (30 meters) from your dive flag.

A compass provides correct directional reference information when it is not affected by nearby objects. Metal objects, other compasses, and electrical fields within a couple of feet of a compass can cause it to deviate from its correct reading. Keep metal, magnets, dive lights, and other compasses away from your compass to help ensure accuracy.

## Monitoring Instruments

Most diving instruments are passive; that is, they do not provide information unless you look at them. Some instruments emit an audible beep (one dive computer talks), but most require observation to provide information. Develop the habit of checking your instrumentation frequently while diving so that you can control your depth, dive time, and direction and avoid running out of air. You should be able to accurately estimate your tank pressure at any time during training. If you cannot estimate the pressure within 300 psi (20 atmospheres) at any time, you need to monitor your SPG more frequently.

When you are planning to dive in open water, look at your instruments when you assemble your equipment. Look at your instruments again when you inspect your equipment. Look at your instruments again before you descend and again while you descend. Refer to your compass for directional reference before you begin moving underwater. Monitor your gauges every few minutes while diving, and compare your air pressure with your buddy's several times during a dive. At any given time during a dive, you should be able to estimate accurately your depth, your dive time, your direction, your tank pressure, and your buddy's tank pressure. If you cannot do this, you need to improve your instrument-monitoring skills.

## Using Scuba Diving Hand Signals

Scuba divers use several hand signals that are not used for skin diving. The signals specific to scuba diving relate to air supply. Learn and use the standard hand signals shown in figure 3.28. Remember to display hand signals clearly and deliberately and also to acknowledge them.

## Ascending

Scuba ascents are different from skin diving ascents, although there are a few similarities. The procedures you need to learn become automatic with practice and experience.

To initiate an ascent, one member of a buddy team gives the ascent signal, which the other acknowledges. Always obey the ascent signal. Prepare to ascend by noting your time, depth, and remaining air. Locate and hold your BC inflator-deflator assembly in your left hand. Begin the procedures for the open-valve ascent previously described under the "Controlling Buoyancy" on page 72.

Begin ascending slowly with your buddy while breathing continuously. Monitor your depth gauge and keep tabs on your buddy. The maximum rate of ascent is 0.5 feet

Figure 3.28  Scuba diving hand signals.

(0.15 meters) per second, which is quite slow. Some instruments warn you when your rate of ascent is too rapid. You need training, practice, and awareness to avoid exceeding the maximum rate of ascent.

Stop and decompress (outgas) for one to three minutes at a depth of 15 feet (4.6 meters) to help prevent decompression sickness (DCS). The procedures for decompression are described in chapter 5. As you ascend, look up and around. Extend one hand above your head for protection against overhead obstacles. Make one full rotation to view the surrounding area as you near the surface. When you reach the surface, make another rotation to view the area, and then inflate your BC to establish buoyancy. Exchange your regulator mouthpiece for your snorkel.

## Handling Equipment

Sometimes you need to remove, adjust, and replace scuba equipment while you are in the water. You may need to remove equipment to exit the water onto a boat, to make an adjustment, or to free the equipment from an entanglement. With training and practice, you should be able to handle your equipment easily.

Removal of the scuba unit is easy because it is similar to removing a coat. Open the releases, slip your left arm free, swing the scuba tank forward under your right arm, hold the scuba unit with your left hand, and pull your right arm free. It is easier to free your left arm by inserting your hand and wrist through the armhole of the BC first and removing it hand first than by pulling your arm through first. If you are at the surface in water too deep to stand when you want to remove your scuba unit, remove your weight belt first and place it on a surface float or support station. Don the scuba unit in the water according to the in-water donning procedures previously presented in this chapter.

## Exit Techniques

The technique you use to exit the water depends on the situation. To exit from shallow water in a swimming pool, begin by removing your weight belt, tank, and fins, in that order. Carefully place the equipment on the side of the pool; then climb out by using the ladder or lifting yourself up onto the edge of the pool (see figure 3.29).

To exit from the deep end of a swimming pool, as shown in figure 3.30, begin with your BC inflated partially. If you exit on a ladder, grasp the ladder with one hand and remove your fins with the other; maintain contact with the ladder at all times. Place your fins on the edge of the pool or slide the heel straps over your wrists; then climb the ladder to exit the water. Clear the exit area at once, and take your fins with you. Remove your scuba system and weight belt when you are well clear of the exit area.

To exit from deep water without a ladder, begin by removing your weight belt and carefully placing it out of the water. Remove the scuba unit and use one hand to trap the regulator hose against the surface onto which you will exit. Use your other hand to remove your fins, and place them out of the water. Place both hands on the exit edge. With the regulator hose trapped under one hand, lower yourself to about chin level in the water while you extend one leg forward and one leg backward. Pull yourself upward with your arms and pull your legs together forcefully in a strong scissors kick to provide upward momentum. Pull with your arms until you are far enough out of the water to push downward and lift yourself from the water (see figure 3.31). Immediately after your exit, turn around and pull your scuba unit from the water carefully.

▶ Figure 3.29   Exiting from shallow water in a pool.

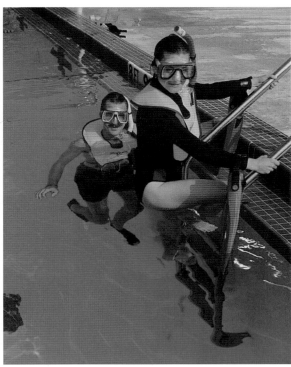

▶ Figure 3.30   Exiting from the deep end of a pool.

▶ Figure 3.31   Exiting from deep water without a ladder.

If you are exiting onto a boat that has a ladder, wear your tank and mask and keep your regulator in your mouth in case you should fall back into the water. Use the ladder exit technique described to exit the deep end of the pool (see figure 3.32). Maintain contact with the ladder at all times when you are in the water. If the boat has a platform at the rear, you usually swim onto the platform, remove your fins, and then stand on the platform and board the vessel.

Techniques for wading exits in open water vary with the environment. Usually it is a good idea to wear all your equipment until you are clear of the water. Shuffle your feet along the bottom while moving backward. Surf exits require training and practice. Stop outside the breaking waves and evaluate the surf. Approach the surf zone with your regulator in your mouth and your BC deflated. Hold your mask continually in the surf zone. Follow a breaking wave, and allow additional waves to pass over you until the water is only a couple of feet deep. If the surf is mild, you can stand at that point and back out of the water. If the surf is strong, swim until you can crawl; then crawl clear of the water (see figure 3.33).

When you are clear of the water, work with your buddy to remove your fins. The buddy system is in effect even when you are out of the water.

▶ Figure 3.32   Exiting onto a boat with a ladder.

▶ Figure 3.33   Surf exit.

## Disassembling Equipment

The first step in disassembling your scuba equipment is to turn off the air by turning the valve in a clockwise direction. Release the pressure in the hoses by depressing the purge on the regulator second stage. Keep the purge depressed until you bleed all the air from the system. Next, disconnect all hoses connected to the scuba unit: the low-pressure inflator, the extra second stage, and the SPG. Loosen the yoke screw and remove the regulator from the tank. Dry the first-stage dust cover thoroughly and replace it. Loosen the tank band and remove the BC from the scuba tank. Be sure to rinse and care for your equipment as soon as possible, following the procedures described in chapter 2.

# PROFICIENCY TESTING

After you have learned and practiced the skills of skin and scuba diving, you must demonstrate your competence at a level established by the agency sponsoring your training. Proficiency testing may include skin and scuba diving exercises that are challenging and fun. Examples include skin diving mask recovery and clearing, simulated boat exit for scuba diving, alternate air source breathing, buddy breathing, equipment handling, and a surface entry and equipment donning sequence known as a bailout.

# MANAGING PHYSIOLOGICAL PROBLEMS

If you do everything you are trained to do as a scuba diver, you can avoid problems. But it is not a perfect world. If you fail to pay attention or forget to do something, a problem can occur. Good divers can deal with nearly any problem. This section introduces you to proven ways of dealing with potential diving difficulties. Do not be overly concerned about the problems presented. You can prevent them, but knowing how to deal with them helps reduce your apprehension.

Difficulties affecting your physiology include seasickness, dizziness, stress and panic, overexertion, coughing, and cramping. When you have one of these problems, your body sends messages that something is wrong. You need to know the messages and the actions you can take to overcome physiological difficulties.

## Seasickness

It is best to prevent seasickness (see the description under the heading "Equilibrium Adaptations and Seasickness" in chapter 5) because taking medication after you are seasick is usually ineffective. If you do get seasick, you are likely to vomit. Vomiting underwater can be dangerous due to involuntary gasping that can cause you to choke. Only you can determine your degree of nausea. If you throw up or feel you are on the verge of doing so, do not dive. If you feel queasy, getting into the water may help you overcome the feeling. Some divers who feel slightly nauseated find that they feel better if they get into the water quickly and dive. After that first dive, they are fine for the remainder of the day.

Surface if you feel nauseated while diving. If you must vomit underwater, do not vomit through your regulator. Hold the second stage against one corner of your mouth and depress the purge fully while you vomit. You should get air instead of water if you gasp. When you have finished throwing up, place the second stage in your mouth, clear it, and resume breathing. The purge method should be a last resort.

If you are seasick and have to throw up while aboard a boat, do it over the rail on the side of the vessel opposite the wind. Do not use the rest room (or head, as it is called on a boat). The best remedy is to get to land, rest until you feel better, and take seasickness medication before returning to the vessel. If you are ill from motion sickness, the dive boat has a dinghy, and there is land nearby, request to be taken to shore for a while.

## Dizziness

The absence of visual clues in a weightless environment can cause temporary dizziness. Visual references can help you prevent disorientation (see chapter 5). Injury, temperature changes, and pressure changes affecting the inner ear also can cause a whirling feeling called vertigo, which may be more difficult to overcome than dizziness caused by disorientation.

To cope with either dizziness or vertigo, first seek a fixed visual reference. If possible, make physical contact with something solid for a point of reference. If there is nothing to see or to grasp, close your eyes and hug yourself. In most cases, dizziness passes in a minute or two. If you then move slowly and keep your head still, you should be able to surface. A good buddy can recognize your difficulty and assist you.

## Stress and Panic

Stress is the perception of a substantial imbalance between environmental demand and response capability, under conditions where failure to meet demand is perceived as having serious consequences. Stressors are conditions or attitudes that cause stress. Dive stressors, which can be internal or external, include cold, illness, exhaustion, injury, fear, equipment problems, loss of air supply, buddy separation, depth, darkness, currents, and disorientation. Stress is not always bad. Moderate stress can cause a feeling of exhilaration, improve performance, and lead to a positive condition called eustress. Excessive stress causes anxiety, decreases performance, and leads to a negative condition called distress.

WHEN IN DOUBT . . . GET OUT

Knowledge and appraisal of a situation affect your reaction to stress. Training, experience, and your predisposition toward a situation affect your knowledge and appraisal. Thus, your perception of the circumstances is determined by what you know and are able to do, by what you have done, and by any inherent fears about the circumstances that you might have.

The problem with stress in diving is that it can lead to panic: a sudden, uncontrolled, irrational reaction to a perceived danger. Divers who panic often perish. We must manage stress to prevent panic. Dr. Tom Griffiths, who has researched stress, said, "The most critical factor in the progression of panic after stress increases is whether or not a problem arises." Divers who can recognize and manage stress can overcome problems and are far safer than those who cannot cope with the effects of stress.

There are two components to stress: the physiological and the psychological. Anxiety causes involuntary physiological changes. When stress leads to anxiety, your breathing rate and heart rate increase, your nervous system becomes more active, and your awareness decreases. These factors decrease your performance and increase your anxiety. Then heightened anxiety begins the cycle again. Unless you interrupt the cycle, anxiety escalates into panic. Psychological difficulty is every bit as critical as the physical problems. Frank Pia, a chief lifeguard, says, "Much of the distress that a person experiences when difficulty arises stems from what the person tells himself about the situation." You can be exhilarated by a situation or allow it to cause anxiety and distress. Pia continues, "The difference between panic and a heightened physiological state is the thought process."

Michael J. Asken, who has written books about stress, encourages the use of task-relevant instructional self-talk (TRIST). You determine your emotional state when in distress by what you tell yourself. Asken says that in a stressful situation, "Success is not achieved by focusing on the outcome, hoping for a good outcome, or even telling yourself that the outcome will be okay. The most effective self-talk involves imagining that your instructor is sitting on your shoulder guiding you through your response."

With the foregoing concepts in mind, you can recognize and manage stress. The first steps are to sense your breathing rate and your self-talk when a problem occurs. If your breathing rate is fast and you are having negative thoughts about the situation, it is time to break the stress cycle. Stop all physical activity, establish buoyancy, and breathe deeply. Divers in distress usually have an adequate supply of air! As you gain control of respiration, you can think more clearly. Take control of your thoughts before they take control of you. Imagine that you are telling someone else how to deal with this situation. Assess your options, determine the best course of action, and then take deliberate action. As you begin to overcome the difficulty, your confidence increases and your physiological condition begins to return to normal. Figure 3.34 shows how to break the stress cycle that leads to panic.

Now you can understand why some divers are thrilled by the same situation that causes another diver to panic. Remember that stress is simply a matter of perception and that you can change your perception

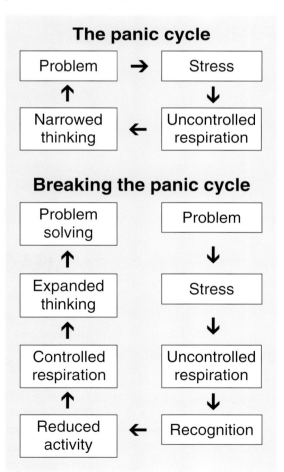

▶ Figure 3.34 The panic cycle and how to break it.

**The panic cycle**

| Problem | → | Stress |
| Narrowed thinking | ← | Uncontrolled respiration |

**Breaking the panic cycle**

| Problem solving | | Problem |
| Expanded thinking | | Stress |
| Controlled respiration | | Uncontrolled respiration |
| Reduced activity | ← | Recognition |

with training and experience. You can also learn to manage difficult situations by imagining them vividly in your mind. Your body cannot distinguish the difference between an actual event and one that you imagine. As you learn to solve problems in your mind, you can learn to recognize and manage stress.

## Overexertion

If you work too hard while scuba diving, the equipment may not be able to supply enough air to meet your respiratory needs. You experience a sudden feeling of suffocation, and you may suspect that your equipment has malfunctioned. It is unlikely that scuba equipment will cease to function suddenly in a way that restricts airflow. More likely than not, overexertion is causing the feeling that you cannot get enough air. You manage overexertion similarly to the way you manage stress. Stop all physical activity and breathe deeply; you should overcome your respiratory problem within a minute or two.

## Coughing

When water strikes your larynx, a reflex coughing action tries to clear the foreign matter from your airway. When you cough while in water, you may inhale additional water, which can complicate the situation. You need to overcome the reflex as quickly as possible. The best way is to swallow hard three times in rapid succession. If you must cough, try to do so through a regulator so that you inhale air rather than water if you gasp. You can lose buoyancy as you expel air when coughing, so you may need to establish positive buoyancy if you cough excessively.

## Cramps

When your muscles get cold or when circulation to your muscles is inadequate, cramping can occur. A cramp is a sudden, strong, involuntary, persistent, painful muscle contraction. Divers tend to get cramps in the lower legs and the feet. To alleviate a cramp, stretch the affected muscle and rub it to increase circulation. Pounding a cramped muscle is ineffective and causes tissue damage. If you experience a cramp in your leg or foot in the water, you may be able to get rid of it by grasping the tip of your fin and pulling it toward you. Buddies should assist one another with getting rid of cramps. Figure 3.35 shows a diver relieving a cramp.

# MANAGING PHYSICAL PROBLEMS

Potential physical diving difficulties include entanglement; loss of buoyancy control; loss of air supply; and a distressed, injured, or incapacitated buddy. As with physiological problems, you can overcome these problems, but it is better to avoid them.

## Entanglement

You probably will encounter fishing line, nets, wire, string, and rope in water, and these items can entangle you. Underwater plants can also entangle divers in some areas. Streamlining your equipment to minimize places where things can get caught helps reduce the chance of entanglement. Being aware also helps. When you encounter something that can entangle you, swim around it or push it beneath you and swim over it. Avoid swimming beneath things that can cause entanglement. The area of your tank valve and regulator first stage is one of the easiest places to become entangled and also one of the most difficult areas to free from entanglement.

If you become entangled underwater, stop. Then try to examine the problem without turning because turning often compounds the problem. If you can reach the entanglement, free yourself. If not, signal your buddy to help you get free. If you can see what you are doing, you can use your dive knife to cut yourself free. Trying to cut yourself free from something in the area of your tank valve is an obvious mistake. If your tank is entangled and you can't reach the entanglements or your buddy is not nearby to lend assistance, remove your scuba unit, free it from entanglement, and put it back on.

## Loss of Buoyancy Control

You can lose control of buoyancy underwater if you lose weights, if a low-pressure inflator on your BC or dry suit sticks, or if the $CO_2$ cartridge on your BC accidentally detonates. You can take steps to prevent loss of buoyancy control. Check your weight system from time to time while diving to make sure it is secure. Inspect your low-pressure inflators before each use, and have them serviced at the first sign of unusual operation. Don't opt for a $CO_2$ detonator on your BC.

If your weights fall off while underwater, immediately maneuver yourself into an inverted position, swim down forcefully, and retrieve the weights. If you are successful, you can avoid an uncontrolled ascent; if you are unsuccessful, you will float to the surface. Your rate of ascent depends on how buoyant you are without your weights, the type of exposure suit you are wearing, the amount of air in your BC at the time, your depth, and the amount of surface area you can expose to the direction of motion. The greater the cross-sectional area of an object moving in a given direction, the greater the resistance to movement in that direction. (You will learn more about resistance to movement, or drag, in chapters 4 and 5.) If you lose control of buoyancy and your ascent is uncontrolled, you can slow your rate of ascent by **flaring**: arching your back, extending your arms and legs, and positioning your fins parallel to the surface. Flaring (shown in figure 3.36) is the method recommended to slow a buoyant ascent.

**flaring**—A method of slowing an uncontrolled ascent by arching the back, extending the arms and legs, and positioning the fins so they are parallel to the surface.

▶ Figure 3.36 Flaring is an effective way to slow a buoyant ascent.

Unless you care for your BC inflator carefully and have it serviced annually, the inflator valve will stick eventually. If your low-pressure inflator sticks in the open position, first hold your BC deflator valve in the open position. Modern BCs vent air faster than the low-pressure inflator admits air. If the inflator valve remains stuck, disconnect the low-pressure hose. If an uncontrolled ascent results, flare to slow your rate of ascent.

$CO_2$ is more compressible than air. If your BC has a $CO_2$ detonator and it misfires underwater, the resulting buoyancy depends on the pressure (depth), the water temperature, and the size of the cartridge. If your detonator activates accidentally, vent the gas from the BC and flare if an uncontrolled ascent results.

## Loss of Air Supply

You are unlikely to have air supply difficulties if you have your regulator serviced annually, if you maintain your regulator properly, and if you monitor your SPG. Potential problems are a regulator that free-flows, low air pressure, and no air to breathe. There are ways to deal with each of these difficulties.

Sand, dirt, and freezing can cause regulator free-flow. If free-flow occurs, your best course of action is to switch to your extra second stage. You also could use your buddy's extra second stage. If there is no source of air except the regulator that is free flowing, you can breathe from it by pressing your lips lightly against the mouthpiece, taking the air you need, and allowing the excess air to escape. Look down while you breathe from the regulator to keep the escaping air from causing your mask to leak.

You are supposed to end a dive with at least 500 psi (34 atmospheres) of air in your tank. If you are inattentive and breathe nearly all the air from your cylinder while diving, it will become difficult to get air from your regulator. Divers often refer to the situation as being "out of air," but, in reality, they are out of air only at the depth at which breathing is difficult. As you ascend, the lower ambient pressure allows you to obtain additional air from your tank. When breathing becomes difficult and your tank is nearly empty, use your buddy's alternate air source (AAS) or ascend while continuing to breathe shallowly through your regulator.

In the rare event that you should completely lose your primary source of air while underwater, you have five ascent options. Figure 3.37 shows the order of preference of these options.

An extra-second-stage-assisted ascent closely approximates a normal ascent. You ascend while breathing from your buddy's extra second stage. When you require air underwater, get your buddy's attention and give the signals for "out of air" and "give me air," if possible. If your buddy's extra second stage and primary second stage are similar, your buddy will hand you the extra second stage, or you may take it. If your buddy's extra second stage is integrated into the BC low-pressure inflator, your buddy will hand you the primary second stage and breathe from the integrated second stage. If you cannot get your buddy's attention, take the extra second stage, begin breathing, and then signal your buddy that you have no air. After you establish a breathing rhythm, grasp each other's right forearm and ascend normally (see figure 3.38).

An emergency swimming ascent (ESA) is a scuba ascent you do using only the air in your lungs. The ascent rate of an ESA is faster than a normal ascent, but not rapid. Retain your regulator in your mouth, and try to breathe from it from time to time. Do not hold your breath or you risk a lung overexpansion injury. If you exhale too much

## Emergency ascent option hierarchy

5. Make a buoyant emergency ascent (BEA) if the depth is 50 ft (15 m) or greater.

4. Make an emergency swimming ascent (ESA) if depth is less than 50 ft (15 m).

3. Buddy-breathe (only if both divers are trained).

2. Breathe from buddy's alternate air source (AAS).

1. Breathe from a backup scuba unit.

▶ Figure 3.37   Loss-of-air options.

▶ Figure 3.38   Air sharing requires good skills and cooperation.

air, you will have a strong urge to inhale. The key to a successful ESA is to exhale enough air that your lungs remain at a comfortable volume. When you do an ESA correctly, you can ascend 50 feet (15 meters) easily without an overwhelming desire for air. If the depth is over 50 feet (15 meters), discard your weights to initiate a buoyant emergency ascent (BEA). Swim for the first portion of the ascent, but allow yourself to drift up when buoyancy can replace swimming. Flare during the last 15 feet (4.6 meters) of a BEA and keep your lungs at a comfortable—but not maximum—volume.

Buddy breathing—the sharing of a single regulator second stage by two divers—may be a less desirable loss-of-air option because it jeopardizes the safety of two people. You and your buddy should practice buddy breathing at the surface before beginning a dive if buddy breathing is a loss-of-air option for the dive. Not all divers are trained to buddy-breathe, and buddy breathing attempted by two divers who are not proficient with the skill can result in disaster. However, those who are proficient buddy breathers can make a loss-of-air situation a mere nuisance.

Initiate buddy breathing with the "out-of-air" signal followed by the signal for "give me air." Your buddy holds the regulator second stage in the right hand and grasps your shoulder strap with the left hand. Your buddy extends the second stage toward you and holds it in such a way that you have access to the purge. You grasp your buddy's wrist (not the regulator) with your left hand and your buddy's shoulder strap with your right hand. Guide the second stage to your mouth and push your lips against the mouthpiece to make a seal instead of inserting the mouthpiece into your mouth. By not putting the mouthpiece into your mouth to breathe, you can exchange the regulator quickly and reduce mask leakage caused by facial movements. Take several quick breaths initially; then pass the regulator back to your buddy. Exhale a small amount of air continuously when you are not breathing from the regulator. The exhalation helps prevent a lung overexpansion injury during ascent. After the initial contact, you and your buddy each take two breaths before passing the regulator. Do not inhale fully when buddy-breathing because full breaths can cause buoyancy problems or lung injuries. A medium inhalation is adequate because you receive air every few seconds. Do exhale fully after each first breath that you take. The complete exhalation helps expel carbon dioxide and reduces your urge to breathe.

As soon as you and your buddy establish a breathing rhythm, you should swim to the surface, holding on to each other throughout the ascent. Blow bubbles continuously when the regulator is not in your mouth. Remember to control your buoyancy.

Skills for loss-of-air situations require proficiency, so they must be learned well and renewed periodically. Discuss the procedures for a loss-of-air situation with your buddy and agree on the options you will use. You should both be familiar with the signals, positions, and techniques.

## Assisting Your Buddy

You have read about many ways to assist your buddy and how your buddy can assist you, so you should realize the importance of the buddy system while diving.

In addition to helping your buddy handle entanglements, cramps, equipment problems, and loss-of-air situations, you may need to provide assistance if your buddy is incapacitated from exhaustion, illness, or injury.

A buddy who becomes agitated at the surface needs assistance in regaining control. Help such a buddy establish buoyancy, calm down, and breathe slowly and deeply. When the situation is under control, you may be able to help your buddy resolve the difficulty that caused the agitation.

If your buddy becomes exhausted, provide assistance at the surface with a biceps push, a fin push, or a do-si-do (arm-under-arm) push. The three types of pushes are illustrated in figure 3.39. Use the biceps push when your buddy can help and the fin push when your buddy is too exhausted to help at all. Monitor your buddy and offer encouragement while you provide assistance.

▶ Figure 3.39 The biceps push (top), fin push (middle), and do-si-do push (bottom) are ways to assist an exhausted buddy.

# MANAGING EMERGENCIES

Diving accidents occur when divers do not exercise good judgment or when they fail to follow recommended practices. If you do what you are supposed to do, the chances of a diving accident are extremely small. But you may have to render aid to someone else who violates safety rules. This section identifies the aid you should be capable of providing.

## Training and Preparation

Three types of emergency preparedness training are recommended for all divers: first aid, cardiopulmonary resuscitation (CPR), and diving rescue techniques. You can get first aid and CPR training from various public service organizations. You'll learn some diving rescue techniques in your entry-level course, but you should also complete a rescue specialty course.

Emergency preparedness includes having emergency equipment and information available. Emergency equipment desirable at a dive site includes these items:

- Diving first aid kit (see checklist of kit items in chapter 2)
- Oxygen delivery system
- Blanket (if appropriate)
- Drinking water

You may not have all of the emergency equipment yourself, but you can determine whether it is available aboard a boat or as part of an organized dive.

Have a means of communication—a telephone, cellular phone, CB radio, or marine radio—to summon assistance. Have contact information for local emergency medical assistance and for the emergency treatment of divers at the dive site. Have phone numbers and radio frequencies for local emergency support services. Examples of numbers to have include the Coast Guard, paramedics, hospital, ambulance, police or sheriff's office, recompression facility, and the Diver's Alert Network (DAN). The Diver's Alert Network has a 24-hour emergency number, 919-684-8111, to assist with the coordination of response to diving accidents. You need to be a DAN member to use their services.

## Scuba Lifesaving

The principal elements of scuba lifesaving are cognizance, assessment, rescue, and evacuation (CARE). Cognizance is the ability to detect signs that identify or predict an accident. Trained and experienced divers can recognize situations that can lead to accidents before divers enter the water, when they enter the water, at the surface, during descents, underwater, during ascents, and during exits. As your experience increases, you will become more cognizant of potential difficulties.

Assessment is an ongoing evaluation of various factors that can affect a lifesaving situation. Rescuers need to consider their own ability to rescue the victim, the victim's condition, the environmental conditions, equipment, and additional resources.

Rescue techniques include approaches, extensions, throws, assists, establishing buoyancy, defenses, towing, deep-water rescue breathing, equipment removal, and removing the victim from the water. The ability to rescue both conscious and unconscious divers at the surface and underwater is an important skill to develop; you should take a scuba lifesaving or rescue specialty course as soon as possible after completing basic scuba training.

An unconscious diver underwater can drown unless rescued immediately. Illness, drugs, and blows to the head can cause loss of consciousness. If a diver loses consciousness underwater, make the diver buoyant and get him or her to the surface immediately. You need not concern yourself about expanding air if the diver is not breathing because an unconscious person exhales automatically regardless of head position. Do not concern yourself about the diver's decompression status; he or she can be treated for DCS but will die after about four minutes without air. Do not jeopardize your own safety when attempting to rescue another diver.

A diver who is not breathing needs air quickly and must get it at the surface. This is where training in CPR and diving rescue techniques are invaluable. Open the victim's airway. Often this is all an unconscious person needs to be able to breathe. To open the airway, tilt the head and lift the chin. Turn the person's head to the side to drain water from the mouth and throat. Vomiting is common, so be prepared for it. Clear vomit from the victim's mouth and throat at once or the person may inhale it and choke.

A person who is not breathing after you have opened the airway requires rescue breathing and medical assistance. Shout for help. While keeping the victim's airway open, lightly pinch the victim's nostrils to seal them. Seal your mouth over the other person's and fill the person's lungs with air until the chest rises gently. Give the victim one breath every 5 seconds or two breaths every 10 seconds while swimming to safety. A gurgling sound from the victim indicates water or vomit in the airway. Roll the person to the side and drain the fluid before continuing rescue breathing. The preferred method of in-water artificial respiration is with a rescue-breathing mask, which you can carry in the pocket of your BC. Figure 3.40 shows a person doing rescue breathing using such a mask.

▶ Figure 3.40  Rescue breathing with a breathing mask.

You probably will not be able to detect a pulse in the water, so don't bother trying. You cannot administer CPR in the water; you must remove the victim from the water and position him or her on a firm surface.

Evacuation is the final principal element of scuba lifesaving. Evacuation procedures include accident preparedness, communications, and transportation options. Advance planning is essential to evacuate an injured diver to a medical facility.

# First Aid

There are some aspects of diving first aid that standard first aid courses do not teach. This section touches on those aspects, but you need the additional study and training that you can get in rescue specialty and oxygen administration courses.

Nothing is more important than attending to basic life support: breathing and circulation. The next priority for any serious diving injury is treatment for shock. Lay an injured diver who is breathing on the side, keep the person warm (but avoid overheating), and administer sips of water if he or she is conscious. If you suspect an air embolism, DCS, or near drowning, have the person breathe oxygen in the highest possible concentration. Keep any diver who has lost consciousness or who has symptoms of DCS lying down until the he or she can be evaluated at a medical facility. Monitor the victim continuously.

You should be able to recognize signs and symptoms that indicate a serious diving illness. The following signs and symptoms indicate an injury that requires the prompt administration of oxygen and medical treatment.

- Loss of consciousness
- Sudden, extreme weakness
- Numbness
- A pins-and-needles sensation
- Inability to do simple motor skills
- Paralysis
- Unequal pupils

There are venomous marine animals in some parts of the world. A few venomous animals can inflict life-threatening wounds (see chapter 7). The wounds can cause pain, weakness, nausea, shock, mental confusion, paralysis, convulsions, depression, arrest of breathing, and even cardiac arrest. Fortunately, such wounds are rare.

Venomous injuries are either punctures or stings. First aid for venomous puncture wounds involves removing all foreign matter from the wound, applying hot packs to the injured area for half an hour, and keeping the injured area below the level of the heart. Obtain medical attention.

First aid for a venomous sting includes killing any stinging cells that are in contact with the skin, removal of any residue, cleansing the area, applying an analgesic ointment for pain relief, and medical attention. Vinegar is a good solution to apply to all stings to neutralize stinging cells initially.

You may not recall the appropriate first aid procedures in the event of an accident, so it is a good idea to have a diving first aid book to help you identify an injury and administer the appropriate first aid.

# Scuba Wise

*People are creatures of habit, and habits are the result of repetition. If you repeat an action correctly enough times, you form a good habit. On the other hand, if you repeat an action incorrectly enough times, you create a bad habit. Divers need good habits to avoid accidents, but sometimes they fail to take the time to develop them. I watch divers on charter boats and at dive sites when they prepare to dive and notice that some fail to inspect their equipment adequately, fail to plan their dive properly, or fail to follow the practices outlined in this chapter.*

*Usually they know what to do, but because they have bypassed many steps every time they go diving, they have a habit of skipping important items. How safe is a pilot if he or she ignores the preflight checklist? Taking the correct action requires concentration initially, but when repeated until the action becomes a habit, the process becomes automatic. We can make complex processes simple when we repeat them. I strongly encourage you to take the time to form good diving habits. If you do, I assure you that the odds of being injured are extremely small.*

## Managing Accidents

If a serious diving accident occurs, and no supervisory personnel are available to take charge, you have to manage the situation to the best of your ability. Summon help, but do not leave a seriously injured diver unattended. Enlist the aid of others. Try to locate the injured diver's identification and medical information. Write down what happened, the person's dive profile, his or her symptoms, dive times, and so forth. Pin the information in a conspicuous place, and send it with the injured diver to the medical facility. Accompany the diver to the medical facility, if possible.

## SUMMARY

The skills of diving range from simple skin diving procedures to complex scuba skills to problem management. You need to learn the skills correctly the first time, practice them until you can do them easily, and renew them frequently to stay proficient. You also need to be trained and prepared to handle a diving emergency.

# Diving Science 4

## Dive In and Discover

By the end of this chapter, you will be able to do the following:

- List three body air spaces of concern to divers.
- Describe the process of hearing in air.
- Describe the cardiorespiratory process.
- Explain the effect of carbon dioxide on breathing.
- Define the terms *eardrum, middle ear, eustachian tube, nitrogen narcosis, hyperventilation, hypoventilation, density, buoyancy, pressure, gauge pressure, absolute pressure, Boyle's law, Gay-Lussac's law, Dalton's law, squeeze, reverse block, ingassing, outgassing,* and *partial pressure.*
- Explain the principle of buoyancy and the key to controlling buoyancy.

- Explain the effects of pressure and temperature on a volume of air in a flexible container.
- Explain why it is important to vent your lungs when you ascend in water.
- Convert any temperature to absolute temperature.
- Explain the process of ingassing and outgassing.
- State the two primary factors that affect the air consumption of a scuba diver.
- List four methods of heat loss.
- Describe three potential problems for scuba divers that may be caused by humidity.
- Describe the effects of water on vision and hearing.

Your body is a marvelous machine. It performs many complex functions automatically. Just as your body is well adapted to an air environment, it can adapt in many ways to the aquatic environment. In this chapter, you will become familiar with some of the structures and functions of your body that are important for scuba diving. You will learn the differences between the air and water environments and how changes in pressure affect your body.

## Abbreviations

| | | | |
|---|---|---|---|
| ATA | atmospheres absolute | FSW | feet of seawater |
| atm | atmospheres | ft | feet |
| CO | carbon monoxide | m | meters |
| $CO_2$ | carbon dioxide | $O_2$ | oxygen |
| °C | degrees Celsius | psia | pounds per square inch, absolute |
| °F | degrees Fahrenheit | psig | pounds per square inch, gauge |
| FFW | feet of fresh water | | |

# ANATOMY FOR THE DIVER

Inside your body are air-filled spaces that are affected by changes in pressure. The three primary body air spaces of concern to you as a diver are the lungs, the ears, and the sinuses. It helps you as a diver to understand the function of your throat. Figure 4.1 explains the functions of the sinuses, throat, and lungs.

- **The Sinuses.** The sinuses warm and humidify inspired air. They secrete mucus to help protect the body by trapping airborne germs. The small airways that connect the sinuses to the nasal passages normally are open. Congested sinuses pose problems for divers. In the next chapter, you will learn more about sinus problems and their prevention.

- **The Throat.** In addition to being the organ of voice, the larynx helps prevent foreign matter from entering the lungs. If something foreign, such as food or water, comes into contact with the larynx, a reflex action causes a spasm of the larynx. Coughing expels the foreign substance. You have experienced this sensation when something has gone down the wrong pipe. Review the throat section of figure 4.1. During your scuba diving training, you will learn how to keep water out of your larynx to avoid coughing and choking in and under the water.

- **The Lungs.** Healthy lungs are essential for scuba diving. The lungs are large air sacs contained within your chest cavity. Your lungs have a maximum capacity and a minimum capacity. When you exhale completely, your lungs are not empty. They contain about two pints (one liter) of air. The air remaining in your lungs after you have exhaled completely is your residual volume. The amount of air you move in and out of your lungs is your tidal volume. When you are at rest, your tidal volume is small. When you exert

# Function of the sinuses, throat, and lungs

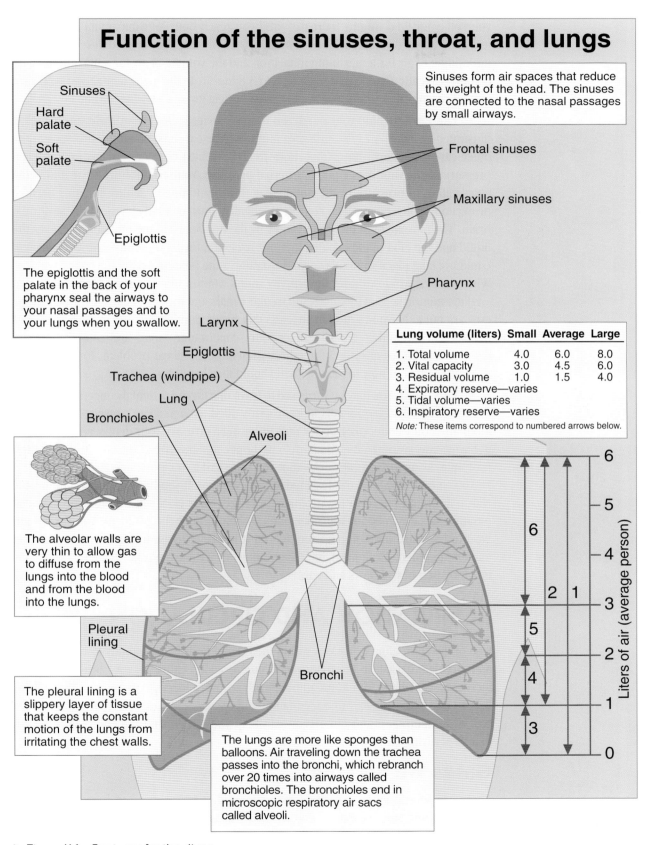

Sinuses

Hard palate

Soft palate

Epiglottis

The epiglottis and the soft palate in the back of your pharynx seal the airways to your nasal passages and to your lungs when you swallow.

Sinuses form air spaces that reduce the weight of the head. The sinuses are connected to the nasal passages by small airways.

Frontal sinuses

Maxillary sinuses

Pharynx

Larynx

Epiglottis

Trachea (windpipe)

Lung

Bronchioles

Alveoli

| Lung volume (liters) | Small | Average | Large |
|---|---|---|---|
| 1. Total volume | 4.0 | 6.0 | 8.0 |
| 2. Vital capacity | 3.0 | 4.5 | 6.0 |
| 3. Residual volume | 1.0 | 1.5 | 4.0 |
| 4. Expiratory reserve—varies | | | |
| 5. Tidal volume—varies | | | |
| 6. Inspiratory reserve—varies | | | |

*Note:* These items correspond to numbered arrows below.

The alveolar walls are very thin to allow gas to diffuse from the lungs into the blood and from the blood into the lungs.

Pleural lining

The pleural lining is a slippery layer of tissue that keeps the constant motion of the lungs from irritating the chest walls.

Bronchi

The lungs are more like sponges than balloons. Air traveling down the trachea passes into the bronchi, which rebranch over 20 times into airways called bronchioles. The bronchioles end in microscopic respiratory air sacs called alveoli.

Liters of air (average person)

▶ Figure 4.1  Anatomy for the diver.

yourself, your tidal volume increases until you reach both your maximum lung volume and your residual volume with each breath. Your vital capacity is the difference between the volume of air for a maximum inhalation and the volume of air for a maximum exhalation—typically about 6 to 8 pints (2.8 to 3.8 liters). In the next chapter, you will learn several reasons that your lungs are the most critical air spaces when diving.

• **The Ears.** Behind your **eardrum** is an air space called the **middle ear,** which is illustrated in figure 4.2. The pressure in the middle ear must equal the pressure in the outer ear or the eardrum cannot move freely. The next chapter explains how to keep pressure inside your ears equal to external pressure. Your **eustachian tube** allows the equalization of pressure in the middle ear. The liquid-filled cochlea contains hairlike projections called cilia, which convert mechanical movement to electrical signals for the brain. The movement of the oval window by the tiny bones of the middle ear causes the liquid and the cilia in the cochlea to move back and forth. The oval-window movement could not take place without a second window in the hearing organ: the round window. When the oval window moves inward, the round window moves outward, and vice versa.

If the motion sensed by your semicircular canals and the visual cues received by your eyes are not in harmony, motion sickness can result. Sudden changes in temperature or pressure in the middle ear can affect your semicircular canals and cause temporary disorientation. (See chapter 5 for a discussion of potential ear problems for divers, how to avoid them, and how to handle them should they happen.)

• **The Teeth.** You may be surprised to learn that there are dental concerns for divers. Pressure can affect air pockets in improperly filled teeth and can cause tooth pain. If a tooth hurts only under pressure or only following a dive, see your dentist and tell him or her what you suspect. The roots of some upper molars extend into the sinus cavities. Postpone diving for several weeks after you have had a tooth extracted.

Your mouth and jaws are designed for an even bite. If you bite hard on a mouthpiece with only your front teeth for prolonged periods, your jaws will become sore. Special mouthpieces designed for a proper bite can help reduce the problem. You should not have to bite hard on a mouthpiece to hold it in place. If you find biting necessary, get lighter equipment. Prolonged, improper biting that irritates your jaws can lead to serious inflammation of your jaws and ears

# RESPIRATION AND CIRCULATION

One of the fascinating processes within the human body is your ability to breathe in air and circulate oxygen to the tissues with no conscious effort. As your level of exertion increases, your heart and lungs automatically adjust to meet the increased demands for oxygen and nourishment. An understanding of the gases involved in respiration and the basics of respiration and circulation can help you understand the effects and the demands of diving on your lungs and heart.

## Gases We Breathe

There are several gases that affect recreational divers. You need to know about their effects on your body. About 80 percent of air is nitrogen ($N_2$). At sea-level pressures, nitrogen has no effect on your body. At a depth of about 100 feet (30 meters), the increased pressure of the gas has a detrimental effect, which is called **nitrogen narcosis.**

▶ Figure 4.2 Process of hearing in air.

Three tiny bones couple vibrations from the eardrum to the inner ear.

Semicircular canals

The semicircular canals sense motion and help maintain balance.

Oval window

Round window

Middle ear cavity

Ear canal

Oval window

Fluid-filled

Round window

To couple sound to the cochlea, the round and oval windows move in opposite directions.

Eardrum

Cochlea

The eardrum (a flexible, airtight barrier) separates the outer ear from the middle ear.

Outer ear  Middle ear  Inner ear

Eustachian tube

Air

The eustachian tube is an airway between the middle ear and the throat.

**Three main parts of the ear**

Excessive nitrogen in your body at the end of a dive can produce a serious illness known as decompression sickness. You will learn more about nitrogen narcosis and decompression sickness in the next chapter.

Oxygen ($O_2$) is the gas that supports human life. Any other gas mixed with oxygen serves only as a vehicle for oxygen to be inspired. Approximately 21 percent of air is oxygen (see figure 4.3). You need to breathe at least 10 percent oxygen to remain conscious, but oxygen breathed under high pressure is poisonous and causes convulsions. You must have compressed air—not pure oxygen—in your scuba tanks. A specialty form of diving uses a nitrogen and oxygen mixture with a higher percentage of oxygen than is found in air. The mixture, which reduces the effects of nitrogen at depth, is called nitrox. The use of special mixed gases, including nitrox, requires special training, equipment, and procedures.

As your tissues use oxygen, they produce carbon dioxide ($CO_2$). Carbon dioxide is the primary stimulus for respiration. The greater the level of carbon dioxide in your body, the greater the urge to breathe. If the level of carbon dioxide in your body becomes too great, unconsciousness results.

Carbon monoxide (CO) is a poisonous gas produced by the incomplete combustion of gas or oil. The exhaust from an internal combustion engine contains carbon monoxide. An oil-lubricated air compressor that overheats can produce carbon monoxide. Even a minute amount of carbon monoxide in your

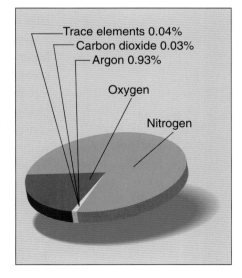

Trace elements 0.04%
Carbon dioxide 0.03%
Argon 0.93%
Oxygen
Nitrogen

▶ Figure 4.3 Composition of air.

scuba tank can poison you and lead to unconsciousness or death. Air filling stations must take care to avoid contamination of air with carbon monoxide.

# Breathing and Circulation Mechanics

When you need to breathe, sensors at the base of your brain send a signal that stimulates your diaphragm to contract. This draws air into your lungs in the same way that an old-fashioned bellows draws in air when you expand it. Your diaphragm and the muscles of your chest expand your chest cavity to inspire air. Figure 4.4 describes how the heart, lungs, and circulatory system work in the process of respiration.

Blood consists of plasma, a colorless liquid, and a variety of cells. Hemoglobin, a blood component, is the primary oxygen-carrying mechanism in the blood. Approximately 45 percent of the blood is hemoglobin. Hemoglobin releases oxygen when it reaches tissues that need oxygen.

When the tissues use oxygen, they produce carbon dioxide. The carbon dioxide enters the venous system. Carbon dioxide diffuses into the lungs in exchange for oxygen. This completes a circulatory cycle, which takes about 30 seconds.

Carotid sinuses on each side of the neck sense blood pressure within the circulatory system. Excessive pressure on the carotid sinuses during exercise causes the heart to slow when it should be working hard to meet the oxygen demands of the body. Decreased output from the heart can lead to insufficient oxygen for the brain, which can cause unconsciousness. A blackout caused by pressure on the carotid sinuses (which figure 4.5 illustrates) is a carotid sinus reflex. Therefore, beware of diving equipment that is tight around your neck.

Exhalation usually is a passive process. To exhale carbon dioxide–laden air from the lungs, the diaphragm relaxes, and the elasticity of the chest cavity forces air from the lungs. You ventilate your lungs approximately 12 to 14 times per minute when at rest. Respiration functions automatically. The key to respiration is the level of carbon dioxide in your circulatory system. When the carbon dioxide in your body reaches a certain level, your brain stimulates respiration. When you voluntarily hold your breath, the buildup of carbon dioxide within your body urges you to breathe. Many people believe the amount of oxygen in the body controls respiration, but it is the level of carbon dioxide that regulates breathing.

**Hyperventilation** is rapid, deep breathing in excess of the body's needs. Limited hyperventilation—three to four breaths—enhances breath holding, but if you hold your breath after excessive hyperventilation, you may lose consciousness without warning before being stimulated to breathe. A breath-holding diver who loses consciousness from lack of oxygen usually blacks out near the surface during ascent. The sudden loss of consciousness near the surface is called shallow-water blackout. Loss of consciousness while in the water can cause drowning. Avoid excessive hyperventilation. Figure 4.6 illustrates shallow water blackout.

If you breathe rapidly and shallowly, carbon dioxide continues to build in your system, but you do not expel it from your lungs. Inadequate breathing is **hypoventilation.** Shallow breathing is dangerous, especially when you exert yourself, because you can lose consciousness from lack of oxygen. It is essential to breathe sufficiently to exchange the air in your lungs.

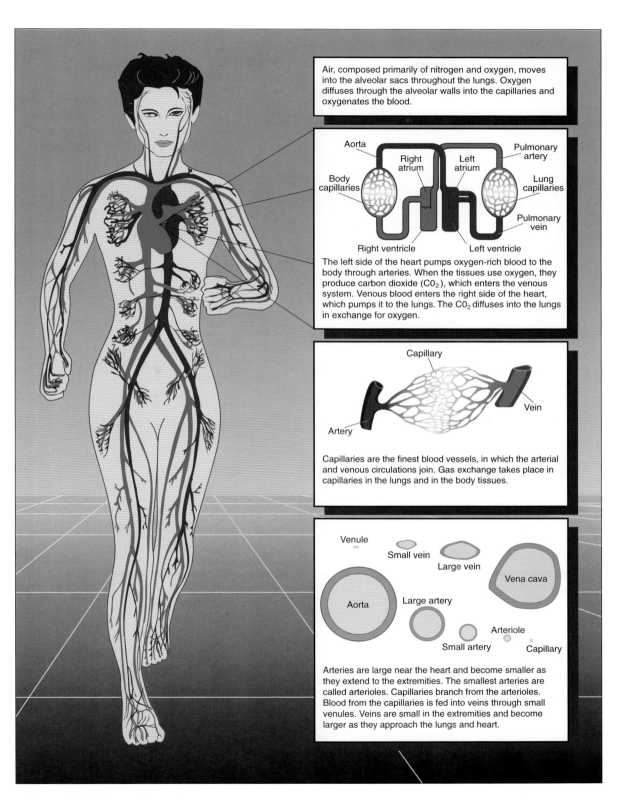

Air, composed primarily of nitrogen and oxygen, moves into the alveolar sacs throughout the lungs. Oxygen diffuses through the alveolar walls into the capillaries and oxygenates the blood.

Aorta
Right atrium
Left atrium
Pulmonary artery
Body capillaries
Lung capillaries
Pulmonary vein
Right ventricle
Left ventricle

The left side of the heart pumps oxygen-rich blood to the body through arteries. When the tissues use oxygen, they produce carbon dioxide ($CO_2$), which enters the venous system. Venous blood enters the right side of the heart, which pumps it to the lungs. The $CO_2$ diffuses into the lungs in exchange for oxygen.

Capillary
Vein
Artery

Capillaries are the finest blood vessels, in which the arterial and venous circulations join. Gas exchange takes place in capillaries in the lungs and in the body tissues.

Venule
Small vein
Large vein
Vena cava
Aorta
Large artery
Arteriole
Small artery
Capillary

Arteries are large near the heart and become smaller as they extend to the extremities. The smallest arteries are called arterioles. Capillaries branch from the arterioles. Blood from the capillaries is fed into veins through small venules. Veins are small in the extremities and become larger as they approach the lungs and heart.

▶ Figure 4.4   The cardiorespiratory system.

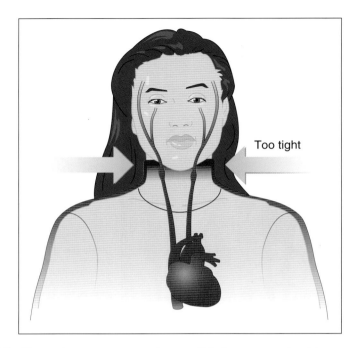

▶ Figure 4.5  Excessive pressure on the carotid sinuses can lead to unconsciousness.

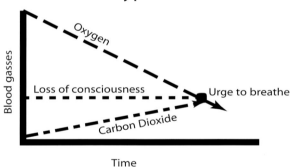

▶ Figure 4.6  Shallow-water blackout.

# CONTRASTS IN AIR AND WATER ENVIRONMENTS

We live immersed in air, which is a fluid. Air has weight and takes up space. We don't pay much attention to our immersion in air because we are adapted to this environment: We have lived in it all of our lives, and we cannot see the air. The weight of the atmosphere does affect us, however.

Air weighs about 0.08 pounds per cubic foot (1.28 milligrams per cubic centimeter) at sea level. As altitude increases, air becomes thinner, so its weight per volume is less in the mountains than it is at the seashore (see figure 4.7). The change in the weight of air upon us affects the air spaces in our ears when we fly or when we drive in the mountains.

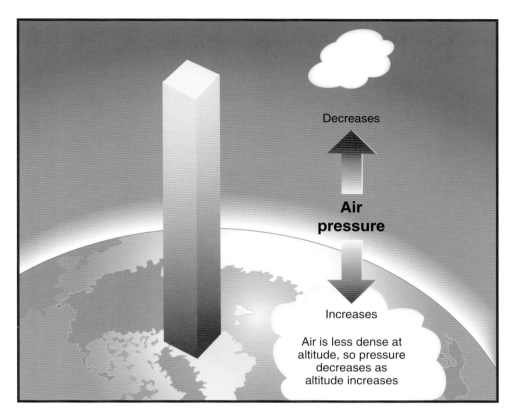

▶ Figure 4.7  Air density and pressure are affected by altitude.

# Density

**Density** is weight per unit volume (for example, pounds per cubic foot). Water is a fluid, but it is much heavier than air. Seawater weighs about 64 pounds per cubic foot (1.025 grams per cubic centimeter), which makes it about 800 times denser than air. Fresh water, because it does not contain salt, weighs a little less than seawater: 62.4 pounds per cubic foot (1 gram per cubic centimeter). Temperature affects the density of water, air, and all fluids; cold water is slightly denser than warm water.

Air can be compressed, but water is essentially incompressible. While air becomes thinner as altitude increases, water density remains constant throughout the water column.

**Drag** is a force that retards movement. Resistance to movement is much greater in water than in air. Factors affecting drag include the viscosity of the fluid, the speed of motion, and the size and shape of the object moving through the fluid. Drag is greater when the fluid is denser, the motion is faster, the object is larger, or the surface of the object is more irregular (see figure 5.9 in chapter 5).

Because of its higher density, the molecules of water are much closer together than those of air. The tightly packed molecules affect the transmission of light, sound, and heat (see table 4.1). Light travels about 27 percent slower in water than in air. Sound travels about 4 times faster in water than in air. Still water conducts heat nearly 25 times faster than air. Moving water can conduct heat hundreds of times faster than air. Water has an enormous capacity for absorbing heat with little change in its temperature. The higher

| Property | Air | Water | Comparison |
|----------|-----|-------|------------|
| Density | 0.08 lb/ft³ (1.3 kg/m³) | 62.4 to 64 lb/ft³ (1,000 kg/m³) | Water is 800 times denser than air. |
| Compressibility | Yes | No | Air density varies; water density is constant (at dive pressures). |
| Speed of light | 186,000 mi/s (300,000 km/s) | 140,000 mi/s (225,400 km/s) | Light travels 27% more slowly in water. |
| Light absorption | Low | High | Water absorbs color quickly. |
| Speed of sound | 1,125 ft/s (340 m/s) | 4,900 ft/s (1,400 m/s) | Sound travels 4 times faster in water. |
| Conductivity | 0.17 | 3.86 to 4.12 | Heat loss is 22 to 24 times faster in water than in air. |
| Heat capacity | 0.24 | 0.94 to 1.0 | The heat capacity of water is 4 times greater than air. |

**Table 4.1  Water Compared With Air**

density of water affects you in many ways when you dive. The next chapter explains how to deal with the effects of water density.

# Buoyancy

An object's ability to float in a liquid depends on the density of the object compared with the density of the fluid in which the object is immersed. Water exerts pressure equally in all directions, even upward. You can feel the upward force **(buoyancy)** of water when you try to push something under water. Buoyancy results from the difference in pressures on the upper and lower surfaces of an object. The weight of an object plus the weight of the fluid (air, water, or both) above the object exert a downward force. Fluid pressure pushes upward from below. The difference between these two forces is the buoyancy of the object.

Archimedes, an ancient Greek scientist, discovered that the force of buoyancy acting on a submerged object equals the weight of the water displaced (this is known as **Archimedes' principle**). A hot-air balloon floats in air because hot air inside the balloon weighs less than the volume of cooler air the balloon occupies. A diver is buoyed upward with a force equal to the weight of the water that the diver displaces (see figure 4.8). If you and your equipment weigh less than the weight of the water you displace, you float, or have positive buoyancy. If you and your equipment weigh more than the water being displaced, you sink. An object that sinks has negative buoyancy. If you and your equipment weigh exactly the same as the water displaced, you neither float nor sink. Instead, you remain at the depth where you are; you have neutral buoyancy.

As a diver, you can float at the surface, sink to the bottom, or hang suspended between the bottom and the surface. If the volume of an object increases with very little change in its weight, buoyancy increases. This happens when you add air to an inflatable jacket or vest. The next chapter addresses the factors affecting buoyancy and the principles of buoyancy control.

**Archimedes' principle**— A body immersed in a fluid is buoyed up by a force equal to the weight of the displaced fluid.

▶ Figure 4.8   Principles of buoyancy.

## Pressure Measurement

Force (often weight) per unit area, such as pounds per square inch or grams per square centimeter, is **pressure.** The envelope of air surrounding the earth is the atmosphere. The weight of one square inch of the atmosphere at sea level is 14.7 pounds (1.03 kilograms per square centimeter), or one atmosphere (atm) of pressure. As you descend in water, the weight of the fluid—the pressure—exerted upon each square inch of your body increases. One square inch of salt water that is 33 feet (10.1 meters) in height weighs 14.7 pounds (1.03 kilograms per square centimeter), 1 atm, or 1.01 bar. One square inch of fresh water 34 feet (10.36 meters) in height also exerts a pressure equivalent to 1 atm. Because 1 bar is almost equal to 1 atm, we consider them identical in this book. Because water does not compress (at the pressures involved with recreational diving), it follows that water pressure increases by 1 atm for every 33 feet (10.1 meters) of salt water (33 FSW) and for every 34 feet (10.4 meters) of fresh water (34 FFW). Figure 4.9 shows how **atmospheric pressure** and water pressure are measured.

The reference for pressure is either the atmospheric pressure at sea level or zero pressure (outer space). A pressure gauge that reads zero at sea level displays only the pressure in excess of one atmosphere. Tire gauges and depth gauges are good examples of instruments that indicate **gauge pressure,** which is measured in pounds per square inch gauge (psig).

**Pressure measurement**

1 in.²

1 atm
gauge
pressure

2 atm
absolute
pressure

3 atm
absolute
pressure

4 atm
absolute
pressure

Each
33 ft of
water
equals 1
atm of
pressure

33 ft

66 ft

99 ft

2 atm gauge
pressure

Absolute pressure equals
gauge pressure **plus**
atmospheric pressure

3 atm
gauge
pressure

| Depth | | Gauge pressure | | | Absolute pressure | | |
|---|---|---|---|---|---|---|---|
| FSW | FFW | In atm | | In psig | In ATA | | In psia |
| 0 | 0 | 0 | = | 0 | 1 ATA | = | 14.7 |
| 33 | 34 | 1 | = | 14.7 | 2 ATA | = | 29.4 |
| 66 | 68 | 2 | = | 29.4 | 3 ATA | = | 44.1 |
| 99 | 102 | 3 | = | 44.1 | 4 ATA | = | 58.8 |
| 132 | 136 | 4 | = | 58.8 | 5 ATA | = | 73.5 |

Gauge pressure compared to absolute
pressure in fresh and salt water.

**Pressure**

1 atm of
air pressure
(14.7 psi)

**Air**
1 in. × 1 in.
×
100 miles

1 atm of
water pressure
(14.7 psi)

**Salt water**
1 in. × 1 in.
× 33 ft

▶ Figure 4.9   Principles of pressure.

The total pressure exerted is what matters to divers. Both the pressures of the atmosphere and the water apply to diving. The reference for the total pressure is zero, as in a vacuum. The total pressure is called **absolute pressure,** which is measured in pounds per square inch, absolute (psia). When we express absolute pressure increments in atmospheres, we use atmospheres absolute (ATA).

You obtain absolute pressure by adding atmospheric pressure to gauge pressure. Be sure you understand the concept because we use absolute pressure when we deal with the effects of pressure in this and later chapters.

# GAS LAWS

When you compress a quantity of gas, you reduce its volume and increase its density. **Boyle's law** states that for any gas at a constant temperature, the volume varies inversely with the absolute pressure, while the density varies directly with the absolute pressure.

## Boyle's Law

If you compress a closed, flexible air space, such as a balloon, you reduce its volume in proportion to the increase in pressure. When you double the pressure, a closed, flexible air space occupies only half the volume that it did at the surface. No air is lost. The molecules compress into a smaller area. The density of the air is twice as great as it was originally. When you return the compressed air space to its original pressure, the air inside expands until the object reaches its original volume. You compress your lungs during a breath-hold descent, and they return to normal volume when you return to the surface, provided that you do not expel air underwater.

Scuba equipment provides air to you at the exact pressure of the surrounding water. This allows you to expand your lungs to their normal volume regardless of the depth. The density of the air inside the lungs is greater in proportion to the water pressure. If the water pressure doubles, the density of the air in your lungs also doubles. Figure 4.10 shows the relationships between pressure, volume, and density.

Boyle's law also applies when you reduce the surrounding pressure. As outside pressure decreases, compressed air in a closed, flexible container expands in proportion to the reduction in pressure; for instance, if the pressure halves, the volume doubles. If a container filled with compressed air at depth is vented correctly during ascent, expanding air escapes through the vent, and the container remains full throughout the ascent. If the container is not vented, pressure inside increases when the container reaches its maximum volume. If the container is weak, the increase in pressure will rupture the container. This concept is important to scuba divers, who have many air spaces filled with compressed air. Vented air spaces do not pose a hazard. But if your lungs are not vented during ascent, life-threatening injuries will result. If you do not vent air from a flotation jacket during ascent, control of buoyancy will be lost as air expands and the jacket volume increases.

| Depth | Pressure | Volume | Density |
|---|---|---|---|
| 0 ft (0 m) | 1 atm | 1.0 | x 1 |
| 33 ft (10 m) | 2 atm | 1/2 | x 2 |
| 66 ft (20 m) | 3 atm | 1/3 | x 3 |
| 99 ft (30 m) | 4 atm | 1/4 | x 4 |

▶ Figure 4.10   Pressure, volume, and density relationships.

Figure 4.10 shows an interesting point about the rate of change of pressure (and volume) in water. The pressure doubles from 1 ATM to 2 ATM in 33 feet (10 meters) of seawater. To double the pressure again requires a depth of 99 FSW (30 meters). Note that you must ascend from 99 feet (30 meters) to a depth of 33 feet (10 meters)—a distance of 66 feet (20 meters)—to experience the same rate of change of pressure that you experience when you ascend from 33 feet (10 meters) to the surface. In other words, the closer you get to the surface, the greater the rate of change of pressure (and of the volume of an air space). You must be more attentive to compressed air in air spaces the nearer you are to the surface.

The change in pressure you experience during descents and ascents in water is perhaps the most significant challenge of diving. Changes in pressure have direct, mechanical effects upon your body. Pressure imbalance in your body air spaces can cause discomfort. You feel pressure changes in air as a result of changes in altitude, although pressure changes in water occur at a much greater rate than in air. You can sustain serious injury unless you keep the pressure in air spaces inside and attached to you equalized with the surrounding water pressure. Boyle's law causes **squeezes** and **reverse blocks,** which figure 4.11 illustrates. Knowledgeable and experienced divers routinely equalize pressures to avoid squeezes and blocks. Keeping pressure in air spaces equalized with the surrounding pressure is one of the main subjects of the next chapter.

## Gay-Lussac's Law

Boyle's law addresses gas at a constant temperature because the temperature affects the pressure and volume of a gas. Jacques Charles, a French chemist, discovered that the volume of gas at a constant pressure changes with temperature. Joseph-Louis Gay-Lussac, a French scientist, defined the effect of temperature: For any gas at a constant volume, the pressure of the gas varies directly with the absolute temperature. Just as absolute pressure must be used for pressure calculations, absolute temperature must be used for temperature computations. The absolute temperature scale for Fahrenheit temperatures is Rankine. To convert a Fahrenheit temperature to Rankine, add 460 degrees. The

**Gay-Lussac's law**—For any gas at a constant volume, the pressure of the gas varies directly with the absolute temperature.

## Squeezes and blocks

If the pressure inside an air space is less than the surrounding water pressure, the outside pressure attempts to compress the air space. This condition is a "squeeze."

During descent, squeezes may occur in ears, sinuses, the mask, and other air spaces in or attached to the body.

During ascent, the pressure surrounding an air space decreases. If the air inside the space, which was equalized to a higher pressure during descent, cannot escape, a situation that is the reverse of a squeeze occurs. When the pressure inside an air space is greater than the surrounding pressure, the condition is a "reverse block."

A "block" describes a situation where some form of blockage prevents compressed air from entering.

Prevention of both squeezes and blocks involves keeping the pressure within an air space equalized with the surrounding pressure.

▶ Figure 4.11 Equalizing pressure.

**Dalton's law**—The partial pressure of a given quantity of gas is the pressure it would exert if it alone occupied the same volume. Also, the total pressure exerted by a mixture of gases is the sum of the pressures that would be exerted by each gas if it alone were present and occupied the total volume.

**Henry's law**—At a constant temperature, the amount of a gas that dissolves in a liquid is directly proportional to the partial pressure of that gas.

absolute temperature scale for a Celsius temperature is Kelvin. To convert a Celsius temperature to Kelvin, add 273 degrees.

You can observe the effect of **Gay-Lussac's law** with a scuba tank, which has a constant volume. Decreasing the temperature of the air in a tank causes the pressure to decrease, while increasing the temperature of the air in a tank causes the pressure to increase. A scuba tank taken from the trunk of a hot car and cooled in water experiences a drop in pressure, although no air leaves the cylinder. Pressure increases or decreases in a standard 80-cubic-foot (2,265 liter) aluminum scuba cylinder at a rate of about 6 psig per degree Fahrenheit temperature change. Pressure increases or decreases in a standard 71.2 cubic foot (2,016 liter) steel scuba cylinder at a rate of about 5 psig per degree Fahrenheit temperature change.

## Dalton's and Henry's Laws

A gas can diffuse into or out of a substance. When a gas comes into contact with a liquid, the gas dissolves into the liquid. The amount of gas that diffuses into the liquid depends on the density and temperature of the liquid, the pressure of the gas in contact with the liquid, and the length of time that the gas is in contact with the liquid. Another term for the process of gas diffusion into a liquid is **ingassing.** Since the human body is primarily liquid, the gases you breathe diffuse into your body tissues.

In a mixture of gases, such as air, the percentage of the total pressure exerted by each gas is the **partial pressure** of that gas. **Dalton's law** states that the total pressure exerted by a mixture of gases is the sum of the pressures that would be exerted by each gas if it alone were present and occupied the total volume. The partial pressure of a gas determines the amount of that gas that dissolves into a liquid. **Henry's law** expresses gas absorption: The amount of a gas that dissolves in a liquid at a given temperature is directly proportional to the partial pressure of that gas. Table 4.2 shows the partial pressures of gases in the air at 1 ATA.

The partial pressure of a gas is the percentage of the gas in the mixture times the absolute pressure of the mixture. The partial pressure of a gas at depth has the same effect as a higher percentage of that gas at the surface. If a mixture of gas contains 2 percent carbon dioxide ($CO_2$) at sea level (14.7 psia, or 1.03 kilograms per square centimeter), the partial pressure of the $CO_2$ is 0.294 psia (0.021 kilograms per square centimeter). If the absolute pressure of the same mixture of gases increases to the pressure found at a depth of 99 feet (30 meters) in the ocean (58.8 psia, or 4.12 kilograms

### Table 4.2 Partial Pressures of Gases in Air at 1 ATA

| Air composition | Percentage of gas | Partial pressure at 1 ATA | Partial pressure at 1 ATA (metric) |
|---|---|---|---|
| Nitrogen | 78% | 11.466 psia | 0.803 kg/cm² |
| Oxygen | 21% | 3.087 psia | 0.2163 kg/cm² · |
| Argon | 0.93% | 0.137 psia | 0.0095 kg/cm² |
| Trace gases | 0.04% | 0.006 psia | 0.0004 kg/cm² |
| Carbon dioxide | 0.03% | 0.004 psia | 0.0003 kg/cm² |
| TOTALS | 100% | 14.7 psia | 1.03 kg/cm² |

per square centimeter), the partial pressure of the $CO_2$ is 1.176 psia (0.082 kilograms per square centimeter). The amount of $CO_2$ sensed by the body at 99 feet (30 meters) is four times greater than the amount that is sensed at the surface. Breathing 2 percent $CO_2$ at a depth of 99 feet (30 meters) is the same as breathing 8 percent $CO_2$ at the surface! A high level of $CO_2$ has a profound effect on respiration. The surface-equivalent effect of partial pressures makes minute amounts of contaminants in breathing gases unsafe at depth. Table 4.3 shows the surface-equivalent effect of partial pressures at various depths.

When a liquid has absorbed all of a gas that it can hold, the liquid is saturated. When you reduce the partial pressure of the gas in contact with the liquid, gas diffuses out of the liquid. This process is **outgassing.** Ingassing and outgassing provide a foundation for the dive tables used to prevent decompression sickness; these tables are presented in chapter 6.

### Table 4.3 Surface-Equivalent Effect of Partial Pressures

| Depth | Pressure | $O_2$[a] | CO[b] | $CO_2$[c] |
|---|---|---|---|---|
| 0 ft (0 m) | 1 ATA | 20% | 1% | 2% |
| 33 ft (10 m) | 2 ATA | 40% | 2% | 4% |
| 66 ft (20 m) | 3 ATA | 60% | 3% | 6% |
| 99 ft (30 m) | 4 ATA | 80% | 4% | 8% |
| 132 ft (40 m) | 5 ATA | 100% | 5% | 10% |

[a] Breathing 20% oxygen at 132 ft (40 m) has the same effect as breathing 100% oxygen at the surface.

[b] Breathing a (toxic) mixture containing 1% CO at 66 ft (20 m) is the same as breathing 3% CO at the surface.

[c] Breathing a mixture containing 2% $CO_2$ at 99 ft (30 m) is the same as breathing 8% $CO_2$ at the surface and causes labored breathing.

# Additional Information About Gas Laws

The following gas formulas can be used to make precise mathematical calculations of pressure, volume, and temperature.

Boyle's law: $P_1V_1 = P_2V_2$

$P_1$ = Initial pressure (psia or ATA)
$P_2$ = Final pressure (psia or ATA)
$V_1$ = Initial volume
$V_2$ = Final volume

*Example*: A balloon with 2 pints of air floats from 2 ATA to the surface (1 ATA). What is the volume of the balloon at the surface?

$P_1$ = 2 ATA
$P_2$ = 1 ATA
$V_1$ = 2 pints
$V_2$ = Unknown

Rearranging the formula to solve for $V_2$, we find that

$$V_2 = \frac{P_1V_1}{P_2} = \frac{(2 \times 2)}{1} = 4 \text{ pints}$$

Partial pressure = absolute pressure × percentage of gas

*Example*: What is the partial pressure of oxygen if the gas constitues 20 percent of a gas mixture that has an absolute pressure of 58.8 psi?

PP = 58.8 × 0.2 = 11.76 psia

Gay-Lussac's law: $\dfrac{P_1}{T_1} = \dfrac{P_2}{T_2}$

$P_1$ = Initial pressure (psia or ATA)
$P_2$ = Final pressure (psia or ATA)
$T_1$ = Initial temperature (°R or °K)
$T_2$ = Final temperature (°R or °K)

*Example*: A scuba tank with a pressure of 2,250 psig and a temperature of 70 °F is heated to a temperature of 150 °F. What is the pressure of the scuba tank at the higher temperature? First, convert readings for pressure and temperature to absolute measures.

$P_1$ = 2,250 psig + 14.7 psia = 2,265 psia
$P_2$ = unknown
$T_1$ = 70 °F + 460 = 530 °R
$T_2$ = 150 °F + 460 = 610 °R

Rearranging the formula to solve for $P_2$, we find that

$$P_2 = \frac{P_1T_2}{T_1} = \frac{2,265 \times 610}{530} = 2,607 \text{ psia}$$

2,607 psia – 14.7 psia = 2,592 psig

# AIR CONSUMPTION

The volume of air you breathe per minute during exertion is much more than the volume you breathe at rest: up to 17 times more on land and about 14 times more in the water. Pressure on the torso in the water allows only 85 percent of normal inhalation.

Because the density of the air breathed increases with depth, depth significantly affects the rate at which you consume air. For a given level of exertion, a supply of air lasts only half as long at a pressure of 2 ATA as it does at a pressure of 1 ATA. With heavy exertion at a pressure of 4 ATA (at a depth of 99 feet, or 30 meters), you exhaust an air supply over 40 times faster than you would when at rest at the surface! The rapid depletion of your air supply is one reason that you must avoid heavy exertion while diving.

The rate of air consumption is expressed in cubic feet per minute (or liters per minute) or psig (or atmospheres or bars) per minute. By knowing your consumption rate for various levels of activity, you can plan your dives. When you know your consumption rate and the amount of air available, you can calculate air-supply duration for future dives.

# HEAT, HUMIDITY, LIGHT, AND SOUND

You experience many changes when you enter water. You lose body heat faster, you lose body moisture when you use scuba equipment, what you see is deceiving, and what you hear can cause confusion. When you understand what happens to you and why, you can better manage the differences between the water and air environments.

## Heat Transfer

The net effect of the various forms of heat transfer is that you can chill quickly while diving. Radiation, convection, and conduction transfer heat from one medium to another (see figure 4.12). Heat waves radiate from exposed surfaces, heat travels upward through fluids by convection, and heat is transferred directly via conduction between substances in contact with each other. Metals are good conductors. Water is a poor conductor compared with metal but conducts heat about 25 times faster than air (depending upon density). Conduction and convection are the primary means by which heat is transferred from a diver to the surrounding water. Heat rises from the skin, and water carries the heat away. You also lose body heat through the process of evaporation. Moisture evaporates from your lungs when breathing underwater and from the surface of your skin when you perspire above water. Scuba equipment expands high-pressure air and cools it. Your body heat warms the air you breathe, and you lose the heat with each exhalation.

You can slow the transfer of heat by insulating yourself with a material that is a poor conductor of heat. Exposure suits help insulate you from the environment, but insulation does not help reduce heat lost through respiration. The next chapter presents ways to manage the problems of heat loss.

## Humidity

Scuba divers must guard against the effects of humidity, the amount of water vapor present in a gas. The temperature of the gas determines the amount of water vapor a gas can absorb and retain. The warmer the gas, the more humidity the gas can contain.

You humidify inspired air. The process of compressing the air that is put into scuba tanks dehumidifies the air in the cylinder. You lose moisture from body tissues when you breathe dry scuba air. The resulting fluid loss can cause partial dehydration, an undesirable condition, especially for a scuba diver. In the next chapter, you will learn how to avoid the problems of dehydration.

Diving poses other humidity problems that you must manage. Moisture in the air inside your mask condenses on the faceplate as the air cools. Unless you thoroughly clean your mask lens in advance so that the condensation

▶ Figure 4.12   Heat transfer and loss.

**Radiation** Heat waves radiate to surrounding objects without physical contact.

**Convection** Heat warms surrounding fluid, which rises and is replaced by cooler fluid.

**Conduction** Heat lost through direct physical contact. Water conducts 25 times faster than air!

**Evaporation (in air)** Perspiration cools when it changes from a liquid to a vapor.

**Respiration** Heat added to air in the lungs is lost with exhalation.

**Losing or retaining excessive heat is dangerous!**

# Additional Information About Air Consumption

The following air consumption formulas can be used to calculate consumption rates and air-supply duration. To calculate the rate of air consumption, you need three items of information: the depth at which you have remained for a period of time, the length of time you have remained at that depth, and the amount of air you have used during that time.

1. Determine your depth air consumption rate (DACR). This is simply the amount of air used divided by the time at depth. For example, the DACR for a diver who uses 1,000 psi (68 atm) in 10 minutes is 100 psi (6.8 atm) per minute.

$$\text{DACR} = \frac{\text{Air used}}{\text{Time at depth}}$$

2. Convert the DACR to the surface air consumption rate (SACR). You need to express the rate in terms of volume rather than pressure. After you do this, you can apply the air consumption rate to any depth and to a cylinder of a different size from the one used initially to calculate the air consumption rate. Obtain the surface consumption rate by multiplying the DACR by the ratio of the pressure at the surface to the pressure at depth. Since you can express pressure in terms of depth, you can use the following formula:

$$\text{SACR} = \text{DACR} \times \frac{33 \text{ ft (or 10 m)}}{\text{Diving depth} + 33 \text{ ft (or 10 m)}}$$

If, for example, your depth consumption rate for a depth of 33 feet (10 meters) is 30 psi (2 atm) per minute, your SACR is 30 (33/66) = 15 psi per minute, or 2 (10/20) = 1.0 atm per minute.

3. Convert the rate to volume, establish a ratio of the tank volume and pressure (when the tank is full) to the breathing rate volume and pressure, then solve for the breathing rate volume (BRV) as follows.

$$\frac{V_1}{P_1} = \frac{V_2}{P_2}$$

where

$V_1$ = Full tank volume

$V_2$ = Breathing rate volume (BRV)

$P_1$ = Full tank pressure

$P_2$ = Breathing rate pressure

so

$$\text{BRV} = \frac{V_1 \times P_2}{P_1}$$

For example, the breathing rate volume (BRV) for a diver with an 80-cubic-foot (2,265-liter), 3,000-psi (204-atm) tank and an SACR of 30 psig (2.04 atm) per minute is

$$\text{BRV} = \frac{80 \text{ ft}^3 \times 30 \text{ psi/min}}{3,000 \text{ psi}} = 0.8 \text{ ft}^3/\text{min}$$

$$\text{Metric BRV} = \frac{2,265 \text{ L} \times 2.04 \text{ atm/min}}{204 \text{ atm}} = 22.65 \text{ L/min}$$

4. For the same level of activity, you can calculate the approximate duration (in minutes) of any amount of air from a tank of any size used at any depth. Here is an example: How long will 1,750 psi (119 atm) of air from a 71.2-cubic-foot (2,016-liter), 2,475-psi (168-atm) tank last at a depth of 70 feet (21.3 meters) for a diver with a breathing rate volume (BRV) of 0.8 cubic feet (22.7 liters) per minute?

First, determine the volume of air in the tank at a pressure of 1,750 psi (119 atm). The formula for determining the volume of air in the tank is

$$V_2 = \frac{V_1 \times P_2}{P_1}$$

where

$V_1$ = Full tank volume

$V_2$ = Partially filled tank volume

$P_1$ = Full tank pressure

$P_2$ = Partially filled tank pressure

The air-supply volume for the partially filled tank is therefore

$$V_2 = \frac{71.2 \times 1,750 \text{ psi}}{2,475 \text{ psi}} = 50.3 \text{ ft}^3, \text{ or}$$

$$V_2 = \frac{2,016 \text{ L} \times 119 \text{ atm}}{168 \text{ atm}} = 1,428 \text{ L}$$

The formula for air-supply duration (ASD) is

$$ASD = \frac{\text{Air-supply volume}}{\text{BRV}} \div \frac{\text{Diving depth} + 33 \text{ ft (or 10 m)}}{33 \text{ ft (or 10 m)}}$$

The air-supply duration (ASD) for the question posed above is

$$ASD = \frac{50.3 \text{ ft}^3}{0.8 \text{ ft}^3/\text{min}} \div \frac{70 \text{ ft} + 33 \text{ ft}}{33 \text{ ft}} = 20 \text{ min}$$

$$\text{Metric ASD} = \frac{1{,}428 \text{ L}}{22.7 \text{ L/min}} \div \frac{21.3 \text{ m} + 10 \text{ m}}{10 \text{ m}} = 20 \text{ min}$$

These calculations may seem complicated at first, but the ideas are simple. The calculations become easy with practice. Let's review the four steps of air consumption calculations: (1) Determine your depth air consumption rate (DACR); (2) determine your surface air consumption rate (SACR); (3) determine your breathing rate volume (BRV); and (4) determine the air-supply duration (ASD) for a quantity of air. The abbreviated formulas for the calculations are

$$DACR = \frac{\text{Air used}}{\text{Time at depth}}$$

$$SACR = DACR \times \frac{33 \text{ ft (or 10 m)}}{\text{Diving depth} + 33 \text{ ft (or 10 m)}}$$

$$BRV = \frac{V_1 \times P_2}{P_1}$$

$$ASD = \frac{\text{Air-supply volume}}{\text{BRV}} \div \frac{\text{Diving depth} + 33 \text{ ft (or 10 m)}}{33 \text{ ft (or 10 m)}}$$

runs off in a thin sheet, foggy beads of condensation form and blur your vision. Chapter 2 presents the process for cleaning, or defogging, your mask.

In freezing temperatures, moisture from your exhaled breath can cause a scuba regulator to freeze. Water in other items of diving equipment also can freeze. If you intend to dive in a cold environment, you should complete special training and know how to prepare and use your equipment in those conditions.

# Light and Vision

The density of water makes it challenging to interpret what we see and hear. Light travels faster in air than in water. When rays of light traveling in water pass through the lens of your mask, they accelerate and bend (refract). The effect is that what you see underwater is magnified. Objects appear to be at three-fourths of their actual distance (25 percent closer) and four-thirds of their actual size (33 percent larger). The visual distortion requires adjustments, and you will learn to make these with experience. An object 12 feet (3.7 meters) away appears to be only 9 feet (2.7 meters) away. A fish that appears about 2 feet (0.6 meters) long actually is only 1.5 feet (0.5 meters) in length. Many new divers discover that items they bring back from diving are much smaller than they perceived them to be underwater. Figure 4.13 illustrates how light is perceived differently in water.

One difficulty caused by the refraction of light is that distant objects appear closer than they are. This can create a hazard in clear water when you look downward from a drop-off. You may be tempted to go to a point that appears to be at a safe distance but might in fact exceed your planned maximum depth. You must realize that distance perception is inaccurate and rely on your depth gauge instead of your vision.

You have two types of vision: day vision and night vision. You use different parts of your eyes for each type. When you move from a brightly lit area into a dimly lit area, it takes 15 to 30 minutes for your vision to adapt to the lower level of light. Even after the adaptation, your ability to see fine details is much less than your ability with day vision. In addition, particles in water diffuse, scatter, and attenuate light. The deeper you go, the

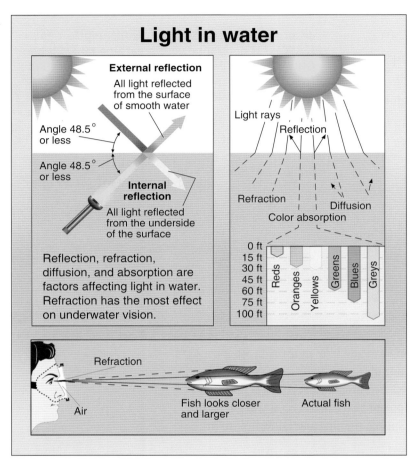

**Light in water**

**External reflection**
All light reflected from the surface of smooth water

Angle 48.5° or less

Angle 48.5° or less

**Internal reflection**
All light reflected from the underside of the surface

Reflection, refraction, diffusion, and absorption are factors affecting light in water. Refraction has the most effect on underwater vision.

Light rays

Reflection

Refraction

Diffusion

Color absorption

0 ft
15 ft
30 ft
45 ft
60 ft
75 ft
100 ft

Reds
Oranges
Yellows
Greens
Blues
Greys

Refraction

Air

Fish looks closer and larger

Actual fish

▶ Figure 4.13 Vision in water.

less light there is. The amount of light decreases very quickly with depth in turbid water. A dive in turbid water involves a change from day vision to night vision.

Water affects light in many ways. The surface of water reflects light. When light strikes the surface of calm water at an angle less than 48 degrees, the water reflects all the light. Early morning and late afternoon sunlight do not penetrate calm water. Light rays going toward the surface from underwater also reflect from the interface, making the underside of the surface appear like a mirror when viewed at the proper angle.

Objects you view underwater often lack their natural colors. White light, such as sunlight, comprises all the colors of the spectrum. Increasing depth absorbs various colors. The water absorbs warm colors, such as red and orange, with only 30 feet (9 meters) of depth. Cooler colors, such as blue, penetrate deepest. This is why deep, clear water is blue. The underwater scene appears drab at depths below 100 feet (30 meters). Fortunately, you can restore all the colors of the spectrum underwater by using an artificial light at close range.

## Sound and Hearing

Sound travels well in water. You can hear many sounds while diving. On land you can determine the direction of a sound by the difference in time that it takes to reach one ear and then the other. This interval is brief but sufficient for your brain to discern it. Underwater you hear sound conducted through water and the bones of your head to your inner ears. Sound travels about four times faster in water than in air. The time delay between the sound's reaching one ear and then the other is so small that directional discernment is difficult underwater.

Sound does not transfer well from air to water. Only 0.01 percent of sound can travel directly between air and water. You must use special devices to make voice communications effective underwater.

## SUMMARY

The aquatic environment affects your body in several ways. Pressure affects your air spaces: your ears, sinuses, and lungs. The rate of change of pressure in water is many times greater than in air and increases as you approach the surface during ascent. Changing pressures also affect the diffusion of gas into and out of liquids. The level of carbon dioxide in your body controls your respiration, and its partial pressure is affected by depth. Temperature also affects the pressure of a constant volume of gas. Depth and activity have the greatest effect on air consumption. Water absorbs heat from the body, so divers need insulation to help prevent excessive heat loss. Humidity can cause several problems for scuba divers. The difference in density between air and water affects your buoyancy, mobility, heat loss, vision, and hearing. Now that you are aware of the effects of the aquatic environment on your body, you are prepared to learn to adapt to the underwater environment.

## Scuba Wise

*There is an old joke about a young woman who returned home from her first session of scuba diving training and was unenthusiastic when asked whether she enjoyed the class. Her reply was, "First the instructor told us all the ways that we could die, then he worked us in the water until I thought that I was going to die." Thankfully, instructors do not teach classes that way today. The reason for learning about potential injuries is to understand how to prevent them. Armed with knowledge that you can convert to wisdom through proper application, you can avoid all of the potential problems identified in this chapter. The use of scuba diving instruction for fitness training also is outdated. Reasonable physical fitness is a prerequisite for scuba diving. Any healthy person who can swim 200 yards (61 meters) continuously is fit enough to dive. The objective of modern scuba training is to help you learn to relax in and under water, not to whip you into shape.*

# Diving Adaptations 5

## Dive In and Discover

By the end of this chapter, you will be able to do the following:

- Define *hypothermia, hyperthermia, vasoconstriction, heat exhaustion, heatstroke, equalization, Toynbee maneuver, Valsalva maneuver, trapdoor effect, skip breathing, barotrauma, pulmonary barotrauma, arterial gas embolism, mediastinal emphysema, subcutaneous emphysema, pneumothorax, vertigo, perfusion, ambient pressure, half-time, compartment, controlling compartment, decompression illness, dehydration,* and *nitrogen narcosis.*

- State the cause, effect, signs and symptoms, first aid treatment, and prevention of hyperthermia, hypo-
thermia, squeezes, reverse blocks, respiratory distress, pulmonary barotrauma, vertigo, seasickness, decompression illness, and nitrogen narcosis.

- Explain three ways to control buoyancy while scuba diving.

- Explain when to equalize pressure in your ears during descent and what to do if the pressure does not equalize.

- Explain how to minimize resistance to movement for underwater swimming.

In chapter 4, you learned about the effects of water on your body. In this chapter you learn how to deal with those effects. Most people with average intelligence and normal health can make aquatic environment adaptations, such as buoyancy control and the equalization of pressure. You make many adaptations automatically, but some you must make consciously. Learning to make the transition from an air environment to an underwater environment requires professional instruction and guidance. You need to learn what to do, then do what you have learned.

To function effectively underwater, you need specific attitudes, equipment, knowledge, and skills. This chapter provides the fundamental knowledge and begins shaping the attitudes required to minimize the risk of injury. You will apply the basic aspects of anatomy, physiology, and physics you have learned to a typical person descending into the depths and ascending back to the surface.

# THERMAL ADAPTATIONS

Maintaining body core temperature within a few degrees of normal is challenging in water. When you are immersed in water, you lose body heat. A water temperature of 50 °F (10 °C) can incapacitate an unprotected diver within 15 minutes. Even water at a temperature of 80 °F (27 °C), which feels relatively warm, can chill a diver within an hour. Wearing only a bathing suit in 80 °F (27 °C) water is the same as being without any clothing in air that is 42 °F (6 °C).

**hypothermia—**
Excessive loss of heat from the core of the body.

Your brain regulates your body functions to maintain your body temperature. If your core temperature is less than 95 °F (35 °C), you will suffer from **hypothermia.** You need to guard against mild and severe hypothermia, both of which can be dangerous. If your core temperature is higher than normal, you experience the effects of **hyperthermia.** You need to understand the effects of two types of hyperthermia—heat exhaustion and heatstroke—and prevent them. They both can be dangerous.

**hyperthermia—**
Higher-than-normal body core temperature.

## Heat Loss

Your body has a variety of physiological responses to the loss of heat. Respiration increases automatically when you get chilled, which is undesirable because as you heat and moisturize inspired air, you lose the heat and moisture with each exhalation. The more you breathe, the more heat and moisture you lose to the environment. Water depth compounds the problem because the greater the surrounding pressure, the greater the density of the air that you breathe. Denser air absorbs more heat than air that is less dense. The deeper you dive, the quicker you get cold.

Anything that affects the function of your body—excitement, fear, seasickness, and other forms of illness—can increase heat loss. This is why good health and a confident state of mind are safety recommendations.

**vasoconstriction—**
Narrowing of the blood vessels.

One way your body responds to cold is to shunt blood from the extremities through **vasoconstriction.** The circulatory shunting reduces heat loss because it keeps warm blood from passing through areas of your body that have little insulation. Your head, underarms and sides, groin, and hands and feet are the areas of your body most prone to heat loss underwater (see figure 5.1). Fortunately, you can insulate these areas easily. You can lose considerable heat from your head in cold water because the head receives a large supply of warm blood and lacks natural insulation. Your body does not shunt blood from your head as it does from other body extremities. In water at a temperature of 70 °F (21 °C) or less, it is important to insulate your head.

Hands have large surface areas relative to their volume. To prevent excessive heat loss from your hands when you get cold, your body shunts blood from them until they reach a temperature of 50°F (10°C). At this temperature, your body restores circulation to your hands to rewarm them partially. Hands quickly lose their warmth to the water. If you dive without hand protection in cold water, you lose body heat through your hands. Since your hands may become numb when they get cold, you should insulate them to conserve body heat.

Small people chill more quickly in water than large people. Small people have less muscle mass to generate and store heat. Insulation is important for all divers, but protection against heat loss is more critical for those of smaller stature.

Failure to wear adequate insulation leads to hypothermia. So does repeated or prolonged exposure. Slow chilling of your body is undesirable. You lose muscle strength and feeling, and your muscles may cramp. Severe heat loss also affects your ability to reason. Another body response to heat loss is shivering, which restores heat through muscular activity. Shivering generates about five times as much heat as your body produces at rest. Shivering is helpful on land, but it is not beneficial in water. Water conducts away the heat you produce by shivering, and you get colder. Uncontrollable shivering indicates that you have lost too much heat from the core of your body and that you cannot rewarm yourself without getting out of the water. When you are shivering, terminate the dive. Rewarm yourself thoroughly before diving again. Warm, dry clothes; warm surroundings; and warm, nonalcoholic drinks help your body temperature return to normal.

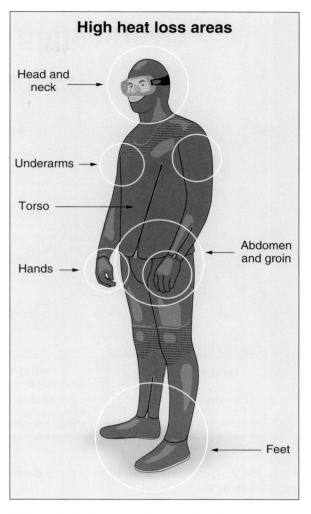

**High heat loss areas**

Head and neck

Underarms

Torso

Hands

Abdomen and groin

Feet

▶ Figure 5.1   Hands and feet are low heat loss areas in air, but they can be high heat loss areas in cold water if unprotected.

There is a difference between warming the surface of your body and warming the core of your body. You may feel rewarmed, but your deep core temperature may remain below normal. If you return to the water in this condition, you quickly will become chilled. The only way to be sure that you are thoroughly rewarmed is to keep warming yourself until you begin to perspire. Perspiration occurs when the core temperature begins to rise above normal.

## Overheating

You can prevent excessive loss of body heat by insulating your body with an exposure suit, but insulation can cause another problem. When you insulate your body to reduce heat loss in water, you reduce your body's ability to rid itself of excess heat above water. The evaporation of the perspiration helps cool your body, but if you cover your body, perspiration cannot evaporate. You may become overheated in warm climates when you are preparing to dive. It is a challenge to maintain your body temperature within acceptable limits before, during, and after dives. Figure 5.2 describes the effects of overheating.

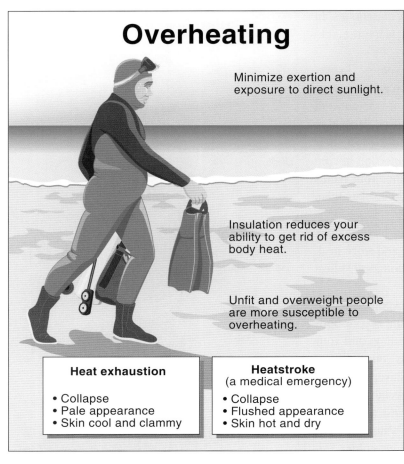

# Overheating

Minimize exertion and exposure to direct sunlight.

Insulation reduces your ability to get rid of excess body heat.

Unfit and overweight people are more susceptible to overheating.

**Heat exhaustion**
- Collapse
- Pale appearance
- Skin cool and clammy

**Heatstroke**
(a medical emergency)
- Collapse
- Flushed appearance
- Skin hot and dry

▶ Figure 5.2 Don't allow yourself to become overheated when preparing to dive.

When a person is unable to stop the rise of core temperature, **heat exhaustion** occurs. This condition is serious. A person affected by heat exhaustion becomes weak and may collapse. The victim looks pale and feels sweaty. Place a person with this condition in a cool place, and take steps to lower his or her body temperature.

A more serious form of hyperthermia is a **heatstroke,** which occurs when the body temperature becomes so high that the body's temperature-regulating ability shuts down. A victim of heatstroke looks flushed and has hot, dry skin. This condition is extremely serious. Cool the patient's body immediately and summon medical assistance.

Preventing hyperthermia is much better than treating it after it occurs. Avoid prolonged exposure to warm temperatures when wearing insulation. If the air temperature is warm, douse yourself with water after donning your exposure suit and before donning the remainder of your diving equipment. Stay out of direct sunlight if possible. All thermal considerations for diving are especially important for divers whose physical fitness is marginal.

# BUOYANCY ADAPTATIONS

Exposure suits and other equipment affect your buoyancy. You must adjust your weight to control your depth in the aquatic environment. When you are too buoyant, you must fight to remain submerged; when you are overweighted, you must work hard to keep from sinking or to stay off the bottom. You need to maintain neutral buoyancy underwater and positive buoyancy at the surface. In chapter 4 you learned the principle of buoyancy and the three states of buoyancy: positive, negative, and neutral. Now you will learn some practical applications of buoyancy.

Your body, composed of solids, liquids, and air spaces, has an average density nearly the same as water. A typical human body immersed and relaxed in water has a positive buoyancy of a few pounds when the lungs are filled with air and negative buoyancy of a couple of pounds when the lungs contain the minimum amount of air.

## Factors Affecting Buoyancy

Usually you wear some type of exposure suit when diving. Most exposure suits increase buoyancy, so you wear weights to offset the buoyancy of the suit and achieve neutral buoyancy. The weights you use are made of lead, which is about 12 times denser than water.

Your initial state of buoyancy in water varies, depending on the volume of water you and your equipment displace. You can vary your volume—with a negligible increase or decrease in your weight—by adding air to or venting air from your BC. Increasing BC volume increases buoyancy, while decreasing BC volume decreases buoyancy.

Your buoyancy is affected by your physical size, your lung capacity, the equipment you wear, and the items you carry (see table 5.1). Exposure suits use air or small bubbles of gas for insulation. When you wear an exposure suit and descend, pressure compresses your suit and reduces its volume, so you become less buoyant. You must add air to your BC to compensate for buoyancy lost from suit compression. On the other hand, buoyancy increases as you consume air from your scuba cylinder. Remember that air weighs 0.08 pounds per cubic foot (1.3 grams per liter). A typical scuba tank contains 80 cubic feet (2,265 liters) of air. A full tank weighs 6 pounds (2.7 kilograms) more than an empty tank. As you consume air from your scuba tank, you can vent some of the air that you added to your BC to compensate for suit compression. The trade-off helps you keep buoyancy constant during a dive.

Inflating your lungs increases your buoyancy, while deflating them reduces buoyancy. A high average lung volume makes you float; a low average volume makes you sink. When you become excited or begin moving quickly, your respiration increases and affects your buoyancy. For optimal control of buoyancy, maintain a calm, relaxed state.

The density of water also affects buoyancy. Salt water is denser than fresh water, so you are more buoyant in the ocean than in a lake. This means that if you are weighted for neutral buoyancy in the ocean, you must remove some weight to achieve neutral buoyancy for freshwater diving. The amount of weight you remove is about 3 percent of the combined dry weight of you and your equipment. For example, if a neutrally weighted 160-pound (73-kilogram) diver with 60 pounds (27 kilograms) of equipment, including 16 pounds (7 kilograms) of weights, wants to dive in fresh water instead of seawater, the diver must remove about 7 pounds (3 kilograms) of weight in order to be weighted correctly.

## Table 5.1 Factors Affecting Buoyancy

| Factor | Effect |
| --- | --- |
| Size and weight of diver | Larger divers are more buoyant. |
| Type and amount of equipment | Larger equipment is more buoyant (due to increased volume). |
| Amount of weight worn | Weights decrease buoyancy. |
| Amount of air in BC | Increasing volume increases buoyancy. |
| Amount of air in tank | Buoyancy increases as air decreases. |
| Amount of air in lungs | Exertion or excitement increases volume and buoyancy. |
| Suit compression | Pressure decreases volume and buoyancy. |
| Items carried | Added weight decreases buoyancy. |
| Type of water | Denser water increases buoyancy. |

## Ways to Control Buoyancy

You control buoyancy three ways: (1) by the amount of weight you wear, (2) by the amount of air in your BC, and (3) by the amount of air in a your lungs. These means of control are coarse, medium, and fine adjustments, respectively. The skills you need to learn to adapt to the aquatic environment include determining the correct amount of weight to be worn, regulating the amount of air in your BC, and varying your breathing for minor buoyancy adjustments. Chapter 3 described these skills.

# PRESSURE EQUALIZATION

One of the most important adaptations you must learn is how to handle the effects of pressure changes in water. Pressure changes rapidly as you descend and ascend. You must keep pressure in the air spaces inside and on your body equalized with the outside pressure to avoid discomfort and injury. This section gives the procedures for pressure equalization.

## Equalizing Pressure in the Sinuses

Your sinuses equalize pressure automatically as long as they are healthy. But when you have a cold or respiratory illness, the membranes lining your sinuses become swollen. The swelling can close the narrow air passages leading to the sinuses. If you descend with swollen sinus membranes, a sinus squeeze will result. Because the sinuses are formed in bone, they do not compress as a flexible container does. When the pressure inside the sinuses is less than the surrounding pressure, the outside pressure forces fluids into the cavities, reducing their volume and compressing the air that is there. Do not attempt this painful method of equalization because your problems are not over after you descend. When you ascend in this condition, the compressed air in the sinuses expands to its original volume. The expansion can force the fluid in your sinuses out through the openings, which are swollen shut. Avoid this painful process; don't dive unless your sinuses are clear and normal. Figure 5.3 shows what happens to both healthy and congested sinuses under pressure.

Do not use medications to relieve stuffiness and congestion caused by an illness before diving. Increased pressure can reduce the medication's effects and the duration of its effectiveness. Decongestants do not cure an illness; they simply mask its symptoms. When medication taken to open swollen airways wears off, a rebound effect occurs. The airways become more swollen than they were before you took the medication. If the rebound occurs while diving, you can trap high-pressure air in your sinuses. If you are not well enough to dive without medications, do not dive.

## Equalizing Pressure in the Ears

You must equalize the pressure in your ears more often than any other air space. Whereas the air passages to your sinuses normally are open, the eustachian tubes leading to your ears normally are closed. You need to learn how to open the tubes at will to allow air to pass through them and equalize pressure in the air spaces of your middle ears.

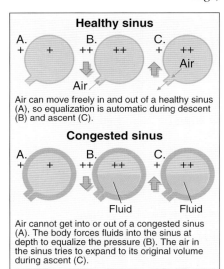

**Healthy sinus**

Air can move freely in and out of a healthy sinus (A), so equalization is automatic during descent (B) and ascent (C).

**Congested sinus**

Air cannot get into or out of a congested sinus (A). The body forces fluids into the sinus at depth to equalize the pressure (B). The air in the sinus tries to expand to its original volume during ascent (C).

▶ Figure 5.3 How pressure is equalized in the sinuses.

You can make several movements to open the ends of the eustachian tubes where they connect with the throat. Swallowing, yawning, lifting the base of your tongue, and jutting the jaw forward (either individually or in combination) should produce a cracking sound in your ears. The opening of the tubes causes the sound. Some divers are fortunate because they can use simple movements to equalize pressure in their ears during descent. Most people require a more forceful means of equalization. Many divers use a technique known as the **Toynbee maneuver,** which you do by blocking your nostrils, closing your mouth, and swallowing. The **Valsalva maneuver** is even more forceful and is done by blocking your nostrils, closing your mouth, and gently attempting to exhale.

You must avoid excessive force when you use the Valsalva method or you can damage your ears permanently by rupturing the round window. When pressure in the outer ear increases, the eardrum bulges inward. The bones of hearing in the middle ear transmit the movement to the oval window in the inner ear. When you attempt to exhale against closed airways, you create an internal pressure on your inner ears. The attempted exhalation pressure in conjunction with the external pressure exerted on the oval window can cause the round window to rupture, a serious injury that can result in a permanent high-frequency hearing loss and constant ringing in the ear. Because you control how hard you attempt to exhale in a Valsalva maneuver, you can prevent this injury. Be careful!

You must equalize pressure in your middle ear air spaces early (prior to descent) and frequently. If you delay equalization during descent, increasing pressure holds your eustachian tubes closed, and attempting to force air through them only closes them tighter. This is the **trapdoor effect,** a difficulty you can avoid by keeping the pressure in your middle ears and your throat equal. You can then open your eustachian tubes and allow air to pass through them. Figure 5.4 shows the trapdoor effect.

Equalize pressure in your ears before descending and about every 2 feet (0.6 meters) for the first 15 feet (4.6 meters) of descent, about every 3 feet (0.9 meters) from 15 to 30 feet (4.6 to 9.1 meters), and as needed thereafter. You can feel and hear air enter your ears when you eliminate any difference in pressure. If you attempt to equalize pressure but cannot get air into your ears, ascend several feet to reduce the pressure on your eustachian tubes and try again. If that works, continue your descent. If that does not work, ascend a few more feet and try again. Your initial descents may be somewhat jerky until you become accustomed to equalization techniques.

Failure to equalize pressure in your middle ears is as bad as trying to equalize forcefully. Pressure bows the eardrum inward in an unequalized middle ear. If the squeeze continues, pressure forces blood and fluid into the middle ear. The process takes time, but it usually is painful and damages the ear. If you feel discomfort or pressure in your ears during descent, reascend until the pain is gone, then ascend another couple of feet before trying to equalize.

**Toynbee maneuver**—A method of opening the eustachian tubes by blocking the nostrils, closing the mouth, and swallowing.

**Valsalva maneuver**—A method of opening the eustachian tubes by blocking the nostrils, closing the mouth, and gently trying to exhale.

Methods:
- Blowing gently with mouth closed and nostrils blocked.
- Swallowing with mouth closed and nostrils blocked.
- Jutting the jaw forward while yawning with mouth closed.

**Trapdoor effect**

When pressure is not equalized often during descent, the pressure difference holds the end of the eustachian tube closed and prevents any further equalization until the diver ascends enough to relieve the pressure.

▶ Figure 5.4  Ear pressure equalization techniques.

If you ignore an ear squeeze and continue your descent, the pressure differential can rupture your eardrum. The rupture instantly equalizes the pressure in your middle ear but damages your ear in the process. A rupture of your eardrum causes a temporary loss of hearing and a feeling of fullness in your ear. Cold water rushing into the middle ear can also cause temporary disorientation. See the section on vertigo later in this chapter. If you suspect an ear injury, see a physician; prompt treatment can minimize the risk of permanent injury.

You can cause an outward rupture of an eardrum if you block the ear canal with a plug or cover your ears with a watertight covering. When you obstruct an ear canal, the air in your outer ear remains at surface pressure while the pressure in your middle ear increases with equalization during descent. The difference in pressure between the middle and outer ear pushes the eardrum outward until it breaks. You can prevent such an injury. Do not wear earplugs while diving, and avoid waterproof seals over your ears.

It is easier to equalize when you descend in an upright position than in a head-down position. Membranes line the airways in your head, and gravity affects blood in the vessels within the membranes. When you are upside down in water, the membranes of your air passages swell and narrow.

Ear equalization difficulties during ascent are uncommon. Air expanding inside the middle ear escapes through the eustachian tube. Air passes out through the tube much more easily than it goes in; you do not have to do maneuvers to open your tubes so the air can escape. But if a plug of mucus happens to block a tube, pressure can build up in the middle ear and cause an uncomfortable reverse block. If you feel pain or pressure in an ear during ascent, stop the ascent. Excess pressure inside the ear usually works its way out if given time. If you are forced to surface, the pain will increase and an injury can result. Have the ear examined by a physician, especially if you have recurring reverse blocks.

## Equalizing Pressure in the Mask

The air space inside the dive mask is affected by changes in pressure. If you descend without increasing the amount of air inside your mask, pressure pulls your face and eyes into the mask slightly. The pulling sensation, if ignored, ruptures capillaries in your eyes and on your face and causes a mask squeeze. After a mask squeeze, the whites of your eyes will be red, and your face will be red and puffy. There is no excuse for a mask squeeze. You can prevent the problem by exhaling through your nose as needed during descent to keep the pressure inside your mask equal to the surrounding pressure.

# BREATHING ADAPTATIONS

Breathing while in water differs from breathing while on land in several ways. You cannot breathe as freely in water as you can on land. Pressure on the lungs from immersion in water prevents you from breathing as fully as you can in air. Also, it is not as easy to get large quantities of air from a scuba system as it is to breathe deeply above water.

When you ascend, compressed air in your lungs expands, which can cause your lungs to rupture unless you allow the excess air to escape. A normal breathing pattern allows expanding air to escape; breath holding does not. A primary rule of scuba diving is to always breathe continuously.

There is a chance that you will inhale some water, which will cause you to choke and gasp when the water strikes your vocal chords. You need to learn the correct methods of breathing while in and under the water.

## Lung Overexpansion

The most important aquatic breathing adaptation is overcoming the instinct to hold your breath underwater. When you breathe compressed air at depth, the density of the air in your lungs is greater than it is at the surface. When you ascend, the air in your lungs expands as the surrounding pressure decreases. If you hold your breath, your lungs expand until they reach their maximum volume, then rupture with an ascent of as little as four feet (1.2 meters). It is imperative that you avoid breath holding when breathing compressed air underwater. You should breathe continuously or exhale a small amount of air continuously, but never hold your breath during ascent after breathing compressed air. Figure 5.5 illustrates why you must breathe continuously. Table 5.2 describes the possible consequences of breath holding while ascending with compressed air in your lungs.

## Skip Breathing

Some divers attempt to extend their air supplies by holding each breath for several seconds. This dangerous practice is called **skip breathing.** When you hold your breath, you increase the amount of carbon dioxide in your circulatory system. A high carbon dioxide level in your body reduces your ability to cope with a difficulty, should one arise. And if you skip breathe, you can forget to exhale while ascending or have a headache after the dive. It is important to breathe continuously when breathing compressed air.

## Breathing Problems

Divers can encounter respiratory difficulties if they overexert themselves, breathe contaminated air, inhale water, or run out of air. Fortunately, you can prevent all of these problems.

### Overexertion

Scuba equipment allows you to breathe comfortably while underwater. A regulator delivers air with little respiratory effort, but breathing underwater requires more effort than breathing above water. If you do not maintain your scuba equipment properly, the effort required to inhale and exhale can be excessive and can cause respiratory distress.

Scuba regulators have a limited capacity to supply air. Regulators are not for activities involving heavy exertion. Commercial divers use helmets with air hoses to supply large amounts of air to meet their requirements while working underwater. You must avoid strenuous activities underwater because you can overbreathe your equipment and experience air starvation, a suffocating feeling of not being able to get enough air.

While diving, make your breaths longer and slower than your breaths on land. Pace your activity to keep respiration at a slow, controlled rate. If breathing becomes rapid or labored, cease all activity immediately and exhale deeply until your respiration returns to a controlled rate.

### Contaminated Air

If the compressed air in your tank comes from an air compressor that is not operated or maintained properly, your tank can contain contaminated air. The contamination is likely to be carbon monoxide (CO), a gas produced by

**The most important rule of scuba diving:**
*Always keep breathing. Do not hold your breath.*

**125**

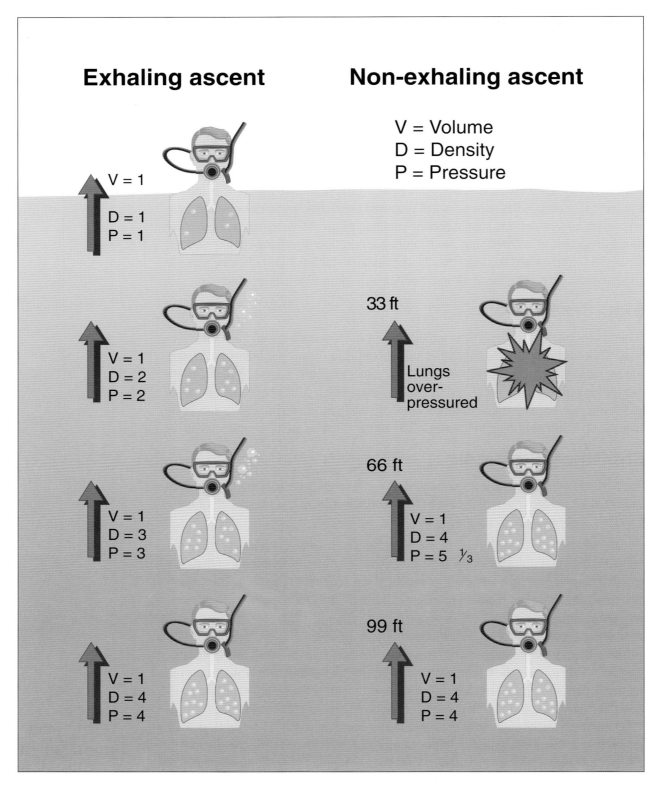

▶ Figure 5.5  A breath-holding ascent after breathing compressed air can cause lung rupture. Breathe continuously while ascending.

**Table 5.2 Potential Lung Injuries**

## Pulmonary Barotrauma

**Barotrauma** is trauma or injury caused by pressure. **Pulmonary barotrauma** is any lung injury caused by pressure. Failure to allow expanding air to escape from the lungs during ascent can cause several forms of pulmonary barotrauma, either singularly or in combination.

## Arterial Gas Embolism

An *embolism* is a blockage of circulation. An embolism resulting from an air bubble blocking the arterial circulation is an **arterial gas embolism** (AGE). This occurs when air expanding in the lungs forces bubbles of air into the circulation. Air bubbles enter the capillary beds of the lungs and pass through the heart, which pumps the bubbles into arteries supplying blood to the body. The diameter of an artery decreases as the distance from the heart increases. At some point a bubble lodges in an artery and becomes an embolus (plug). It is common for an arterial gas embolism to occur in an artery leading to the brain. The embolus has the effect of a stroke, causes unconsciousness, and is an extremely serious injury. Anytime a diver loses consciousness after a dive, you should suspect AGE. The temporary obstruction of an airway, such as that caused by a cold, increases the risk of AGE. Healthy lungs are a prerequisite for diving.

**Air embolism**

## Mediastinal Emphysema

If a rupture of the lung does not force air into the circulation, the air may travel along the bronchi and enter the middle area of the chest, called the *mediastinum*. This results in a **mediastinal emphysema,** which means air in the tissues in the middle of the chest. The injury causes a dull ache or tightness that worsens with coughing, swallowing, or taking a deep breath. Expanding air can interfere with the circulation of the heart and cause loss of consciousness.

**Mediastinal emphysema**

## Subcutaneous Emphysema

Expanding air in the mediastinum can migrate upward along the breastbone. The air then swells the tissues around the neck, producing an injury known as **subcutaneous emphysema,** which is air in the tissues under the skin. The injury can cause changes in the voice, crackling of the skin, and a feeling of fullness in the neck.

**Subcutaneous emphysema**

## Pneumothorax

If a lung rupture forces air into the space between the lungs and the lining of the chest wall, a condition known as **pneumothorax** occurs. The term means air trapped in the chest cavity. As air trapped in the pleural space expands during ascent, it collapses the lung and can affect the action of the heart. Symptoms are severe pain and breathing difficulty.

Lung injuries are serious and can be life threatening. Life support may be required. This is one reason that you should complete a course in cardiopulmonary (heart and lung) resuscitation (CPR). You may have to administer first aid until professional medical treatment (which all lung injuries require) is available.

Failing to allow excess air to escape causes nearly all lung overexpansion injuries. You can prevent injuries by breathing continuously. If you remove the scuba regulator from your mouth for any reason, exhale lightly and continuously to avoid breath holding.

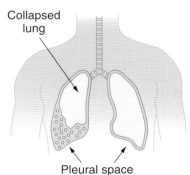

Collapsed lung

Pleural space

**Pneumothorax**

incomplete combustion. CO in the body impedes the blood's ability to transport oxygen. Blood hemoglobin's affinity for CO is 210 times greater than its affinity for oxygen. Hemoglobin normally exchanges oxygen for $CO_2$ about every half minute, but when CO attaches to hemoglobin, the contaminant remains bonded to the hemoglobin for hours. Breathing contaminated air under pressure can make you ill and render you unconscious. Avoid contaminated air by having your tank filled only with pure air. CO is an odorless, tasteless gas, but usually other gases that have a foul taste and odor accompany it. If the air from a scuba tank smells or tastes foul, do not use it. Report the situation immediately to the facility that filled the cylinder. Good air stations have their air tested regularly to ensure purity.

### Water Inspiration

If you inhale water, your larynx spasms as a reflex action to keep the liquid out of your lungs. Avoid coughing and choking in water; not only are these reflexes unpleasant, but they can cause you to inspire more water and lose buoyancy. You need to breathe differently underwater than you do on land. Avoid quick inhalations. Begin a breath with a light, slow inhalation to ensure that you are inhaling air and not water. Once air begins flowing, the remainder of your inhalation can be normal.

You also can prevent droplets of water from going down your throat by placing the tip of your tongue on the roof of your mouth behind your upper teeth to act as a splashboard. If, in spite of all you do to avoid it, you inhale some water and start coughing, try swallowing hard three times in rapid succession. The swallowing helps you overcome your coughing reflex.

If water does enter your lungs, it interferes with respiration. If an extensive area of the lungs is irritated by water, you can drown. This is a risk you face in any aquatic pastime. The purpose of your training is to allow you to enjoy the aquatic environment with the minimum risk of injury, especially of drowning. When you follow the rules and practices that you are taught, the risk of injury while diving is negligible.

An automatic response to the inhalation of water is to swallow it in an effort to keep your airways dry. When you swallow salt water, you can experience illness, nausea, or diarrhea. If you swallow several mouthfuls of salt water while diving, terminate the dive.

### Running Out of Air

Some divers do not monitor their air supplies and run out of air at depth. There is no more excuse for running out of air underwater than there is for running out of gas on the freeway when you have a working gauge. There are ways to manage an out-of-air situation, but it is much better to avoid the problem by monitoring your instruments and keeping them in working order.

# HEART AND LUNGS

ONLY FOOLS STRETCH THE RULES

Immersion changes your cardiac workload. When you are upright in water, there is greater pressure on your lower limbs than on the upper part of your body. The pressure differential shifts more blood than normal into the upper part of your body. Your heart pumps a greater volume with each beat and works from 1.3 to over 1.5 times harder in this situation than it does on land.

Water temperature alters the rate and rhythm of your heart, and physical and emotional stress make it work harder. The combined effects of water pressure, exercise, cold, and stress can cause serious problems if your heart is not healthy. If you have heart problems and wish to dive, you should first obtain medical approval from a diving physician. Even minor heart problems can cause you to suddenly lose consciousness in the water, and you could drown. Fitness for diving is an important safety issue.

Your ability to exert effort in water is not as good as it is on land. Your heart and lungs do not function as well as normal when under pressure. Trying to work hard underwater leads to overexertion and a frightening sensation of suffocation. To adapt to your cardiopulmonary limitations, you must learn to limit your activities and pace yourself.

# EQUILIBRIUM ADAPTATIONS AND SEASICKNESS

If you rupture an eardrum, water colder than body temperature can come into contact with the semicircular canals of your inner ear. The canals are your center of equilibrium and are sensitive to temperature and pressure changes. Cold water cooling the semicircular canals can cause **vertigo,** a feeling of dizziness and disorientation, which passes when the water in the middle ear warms to body temperature. Obviously, it is better to prevent vertigo than to deal with it.

A sudden change in pressure in the middle-ear air space of one ear that affects the semicircular canals can also produce a dizziness called alternobaric vertigo. The disorientation from alternobaric vertigo passes quickly when the inner ear recovers.

There are many causes of vertigo. Fortunately, instances of severe disorientation are rare in diving. If you experience disorientation while underwater, try to grasp a solid object for a point of reference until the feeling passes. If suspended in the water, close your eyes and hug yourself to reduce the effects of the vertigo. Avoid panic by telling yourself that the sensation will not last long.

Motions detected in your inner ears, visual references, and pressures on the joints of your limbs all affect your equilibrium. When your brain receives mixed signals from your inner ears, eyes, and body, you can experience motion sickness. You must avoid seasickness—motion sickness experienced aboard a vessel—because vomiting in or under the water is hazardous.

Medications can help reduce the tendency to be seasick. The medicine dulls the senses of the organs of balance in your ears. Unfortunately, the medications can have other undesirable effects. If you are prone to seasickness, consult a diving physician about the type of medication you should try. Take some of the medicine several days before you plan to dive, and note the effects, if any. If the medication produces drowsiness or blurred vision, do not use it while diving. Seek an alternative that does not produce side effects. Medications that cause dizziness, drowsiness, changes in heart rhythm, or blurred vision can cause you to lose consciousness under pressure. Many divers do successfully use medications to prevent seasickness; you need to find a type that works for you. Take motion-sickness medication at least 30 minutes before you are exposed to motion.

If you do not want to use medication, there are other techniques you can use to reduce the likelihood of seasickness. Eat a good, nonspicy meal before diving. An empty, acid-filled stomach becomes upset more easily than a full one. People whose breakfast before diving consists of coffee and orange juice are good candidates for motion sickness. When aboard a vessel, position yourself as near the center of the boat as possible. Avoid the front end of the boat, breathing engine fumes, and reading. You can reduce your reaction to the boat's motion by lying down for a while with your eyes closed. Being still allows your inner ears to adapt to the motion without visual signals confusing your brain.

You can become disoriented when you are weightless in a dimly lit environment. Under some conditions it can be difficult to tell which way is up if you rely only on your sense of balance. To prevent disorientation, learn to recognize clues about your orientation in the water. Water in your mask settles to the lowest point, bubbles ascend, and heavy objects you hold (such as your weight belt) orient themselves up and down.

# VISUAL ADAPTATIONS

Experience will help you adapt to magnified vision underwater. You can adapt so quickly to distance corrections in water that you have to readapt when you surface from a dive. At the end of a dive, the distance to a boat or to the shore can look much greater than it is. You may be surprised to find that you require less time than you think to swim to a destination.

Your vision also compensates for color differences. If you know a thing's true color, it looks more like that color. The use of artificial light at close range makes it easier to view the rich and magnificent colors in the underwater world.

Your vision adapts to low light levels, but the process takes time. Short, deep dives in turbid water do not allow your visual adaptation to complete, and details will not be clear. You cannot see well without artificial light. You can improve your ability to see while diving by avoiding bright light and glare before a dive. Wear good, dark sunglasses above water during the day. When you complete training for night diving, you will learn other techniques to help your eyes adapt for diving at night.

Humidity can cause condensation to form on the lens of your mask and obscure your vision. A clean glass surface will not fog, so make sure you clean the lens or lenses of your mask thoroughly before diving.

# INGASSING AND OUTGASSING ADAPTATIONS

Your body absorbs nitrogen underwater, and there are limits to the amount of nitrogen that you can safely eliminate at the end of a dive. If you exceed these limits, you can be injured.

## Decompression Theory

Gases diffuse by moving from areas of greater concentration to areas of lesser concentration. When external pressure increases, gases diffuse from your lungs into your blood and then from your blood into your tissues. When the **ambient** (surrounding) **pressure** decreases, diffusion occurs in the reverse sequence.

Two factors affecting diffusion of gases in your body are time and **perfusion** (the circulation in a tissue). The greater the circulation in a tissue, the sooner the pressures of the gases in that tissue come into balance with the pressures of the gases you breathe. Reaching this state of equilibrium takes time. The amount of time it takes a tissue to accumulate half of the gas it can hold at a given pressure is a **half-time.** A tissue is saturated (holds all the gas it can at a given pressure) after six half-times. If perfusion permits 50 percent of a gas to diffuse into a tissue in 5 minutes, the tissue saturates in 30 minutes. Outgassing also occurs in six half-times.

Air is primarily nitrogen and oxygen. The oxygen in the air you breathe is of no concern during decompression within the limits of recreational diving (130 feet or 39.6 meters maximum) because you use the oxygen. Nitrogen, the primary component of air, is inert. Your body cannot use the nitrogen, so when you ascend, you must eliminate the excess nitrogen that you absorbed at depth. Because nitrogen diffuses from your body, there is no problem unless the reduction in pressure is so great that you cannot eliminate the nitrogen fast enough. When you reduce the pressure on a liquid rapidly and there is sufficient gas dissolved in the liquid, the gas forms bubbles. An excellent example of this is $CO_2$ dissolved in carbonated beverages (see figure 5.6). The gas remains dissolved in a sealed, pressurized container. When you reduce the pressure suddenly by opening the container, the gas forms bubbles because it cannot diffuse out of solution slowly. If a beverage container has a tiny leak, however, the carbon dioxide comes out of solution slowly without bubbling. There is no bubbling when you open a container that has a slow leak because the gas has already diffused out of solution.

You must be concerned about the amount of nitrogen in solution in your body and the rate at which you eliminate it. If you absorb too much nitrogen while diving and do not ascend in a manner that allows the excess nitrogen to be eliminated without forming bubbles, the bubbles are likely to cause decompression sickness, a serious diving illness.

Mathematical models provide estimates of the amount of nitrogen in different parts of your body. Because perfusion varies, tissues absorb nitrogen at differing rates. Decompression experts use mathematical models, called **compartments,** to estimate gas absorption and elimination by various areas of the body. A compartment is identified by its half-time. A 5-minute compartment has a half-time of 5 minutes. Experts use compartments ranging from 5 minutes to as long as 960 minutes when calculating gas absorption and elimination.

A compartment that has absorbed gas can withstand some lowering of pressure before bubbling occurs. Originally scientists believed that a reduction in pressure by a ratio greater than two to one would cause bubbling to occur in divers whose tissues were saturated at a particular depth. This ratio was considered a surfacing limit that could not be exceeded. Then scientists discovered that, due to differences in perfusion, the surfacing ratios are different for various compartments. Those that eliminate gas quickly have a higher surfacing ratio than compartments that eliminate gas slowly. The difference in ratios poses an interesting and complex problem for divers because one tissue controls how long a diver can remain at one depth, while another tissue controls how long the diver can remain at another depth. The **controlling compartment** was used to establish our modern time limits for diving. Do not remain at any depth longer than the time it takes the controlling compartment to exceed its surfacing ratio. If you do, you must prevent bubble formation by stopping during the ascent to allow time to eliminate the excess gas. The time limits for various depths have been conveniently arranged into tables and included in dive computer software to help you keep the amount of nitrogen in solution in the various tissues of your body within the surfacing ratio of each and every compartment.

It takes time to eliminate excess gas from tissues. The rate at which you reduce pressure (ascend) is important. The dive tables presented in chapter 6 use an ascent rate, or

▶ Figure 5.6    When you reduce the pressure on a liquid rapidly and sufficient gas is dissolved in the liquid, the gas forms bubbles.

**controlling compartment**—The area of the body that determines how long a diver can remain at a given depth. The determination is made by how quickly a gas diffuses from that compartment.

pressure reduction rate, no greater than 30 feet (9 meters) per minute. Some dive computers' mathematical models use rates two to three times slower than the dive tables. It is important to ascend slowly to prevent the formation of bubbles in your body tissues.

# Decompression Sickness

Commonly known as the bends, decompression sickness (DCS) is the result of a reduction in pressure (decompression) that is too rapid for the amount of gas in solution in body tissues. The gas forms bubbles in the tissues or in the blood before it can diffuse into the lungs and be eliminated. Scientists do not fully understand what occurs when DCS strikes. The symptoms may appear immediately after surfacing from a dive or days after diving. About half of all DCS cases occur within one hour after diving. The symptoms vary, depending on the amount and location of the bubbles. Severe cases of decompression sickness can have severe neurological effects and produce permanent paralysis. These are common symptoms:

- A mottled skin rash
- Joint pain
- Numbness
- Tingling
- Weakness
- Paralysis

These factors can increase the chances of DCS:

- Lack of sleep
- Alcohol and its aftereffects
- Dehydration
- Illness
- Age
- Cold water
- Exercise during and after diving
- Altitude after diving

Some experts believe that you should avoid postdive activities that stimulate circulation because increased perfusion may contribute to DCS. Specific activities to avoid include physical exercise, drinking alcoholic beverages, and taking hot showers or baths. Reduced pressure at altitude, such as flying in a plane or driving into the mountains, too soon after diving is an additional risk factor that can cause DCS. Avoid all activities that increase the likelihood of decompression sickness.

A person suffering from DCS requires prompt first aid and medical treatment. The illness worsens with time. The best first aid measure is to administer oxygen in the highest concentration possible. Breathing oxygen eliminates nitrogen in inspired air and enhances the diffusion of nitrogen from the body. The patient should remain still and sip water. Make arrangements to have the patient transported to the nearest medical facility. After initial medical treatment, the medical staff will arrange to transfer the patient to a facility that has a hyperbaric (high-pressure) chamber. The patient is placed inside a large vessel, called a recompression chamber (see figure 5.7). Hyperbaric treatment consists of increasing the pressure in the chamber to reduce or eliminate the symptoms, administering medications, and then slowly decompressing the patient. Recompression must be done in a chamber. Never attempt in-water recompression of a victim of DCS.

Decompression sickness is extremely serious because it can cause permanent injury. To reduce the likelihood of DCS, remain well within the established time/depth limits for diving. Surface at a rate no faster than that specified by the dive computer you use. Stop during every ascent for two to three minutes at a depth between 10 and 30 feet (3 and 9 meters) to eliminate excess nitrogen before surfacing (see figure 5.8). Ascending at the proper rate and stopping are forms of decompression that reduce the likelihood of DCS.

▶ Figure 5.7 Increasing pressure inside a recompression chamber can reduce the symptoms of decompression sickness.

▶ Figure 5.8 Be sure to complete all necessary precautionary decompression stops when ascending.

An initial precaution to avoid DCS is to delay excursions to altitude after diving. The details about planning your ascent and time delays are given in chapter 6.

## Decompression Illness

**decompression illness (DCI)**—A condition in which a diver has minor symptoms of AGE upon surfacing, recovers, and then develops a severe case of DCS.

When a patient has symptoms of both arterial gas embolism (AGE) and DCS, the medical diagnosis is **decompression illness** (DCI). This is a relatively new term used to describe a unique condition: A diver surfaces from a dive, has some minor symptoms of AGE, recovers somewhat, then develops a severe case of DCS. Any diver who has neurological symptoms following a dive should seek medical attention immediately.

## Nitrogen Narcosis

The increased partial pressure of nitrogen can cause a condition known as nitrogen narcosis, or rapture of the deep, at depths of about 100 feet (30 meters) and deeper. Scientists do not know the exact mechanism of nitrogen narcosis, but its effects are similar to those of anesthetic gases. The feelings associated with narcosis range from euphoria to overconfidence to terror. Narcosis impairs thinking, judgment, reasoning, memory, and the ability to do physical tasks. Narcosis is hazardous; it reduces your awareness and ability to respond to an emergency. Susceptibility to narcosis varies from person to person and within an individual from day to day.

Narcosis begins suddenly at depth. You can relieve its symptoms rapidly by ascending to a shallower depth to reduce the narcotic effect.

The following factors predispose a person to narcosis:

- A high level of systemic $CO_2$ caused by exertion
- Alcohol or its aftereffects
- Anxiety
- Cold
- Medications
- Social drugs

Experience, frequent diving, and concentration reduce susceptibility to narcosis, but it is better to prevent narcosis than to attempt to cope with it.

# DEHYDRATION PREVENTION

You need to preserve body fluids to prevent **dehydration.** Getting cold makes you produce more urine than normal. You receive air underwater by creating an inhalation pressure that opens valves in your air delivery system. The inhalation pressure is slight, but it is greater than normal. Inhaling harder than normal is negative-pressure breathing, which also has the physiological effect of increasing urine production. Breathing underwater compounds the problem of dehydration.

Diuretic beverages (such as coffee and alcohol) and some types of medications cause increased urine production. Avoid ingesting anything that makes you urinate more than normal. You must prevent excessive dehydration because the condition predisposes you to diving injuries. Do the following to prevent dehydration:

- Insulate yourself to stay as warm as possible.
- Keep your regulator well maintained so you can breathe as easily as possible.
- Avoid diuretic drinks and medications.
- Replenish body fluids frequently; drink fluids before and between dives.

# MOBILITY ADAPTATIONS

The equipment that you wear for diving limits your mobility. It reduces your range of motion and makes it difficult to walk. The colder the water, the thicker your exposure suit, and the less your range of movement.

Diving equipment is fairly heavy, and it is challenging to lift and move. Improper lifting techniques can cause back injuries. Squat down and lift with your legs to pick up a tank or weight belt instead of bending over. The weight of the equipment changes your center of gravity and affects your balance. Keeping your balance can be challenging on a rocking boat or an uneven bottom during entries and exits. Move carefully and hold on to something or someone for support when you move around out of the water.

You wear fins so that you can use the large muscles of your legs for propulsion. When diving, you need to learn to use your legs for swimming and your body angle to control direction. These techniques free your hands for other uses underwater. Do not use your hands for propulsion. Fins make it difficult for you to walk when you're out of the water. Shuffle your feet while moving backward or sideways, keep your knees bent, and be careful not to fall.

Drag retards your movement in the water. One factor affecting drag is the speed of motion. The greater the speed, the greater the resistance to movement. The average diver can sustain a speed of a little more than one mile an hour (0.9 knot, or 1.6 kilometers per hour). A knot equals 1.15 miles per hour (1.85 kilometers per hour) and is the method of measuring speed in water. Doubling the speed increases the energy requirement fourfold. Trying to move in water as if it were air causes exhaustion quickly. Use a slow, steady pace and slow, deliberate motions to reduce the effects of drag.

Another factor affecting drag is the size of the object in motion. The larger the surface area exposed, the greater the resistance. A swimming diver is under the influence of four forces: weight (negative buoyancy) pulls the diver downward, lift (positive buoyancy) pulls the diver upward, thrust moves the diver forward, and drag retards forward progress (see figure 5.9). Divers usually wear weight around the waist, which pulls the lower half of the body downward. Buoyancy from the BC lifts the upper half of the body. The effect of these forces increases the surface area of the diver and therefore the drag. Adjust the amount of weight you wear so that your body is as horizontal as possible in the water. Correct weighting minimizes drag and the effort required to swim.

Water flows smoothly across a smooth and rounded surface but turbulently across an irregular surface. When the surface is irregular, the turbulent flow increases drag. Just as vehicles designed to travel through fluids are streamlined to reduce the drag caused by turbulent flow, you can choose and configure your equipment so that it presents the smoothest surface possible to the flow of water.

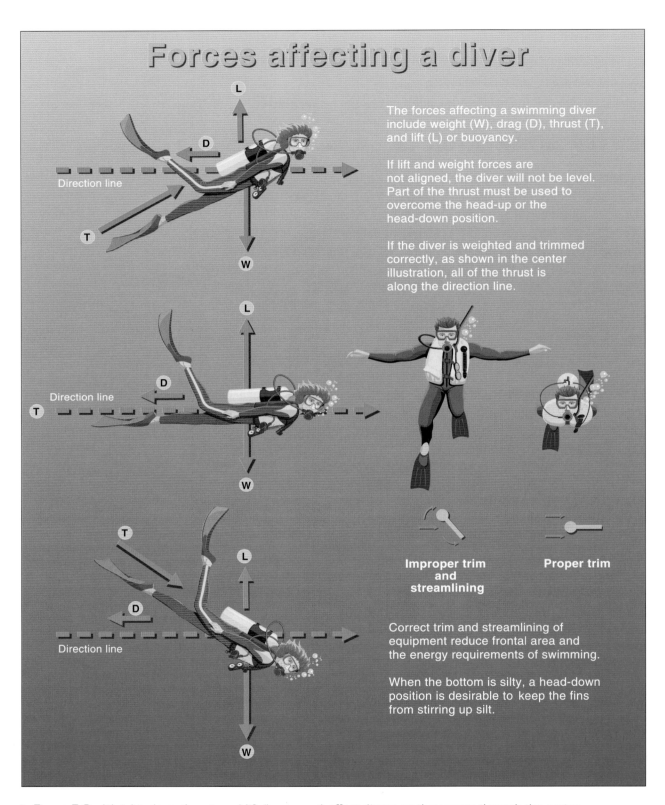

# Forces affecting a diver

L

D

Direction line

T

W

The forces affecting a swimming diver include weight (W), drag (D), thrust (T), and lift (L) or buoyancy.

If lift and weight forces are not aligned, the diver will not be level. Part of the thrust must be used to overcome the head-up or the head-down position.

If the diver is weighted and trimmed correctly, as shown in the center illustration, all of the thrust is along the direction line.

L

D

Direction line

T

W

**Improper trim and streamlining**

**Proper trim**

Correct trim and streamlining of equipment reduce frontal area and the energy requirements of swimming.

When the bottom is silty, a head-down position is desirable to keep the fins from stirring up silt.

T

D

Direction line

L

W

▶ Figure 5.9   Weight, drag, thrust, and lift (buoyancy) affect divers as they move through the water.

# SUMMARY

You have to make many changes in your normal behavior to adapt to the underwater environment. The way you breathe is the most important adaptation. You must breathe continuously and avoid breath holding when you use scuba equipment. You must also limit your activity and pace yourself to avoid overexertion. Managing the mechanical and physiological effects of pressure requires major adaptations. You must keep pressure equalized in your air spaces to avoid pressure injuries and limit your depth and time at depth to avoid nitrogen narcosis and decompression sickness. Being in the underwater environment seems strange at first, but you can adapt to weightlessness and other strange feelings. The sensations of diving become exhilarating as you gain experience in the new world beneath the surface.

# Scuba Wise

At some point in time many divers discover a special feeling of becoming part of the underwater world. I remember vividly an overwhelming feeling—a strange combination of peace and exhilaration—that I experienced during a dive in the Red Sea. The goal of training is to help you adapt to a new environment. When you can adapt, you can relax, and when you can relax, you can focus more on your exciting new surroundings than on yourself. It is challenging to meet the demands of diving, but when you succeed, the exuberance is worth every adaptation you have to make. People can adapt well to new situations. Training helps us adapt more quickly, easily, and safely than we can by trial and error. Study the remaining chapters carefully to learn how to adapt to the subaquatic environment. I want you to feel what I felt in the Red Sea and have felt many times since while diving. The feeling of being one with the sea is powerful, moving, and unforgettable.

# Dive Planning 6

## Dive In and Discover

By the end of this chapter, you will be able to do the following:

- List at least nine factors to consider in dive planning.
- Explain the why, who, where, when, how, and what of advance planning.
- Explain the on-site planning procedures for a dive.
- List at least five methods of obtaining area orientations for scuba diving.
- Use dive tables to plan repetitive dives that do not require decompression.
- Explain the planning procedures for cold or strenuous dives, variations in ascent rate, multilevel dives, omitted decompression, diving after required decompression, going to altitude after diving, exceeding maximum time when doing precautionary decompres-

sion, and a repetitive-dive residual nitrogen time that exceeds the absolute bottom time of the previous dive.

- Define the following terms: *residual nitrogen, repetitive dive, surface interval time, maximum bottom time, decompression stop, repetitive group, safety stop, residual nitrogen time, actual bottom time, total bottom time, emergency decompression, no-decompression-stop limit, dive profile, step dive, spike dive, multilevel dive profile, sawtooth dive profile, scrolling,* and *contingency plan.*
- Explain contingency planning for scuba diving.
- Compare the advantages and disadvantages of dive computers.

First you learn the theory of diving, then the skills of diving, and then you apply what you have learned. Your training objective is to qualify to dive without supervision, which involves planning your underwater excursions.

In this chapter you will learn about all phases of dive planning: advance planning, short-term planning, on-site planning, and postdive planning. You also will learn about area orientations and how to do dive profile planning. An essential part of dive planning is to schedule your time and depth to avoid DCS.

# DIVE-PLANNING FACTORS AND PHASES

A well-planned dive increases enjoyment and satisfaction and decreases the risk of injury. A poorly planned dive can result in disappointment, embarrassment, and discomfort. By the end of this chapter you will understand the significance of the expression, "Plan your dive, and then dive your plan."

## Dive-Planning Factors

Many factors affect your plans for a dive or a diving trip. Keep the following considerations in mind when you are looking ahead to a dive outing.

• Health and fitness are important. Illnesses, required medications, and recent operations probably disqualify you for diving. If your health is not normal, consult a diving physician. If there is any doubt, refrain from diving until you are in good health. If you are prone to motion sickness, try to prevent it.

• Climate is a big factor affecting dive planning. If you dive close to where you live, dive planning is easier than if you intend to dive thousands of miles away. A difference in climate usually means a big difference in diving conditions, which means a difference in your equipment requirements.

• The distance you travel to a diving destination affects your planning. Allow a day to rest and recover from travel before you dive. After two or more days of repetitive diving, wait one full day before flying home.

• Weather affects diving conditions significantly. Storms and sudden changes in the weather can make diving dangerous. Know the weather forecast, and reschedule your dive if poor weather is predicted. Know the expected wind speed, air temperature, and water conditions.

• Seasonal changes affect water movement, water visibility, air and water temperatures, entry and exit areas, and the presence of certain types of animals. You should know what to expect at a dive site at different times of the year. It helps to know the visibility, water temperatures, tides, surf, surge, currents, bottom composition, silt conditions, plants, and animals.

You need to be physically and mentally fit for diving. Fitness for diving implies that you

• are well rested,
• are well nourished,
• have the physical strength and stamina to meet the requirements of the environment and the activity,

- are qualified for the activity,
- are not apprehensive about your plans,
- are not goaded into doing something you are not prepared to do, and
- do not allow pride to affect good judgment.

Your objective for the dive affects your planning. Different diving activities require different plans and different equipment. The planning of an underwater photography dive is not the same as the planning of a dive where you intend to hunt for game.

You must know and observe laws, regulations, and customs. Some areas have laws that require use of a dive flag. Obey fish and game regulations. Some diving professionals discourage the taking of any living thing in an area. You need to know the behavior expected of you. It is better to know the expectations in advance than to be embarrassed at the dive site.

Etiquette is important. Will early diving activities be offensive to residents near the dive site? Will the parking of vehicles at a site irritate people? Be considerate of others who may be in the area where you intend to dive and of those fishing nearby. Consider the impact of noise, changing clothes, and dive site access. Then make your plans using good etiquette.

## Advance Planning and Preparation

The first phase of dive planning is the determination of why, who, where, when, how, and what.

Why?—Determine the objective of the dive. What do you want to do? Take photos? Explore? Look for artifacts?

Who?—Determine with whom you want to dive. Select a buddy who is interested in your dive objective.

Where?—Determine a primary and an alternative site.

When?—Determine the best time to dive. The water usually is calmer in the morning than it is in the afternoon in most areas. Tidal currents and height may affect the best time to dive.

How?—Decide how to reach the dive site. Who will drive? What are the directions?

What?—Determine what equipment is needed for the dive. Who will bring the float and flag? How many tanks do you need? Are there any special needs for the intended activity?

Advance preparation can include

- making reservations,
- paying deposits,
- buying or renting equipment,
- having equipment serviced or repaired,
- getting tanks filled,
- obtaining a fishing license or permit,
- buying film for photography, and
- obtaining emergency contact information.

Your preparations usually include a trip to your local dive facility. Inspect your equipment before you go. You may discover a needed repair that requires some time to complete. Identify your equipment needs early.

## Short-Term Planning and Preparation

The day and evening before you intend to go diving, you need to take two actions. First, find out the weather forecast and current water conditions so you can determine if conditions will be acceptable for your diving activities. Call your dive buddy to discuss and confirm your plans. Last minute revisions, such as going to the alternative site, may be necessary. If you anticipate poor diving or weather conditions, reschedule the dive.

The second step of short-term preparation is packing your diving equipment and your personal items. (See the appendix for an equipment checklist.) Write down your dive plans and schedule, and leave the information with a friend. Instruct your friend to notify the authorities if you fail to return by a certain time.

## On-Site Planning and Preparation

When you and your buddy arrive at the dive site, determine whether the conditions are acceptable for diving. If not, go to an alternative site. If the conditions at the alternative site also are unacceptable, abort the dive.

An important step in the assessment of a dive site is the estimation of the current. Look for telltale signs such as kelp bent over from water movement, a wake around the anchor line or behind an anchored boat, or objects drifting on the surface. Determine the velocity of moving water by measuring how long it takes a floating object to move a known distance, such as the length of your boat. When an object moves 100 feet (30 meters) in one minute, its speed is approximately one knot (1.15 miles or 1.85 kilometers per hour). When a current exceeds about one-third knot (0.4 miles or 0.6 kilometers per hour), you must heed it because you can swim only about 0.75 knots (0.86 miles or 1.4 kilometers per hour). Plan the dive so that the current assists you in swimming to your exit point at the end of the dive. Figure 6.1 includes a table that can help you estimate current velocity.

If the diving conditions are favorable, determine the diving area. Select the entry and exit areas for the dive, and discuss the entry and exit procedures. Agree on the course to be followed during the dive. Agree on time, minimum air pressure, and landmarks for

▶ Figure 6.1 You can estimate the velocity of a current if you time how long it takes a floating object to move the length of your boat.

## Current velocity estimation

Anchor line

20 feet (6 meters)

12 seconds

Measure how long it takes a floating object to travel 100 feet (30 meters). If an object travels 20 feet (6 meters) in 12 seconds, it travels 100 feet (30 meters) in 1 minute.

### Current velocity table
(time to travel 100 feet or 30 meters)

| Time (seconds) | Speed (knots) | Time (seconds) | Speed (knots) |
|---|---|---|---|
| 5 | 12 | 95 | 0.62 |
| 10 | 6.0 | 100 | 0.59 |
| 20 | 3.0 | 110 | 0.54 |
| 30 | 2.0 | 120 | 0.49 |
| 40 | 1.5 | 130 | 0.46 |
| 50 | 1.2 | 140 | 0.42 |
| 60 | 1.0 | 150 | 0.39 |
| 70 | 0.84 | 160 | 0.37 |
| 80 | 0.74 | 170 | 0.35 |
| 90 | 0.66 | 180 | 0.33 |

changes in direction. You and your buddy should know in advance approximately where you will be at any time during the dive.

An important part of your planning is discussion and agreement on buddy-system procedures. Decide who is in charge of the team, where you will position yourselves relative to each other, how you will move (steadily or start-and-stop), and what reunion procedures you will follow in the event of separation. Remember that communication is much easier on land than it is underwater, so take advantage of the opportunity you have to communicate and coordinate while preparing for a dive.

Always plan for emergencies. Agree on air-sharing procedures. Discuss what to do in the event of a serious diving emergency. Know where, how, and whom to call for help. Make sure you both have access to a first aid kit and other emergency equipment. A few minutes spent coordinating procedures before an emergency can save precious seconds if an accident should occur.

Scuba diving requires dive profile planning. You and your buddy need to agree on the maximum time and depth for your dive. You must limit time and depth to avoid DCS. We discuss dive profile planning later in this chapter.

## Character Development

Thorough dive planning and diving according to your plan are ways that you can show the character development values of caring, honesty, respect, and responsibility. By planning well and sticking to that plan, you demonstrate that you care about your buddy. You show honesty when you follow the plan that both of you have agreed to. Respect and responsibility for yourselves and the aquatic environment are reflected in planning that ensures your safety and minimizes your impact on the environment.

# AREA ORIENTATIONS

You should recognize the importance of learning about a dive site before diving there. Because orientation is vital and because you want to be a responsible diver, you need to learn how to obtain orientations. Area orientations can be formal or informal. A formal orientation is provided as a service by a diving professional. The professional tells you what to look for and what to look out for in the area and leads you on a dive. A professional dive guide provides suggestions and points out items of interest and potential hazards. When you have completed a formal orientation, ask the professional to sign and stamp your logbook. A continuing education dive course is another excellent form of formal orientation to a new area.

Formal orientations are ideal, but if you cannot arrange to have a professional introduce you to a new region, consider some or all of the following options for an informal orientation.

• Read books, articles, and brochures about diving in the area. Learn as much about an area as you can before you go there.

- Write to dive stores in the region where you intend to dive. Ask if you can participate in a dive class session for your orientation to the area.

- Write to dive clubs in a region where you intend to dive. Ask if you can participate in a club-sponsored dive when you are in the area. Ask for contact information for several club members who dive regularly and may be willing to allow you to go diving with them.

- When you arrive in a new area, find local dive sites and visit them when divers are likely to be there. Ask the divers about the sites while they are preparing to dive or after they exit from a dive. If you have your equipment ready, you may be able to accompany them on a dive. Make sure they have experience in diving at the site.

- Purchase a space on a diving charter boat. When you board the vessel, tell the crew you are new to the area. Ask for advice about diving procedures and ask to be introduced to an experienced diver who can provide additional information.

When you dive with local divers, allow them to go first. Do as they say and do as they do. Procedures vary from region to region. A procedure you use in your area may be inappropriate in a different area. For example, in your normal diving environment, you may be able to enter the water from a boat in a current without holding on to a line. But if you tried to do so in a different area, you might be swept away at once. Be humble, listen to others, and follow their example to avoid embarrassment.

▶ Figure 6.2  If you make a repetitive dive before allowing the residual nitrogen to leave your body, the nitrogen continues to accumulate.

**Residual nitrogen**

A—Normal amount of nitrogen in body
B—Amount of nitrogen in body after first dive
C—Amount of nitrogen in body after first surface interval
D—Amount of nitrogen in body after second dive
E—Amount of nitrogen in body after second surface interval
F—Amount of nitrogen after third dive

# DIVE PROFILE PLANNING

There are limits on how long you may remain at various depths. The amount of nitrogen absorbed by your body determines the limits. You need to be aware of the effects of **residual nitrogen,** which is nitrogen remaining in your system from a dive made within the past 12 hours. Whether you do one dive or a series of dives, it takes time to eliminate nitrogen from your body. If you dive again before the excess nitrogen has had time to outgas, you add to the nitrogen already in your body and reach critical nitrogen levels faster than if you had not already absorbed excess nitrogen. A **repetitive dive** is any dive made within 6 to 24 hours (depending on the dive-planning device) of a previous dive. Figure 6.2 shows how the amount of residual nitrogen in the body builds from repetitive dives. A **safety stop**—a precautionary decompression stop during ascent—reduces the risk of DCS.

Decompression experts use complex mathematical calculations and field testing to establish time limits for various depths for single and repetitive dives. The time limits are published in tables and programmed into calculators and dive computers. You need to know how to use these dive-planning devices to plan your dive profile to minimize the risk of DCS.

No dive-planning device can guarantee that you will not develop DCS. Dive tables, calculators, and computers provide information based on statistics acquired through testing. The statistical probability that a diver who adheres to the profile limits of a device will develop DCS is small. The devices assume that you are in good health, that you do not get cold during the dive, that you do not exert strenuously, and that you ascend at the correct rate.

If you dive to the maximum time limits indicated by any dive-planning device, you increase the likelihood of DCS. The shorter your exposure to pressure, the less the chance that you will develop DCS.

# DIVE TABLES

More than 30 years ago, the U.S. Navy (USN) developed tables for dive planning. The recreational diving community adopted the military tables and has used modified versions successfully for many years. Although the tables were designed for military diving rather than recreational diving, many decompression experts still consider the USN dive tables—with reduced maximum dive times—appropriate tables for recreational use. Variations of the USN tables, such as the YMCA dive tables, are used widely today.

The USN tables use compartments with half-times of 5 minutes, 10 minutes, 20 minutes, 40 minutes, 80 minutes, and 120 minutes. The amount of nitrogen remaining in the 120-minute (two-hour) compartment determines the **repetitive group designations** of the tables and are represented by letters. Because outgassing of a compartment takes six half-times, you can see why the USN tables define a repetitive dive as any dive within 12 hours (6 × 2 hours) of a previous dive.

**repetitive group** or **repetitive group designation**—The letter on a dive table that indicates the amount of nitrogen in a diver's body.

There are four sets of dive tables:

1. Total bottom timetable

2. Surface interval timetable

3. Residual nitrogen timetable

4. Decompression timetable

## Dive Table Modifications

Diving organizations and manufacturers have modified the USN dive tables to make them more appropriate for recreational diving. These are some typical differences between the USN dive tables and modified USN dive tables:

• Reduced time limits—Dive-planning devices today include maximum time limits that are less than the no-decompression-stop limits of the USN dive tables.

• Reduced depth limits—The USN dive tables provide dive-planning information for depths to 190 feet (58 meters). The recommended maximum depth limit for recreational diving is 130 feet (39 meters). New divers should limit diving to depths of about 60 feet (18 meters). Advanced divers qualify to dive to approximately 100 feet (30 meters).

Scuba Diving

Divers who complete a deep-diving specialty course qualify to dive to 130 feet (39 meters). Depth in water is similar to speed on land. When you qualify for a driver's license, you may drive at speeds up to the legal limit. Driving at much higher speeds is hazardous and requires specialized training, special equipment, and controlled situations to minimize the risk of serious injury or death. Deep diving (beyond 100 feet, or 30 meters) is similar to race car driving in many respects. Deep diving is a professional endeavor that unqualified recreational divers should not attempt.

• Revised **surface interval times**—In 1983, a USN study reported a number of errors in the surface interval timetable. The errors usually do not affect the type of diving that recreational divers do, but some modified versions of the tables include the corrections.

• Combined tables—Modified versions of the USN dive tables often combine information to make the tables easier to use. Tables may include the **actual bottom times** (ABT) for repetitive dives along with the **residual nitrogen times** (RNT). Tables may include required decompression information to eliminate a separate decompression timetable.

## Dive Table Terms

**surface interval time (SIT)**—The elapsed time (rounded up to the next whole minute) from when a diver surfaces following a dive to the time the diver begins the descent of a repetitive dive. The minimum SIT is 10 minutes.

**actual bottom time (ABT)**—The elapsed time in minutes (rounded up to the next whole minute) from when a diver leaves the surface in descent until the diver begins a safety stop or surfaces.

**residual nitrogen time (RNT)**—An amount of time, in minutes, that must be added to the actual bottom time (ABT) of a repetitive dive to determine the total bottom time (TBT). RNT compensates for residual nitrogen remaining in a diver's tissues from previous dives.

**total bottom time (TBT)**—The sum of ABT and RNT. For times not indicated at a particular depth, use the next longest time available for that depth.

**repetitive group designation (RGD or RG)**—A letter that indicates the amount of residual nitrogen in a diver's tissues for 12 hours after diving.

**repetitive dive**—Any dive conducted within 12 hours of a previous dive with a minimum 10-minute surface interval. For repetitive dives of less than 40 feet (12 meters), use the table C RNT 40-foot (12-meter) values to determine the TBT.

**no-decompression-stop limit (NDSL)**—The maximum time that a diver may stay at a specified depth, indicated in table A. For repetitive dives, the residual nitrogen time (RNT) from table C must be added to the actual bottom time (ABT) to obtain the total bottom time (TBT), which must not exceed the NDSL specified in table A. Table C also indicates the maximum ABT for various depth and repetitive group combinations that will prevent the TBT from exceeding the NDSL.

146

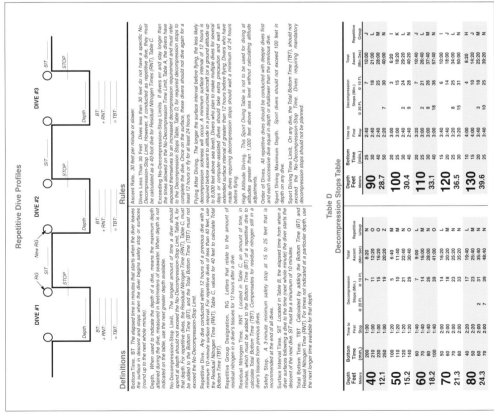

# Dive Table Use

An overview of the YMCA tables makes it easier to understand how to solve specific dive planning problems.

Table A, the **total bottom time** (TBT) table, provides the maximum bottom time without required decompression for various depths and a repetitive group designation for various dive profiles. Table B, the surface interval time (SIT) table, provides information about the duration of the surface interval for each repetitive group. You begin a surface interval with one repetitive group designation, and as you outgas nitrogen over time, you move into a lower repetitive group designation. Table C, the residual nitrogen time (RNT) table, provides the RNT in minutes, which is equivalent to the amount of time you would have to spend at the planned depth to equal the residual nitrogen in your body.

You add RNT to your actual bottom time (ABT) to determine your total bottom time (TBT) for a repetitive dive. Table C also provides precalculated maximum ABTs, which are **no-decompression stop limits** (NDSLs) minus the RNTs. Add the RNT from table C to the ABT for a repetitive dive and return to table A to obtain a new repetitive group (RG) designation. Table D, the **decompression stops** table, specifies time that must be spent at shallow depths during ascent to minimize the risk of decompression sickness when NDSLs are exceeded.

Now it is time to learn how to plan dives using the YMCA dive tables. Refer to the tables for the examples. Rows are horizontal and columns are vertical. Rules for using the dive tables are simple and easy to remember.

Use table A to determine the NDSL for a dive—the maximum time you can spend underwater for the deepest depth you reach during a dive. Enter the table on the row corresponding to the depth to which you plan to dive, and then move across to the third column to determine the NDSL for that depth. To use table A to obtain a repetitive group designation after a dive, enter the table on the row corresponding to the maximum depth of your dive, and then proceed to the right to the first number that the duration of your dive does not exceed. Proceed downward along that column to find the repetitive group designation letter for the dive. For example, a dive to 50 feet (15 meters) for 30 minutes assigns you to group E. A dive to 45 feet (14 meters) for 28 minutes also places you in group E. (Remember that when the depth or duration of your dive exceeds a listed number, you must use the next larger number.)

Use the SIT table, table B, to determine your group designation following SIT, which is the time you spend at the surface between repetitive dives. Enter the table using the group designation you obtained from table A. Move

### Table A
**TOTAL BOTTOM TIME (TBT) IN MINUTES**

| DEPTH Meters | FEET | No-Decompression-Stop Limits | | | | | | | | | | | | | |
|---|---|---|---|---|---|---|---|---|---|---|---|---|---|---|---|
| 4.5 | 15 | | 35 | 70 | 110 | 160 | 225 | 350 | | | | | | | |
| 6 | 20 | | 25 | 50 | 75 | 100 | 135 | 180 | 240 | 325 | | | | | |
| 7.5 | 25 | | 20 | 35 | 55 | 75 | 100 | 125 | 160 | 195 | 245 | 315 | | | |
| 9 | 30 | | 15 | 30 | 45 | 60 | 75 | 95 | 120 | 145 | 170 | 205 | 250 | 310 | |
| 10.5 | 35 | 220 | 5 | 15 | 25 | 40 | 50 | 60 | 80 | 100 | 120 | 140 | 160 | 190 | 220 |
| 12 | 40 | 150 | 5 | 15 | 25 | 30 | 40 | 50 | 70 | 80 | 100 | 110 | 130 | 150 | |
| 15 | 50 | 80 | | 10 | 15 | 25 | 30 | 40 | 50 | 60 | 70 | 80 | | | |
| 18 | 60 | 50 | | 10 | 15 | 20 | 25 | 30 | 40 | 50 | | | | | |
| 21 | 70 | 40 | | 5 | 10 | 15 | 20 | 30 | 35 | 40 | | | | | |
| 24 | 80 | 30 | | 5 | 10 | 15 | 20 | 25 | 30 | | | | | | |
| 27 | 90 | 20 | | 5 | 10 | 12 | 15 | 20 | | | | | | | |
| 30 | 100 | 18 | | 5 | 7 | 10 | 18 | | | | | | | | |
| 33 | 110 | 13 | | | 5 | 10 | 13 | | | | | | | | |
| 36 | 120 | 10 | | | 5 | 10 | | | | | | | | | |
| 39 | 130 | 5 | | | 5 | | | | | | | | | | |

START HERE

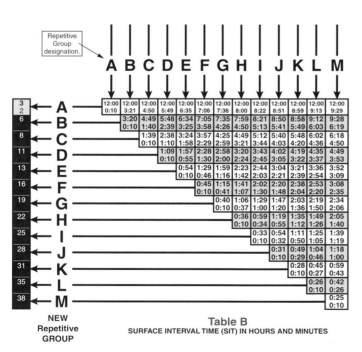

### Table B
**SURFACE INTERVAL TIME (SIT) IN HOURS AND MINUTES**

Repetitive Group designation.

NEW Repetitive GROUP

| New RG | A | B | C | D | E | F | G | H | I | J | K | L | M |
|---|---|---|---|---|---|---|---|---|---|---|---|---|---|
| A (3/2) | 12:00 / 0:10 | 12:00 / 3:21 | 12:00 / 4:50 | 12:00 / 5:49 | 12:00 / 6:35 | 12:00 / 7:06 | 12:00 / 7:36 | 12:00 / 8:00 | 12:00 / 8:22 | 12:00 / 8:51 | 12:00 / 8:59 | 12:00 / 9:13 | 12:00 / 9:29 |
| B (6) | | 3:20 / 0:10 | 4:49 / 1:40 | 5:48 / 2:39 | 6:34 / 3:25 | 7:05 / 3:58 | 7:35 / 4:26 | 7:59 / 4:50 | 8:21 / 5:13 | 8:50 / 5:41 | 8:58 / 5:49 | 9:12 / 6:03 | 9:28 / 6:19 |
| C (8) | | | 1:39 / 0:10 | 2:38 / 1:10 | 3:24 / 1:58 | 3:57 / 2:29 | 4:25 / 2:59 | 4:49 / 3:21 | 5:12 / 3:44 | 5:40 / 4:03 | 5:48 / 4:20 | 6:02 / 4:36 | 6:18 / 4:50 |
| D (11) | | | | 1:09 / 0:10 | 1:57 / 0:55 | 2:28 / 1:30 | 2:58 / 2:00 | 3:20 / 2:24 | 3:43 / 2:45 | 4:02 / 3:05 | 4:19 / 3:22 | 4:35 / 3:37 | 4:49 / 3:53 |
| E (13) | | | | | 0:54 / 0:10 | 1:29 / 0:46 | 1:59 / 1:16 | 2:23 / 1:42 | 2:44 / 2:03 | 3:04 / 2:21 | 3:21 / 2:39 | 3:36 / 2:54 | 3:52 / 3:09 |
| F (16) | | | | | | 0:45 / 0:10 | 1:15 / 0:41 | 1:41 / 1:07 | 2:02 / 1:30 | 2:20 / 1:48 | 2:38 / 2:04 | 2:53 / 2:20 | 3:08 / 2:35 |
| G (19) | | | | | | | 0:40 / 0:10 | 1:06 / 0:37 | 1:29 / 1:00 | 1:47 / 1:20 | 2:03 / 1:36 | 2:19 / 1:50 | 2:34 / 2:06 |
| H (22) | | | | | | | | 0:36 / 0:10 | 0:59 / 0:34 | 1:19 / 0:55 | 1:35 / 1:12 | 1:49 / 1:26 | 2:05 / 1:40 |
| I (25) | | | | | | | | | 0:33 / 0:10 | 0:54 / 0:32 | 1:11 / 0:50 | 1:25 / 1:05 | 1:39 / 1:19 |
| J (28) | | | | | | | | | | 0:31 / 0:10 | 0:49 / 0:29 | 1:04 / 0:46 | 1:18 / 1:00 |
| K (31) | | | | | | | | | | | 0:28 / 0:10 | 0:45 / 0:27 | 0:59 / 0:43 |
| L (35) | | | | | | | | | | | | 0:26 / 0:10 | 0:42 / 0:26 |
| M (38) | | | | | | | | | | | | | 0:25 / 0:10 |

downward along the column until you find the time range (expressed as hours:minutes, for example, 1:26 is one hour and 26 minutes) that your SIT falls into. Remember that whenever you exceed a number on the tables you use the next larger number. Follow the column to the left to find your new group designation. For example, if your group was E at the beginning of a one hour and 58 minute surface interval, you would be in group C at the end of the surface interval. You would be in group C after a surface interval from one hour and 58 minutes up to three hours and 24 minutes.

Use table C, the RNT table, to determine your RNT and maximum ABT limits for a repetitive dive. Residual nitrogen in your body reduces table A NDSLs. Table C provides the reduced time limits. For example, if your letter group is C from a previous dive or dives and you plan to dive to 50 feet (15 meters), your dive time must not exceed 59 minutes.

Use table C, the RNT table, to convert your repetitive group designation letter into a time in minutes that is equivalent to your residual nitrogen, the nitrogen remaining in your body from a previous dive. The amount of time depends on the depth of the dive you plan to make. To determine your RNT, find the column corresponding to the depth to which you plan to dive and the row that corresponds to your letter group after your surface interval. The top number in that entry indicates your RNT. For example, if your repetitive group was C at the end of the surface interval and you were planning to dive to a depth of 70 feet (21 meters), your RNT would be 15 minutes.

Add your RNT to the ABT of your repetitive dive to establish the TBT. Using the TBT, re-enter table A and obtain a new repetitive group letter designation. For example, if your RNT is 15 minutes and your ABT is 20 minutes for a dive to 70 feet (21 meters), your TBT is 35 minutes (20 + 15) and your end-of-dive repetitive group letter is G.

To determine the time for **emergency decompression** for a dive in excess of the NDSL, refer to table D. If the ABT or TBT of your dive exceeds the NDSL for the depth, decompress at the specified depth for the number of minutes indicated to the right of the bottom time. For example, if your TBT for a dive to 70 feet (21 meters) exceeded 50 minutes but was not more than 60 minutes, you would decompress at a depth of 10 feet (3 meters) for 18 minutes. Table D also provides repetitive group letter designations for dives

**emergency decompression**—A required delay in ascent that a diver must take if the actual or total bottom time (ABT or TBT) exceeds the no-decompression-stop limit for a dive.

### Table C
**RESIDUAL NITROGEN TIME (RNT) IN MINUTES**

Repetitive dive depth in feet/meters.

| | 40/12 | 50/15 | 60/18 | 70/21 | 80/24 | 90/27 | 100/30 | 110/33 | 120/36 | 130/39 |
|---|---|---|---|---|---|---|---|---|---|---|
| A | 7/143 | 6/74 | 5/45 | 4/36 | 4/26 | 3/17 | 3/15 | 3/10 | 3/7 | 3/2 |
| B | 17/133 | 13/67 | 11/39 | 9/31 | 8/22 | 7/13 | 7/11 | 6/10 | 6/7 | 6/4 |
| C | 25/125 | 21/59 | 17/33 | 15/25 | 13/17 | 11/9 | 10/8 | 10/3 | 9/1 | 8 |
| D | 37/113 | 29/51 | 24/26 | 20/20 | 18/12 | 16/4 | 14/4 | 13 | 12 | 11 |
| E | 49/101 | 38/42 | 30/20 | 26/14 | 23/7 | 20 | 18 | 16 | 15 | 13 |
| F | 61/89 | 47/33 | 36/14 | 31/9 | 28/2 | 25 | 22 | 20 | 18 | 15 |
| G | 73/77 | 56/24 | 44/6 | 37/3 | 32 | 29 | 26 | 24 | 21 | 19 |
| H | 87/63 | 66/14 | 52 | 43 | 38 | 33 | 30 | 27 | 25 | 22 |
| I | 101/49 | 76/4 | 61 | 50 | 43 | 38 | 34 | 31 | 28 | 25 |
| J | 116/34 | 87 | 70 | 57 | 48 | 43 | 38 | 34 | 32 | 28 |
| K | 138/12 | 99 | 79 | 64 | 54 | 47 | 43 | 38 | 35 | 31 |
| L | 161 | 111 | 88 | 72 | 61 | 53 | 48 | 42 | 39 | 35 |
| M | 187 | 124 | 97 | 80 | 68 | 58 | 53 | 47 | 43 | 38 |

**Note:** For repetitive dives less than 40 feet, use the values for 40 feet.

NEW Repetitive GROUP

### Table D
**Decompression Stops Table**

| Depth Feet / Meters | Bottom Time (min.) | Time to First Stop | Decompression Stops (Min.) @ 20 Ft. | @ 10 Ft. | Total Ascent (Min:Sec) | Repetitive Group |
|---|---|---|---|---|---|---|
| **40** (12.1) | 200 | 1:00 | | 7 | 8:20 | N |
| | 210 | 1:00 | | 11 | 12:20 | O |
| | 230 | 1:00 | | 15 | 16:20 | O |
| | 250 | 1:00 | | 19 | 20:20 | Z |
| **50** (15.2) | 100 | 1:20 | | 5 | 6:40 | M |
| | 110 | 1:20 | | 10 | 11:40 | M |
| | 120 | 1:20 | | 21 | 22:40 | N |
| | 140 | 1:20 | | 29 | 30:40 | O |
| **60** (18.2) | 60 | 1:40 | | 7 | 9:00 | L |
| | 70 | 1:40 | | 14 | 16:00 | M |
| | 80 | 1:40 | | 26 | 28:00 | N |
| | 100 | 1:40 | | 39 | 41:00 | O |
| **70** (21.3) | 50 | 2:00 | | 14 | 16:20 | L |
| | 60 | 2:00 | | 18 | 20:20 | M |
| | 70 | 2:00 | | 23 | 25:20 | N |
| | 80 | 2:00 | | 33 | 35:20 | N |
| **80** (24.3) | 40 | 2:20 | | 17 | 19:40 | L |
| | 50 | 2:20 | | 23 | 25:40 | M |
| | 60 | 2:20 | 2 | 31 | 35:40 | N |
| | 70 | 2:20 | 7 | 39 | 48:40 | N |

| Depth Feet / Meters | Bottom Time (min.) | Time to First Stop | Decompression Stops (Min.) @ 20 Ft. | @ 10 Ft. | Total Ascent (Min:Sec) | Repetitive Group |
|---|---|---|---|---|---|---|
| **90** (28.7) | 25 | 2:40 | | 7 | 10:00 | J |
| | 30 | 2:40 | | 18 | 21:00 | L |
| | 40 | 2:40 | | 25 | 28:00 | M |
| | 50 | 2:20 | 7 | 30 | 40:00 | N |
| **100** (30.4) | 20 | 3:00 | | 3 | 6:20 | I |
| | 25 | 3:00 | | 15 | 18:20 | K |
| | 30 | 2:40 | 2 | 24 | 29:20 | L |
| | 40 | 2:40 | 9 | 28 | 40:20 | N |
| **110** (33.1) | 20 | 3:20 | | 7 | 10:40 | J |
| | 25 | 3:00 | 2 | 21 | 26:40 | L |
| | 30 | 3:00 | 8 | 26 | 37:40 | M |
| | 40 | 3:00 | 18 | 36 | 57:40 | N |
| **120** (36.5) | 15 | 3:40 | | 6 | 10:00 | I |
| | 20 | 3:40 | | 14 | 18:00 | J |
| | 25 | 3:20 | 8 | 25 | 34:00 | L |
| | 30 | 3:20 | 15 | 31 | 50:00 | N |
| **130** (39.6) | 10 | 4:00 | | 4 | 8:20 | H |
| | 15 | 4:00 | | 10 | 14:20 | J |
| | 20 | 3:40 | 3 | 18 | 25:20 | M |
| | 25 | 3:40 | 10 | 25 | 39:20 | N |

# Dive Table Rules

- Ascend at a rate of 30 feet (9 meters) per minute or slower.
- When you consult the tables, use the deepest depth you attained during a dive. If you spend part of the dive at one depth and the remainder of the dive at a shallower depth, treat the dive as if you spent all the time at the deepest depth.
- Enter the tables at a depth that is exactly equal to or the next greater depth than the maximum depth of your dive. The YMCA tables have 5-foot (1.5-meter) increments from 15 to 35 feet (4.5 to 10.7 meters) and 10-foot (3-meter) increments from 40 to 130 feet (12 to 39 meters). For example, if the depth of your dive is 50 feet (15 meters), use the 50-foot (15-meter) listing, but if the depth of your dive is 51 feet (15.5 meters), you must use the 60-foot (18-meter) listing.
- Repetitive dives should be conducted with the deepest dive first; each successive dive should be equal in depth or shallower than the previous dive.
- The TBT must not exceed the NDSL. Dives that require mandatory decompression stops should not be planned.
- Depths shallower than 30 feet (9 meters) do not have an NDSL. When conducted as repetitive dives, calculate all dives shallower than 30 feet (9 meters) using the RNTs for 40-foot (12-meter) dives.
- Select the time that is exactly equal to or the next greater than the time of your dive from the times listed for a specific depth. For example, if you dive to 60 feet (18 meters) for 22 minutes, use the 25-minute listing on the table because there is no 22-minute listing for that depth.
- The minimum time between dives is 10 minutes. When the surface interval time (SIT) is less than 10 minutes, add the times of the dives together and use the deepest depth of the dives when you consult the tables. Do not include the SIT as part of your dive time. Although the dive tables indicate a minimum SIT of 10 minutes, the minimum recommended time between recreational dives is one hour.
- A minimum SIT of 12 hours is required after diving before ascending in a pressurized aircraft or ascending to an elevation greater than 8,000 feet (2,438 meters) above sea level. Divers who make multiple dives for several days or computer-assisted dives (see the "Dive Calculators and Dive Computers" section on page 157) should wait more than 12 hours before flying. When surfacing after required decompression, divers should not dive again for 12 hours or fly in aircraft for 24 hours. Standard dive tables should not be used for planning dives at elevations greater than 1,000 feet (305 meters) above sea level.

with mandatory decompression. The repetitive group for the foregoing dive is M. After a dive requiring decompression, refrain from further diving for at least 24 hours. This example is for emergency purposes only. You should *never* plan a decompression dive.

## Special-Equipment Dive Planning

You must use special dive tables if you dive using oxygen-enriched air (nitrox); you learn how to use the tables when you take a nitrox specialty course. Do not attempt specialized diving without proper training. Exceeding the 130-foot (39-meter) depth limit by a few feet when breathing compressed air is not particularly dangerous, but exceeding the maximum depth limit (which varies with the gas mixture) when breathing mixed gases can cause seizures and drowning. Gas mixtures other than compressed air are only for divers who have the prerequisite training and equipment.

# Dive Profile Terms and Rules

There are several types of **dive profiles**, made by plotting time and depth. Figure 6.3 shows a diagram of a standard profile. A dive to a constant depth for a given period of time is typically depicted as a profile with square corners. A **multilevel dive profile** is a dive that progresses from deep to shallow during a given period of time. When you make a dive in a series of steps, you can refer to it as a **step dive**. A **sawtooth dive profile** is a dive that progresses from deep to shallow and back to deep. Avoid this type of dive. Another profile is the bounce profile. It is a dive with a short ABT, such as a dive to free a fouled anchor. You also should avoid this profile, which is depicted graphically as a spike. Bounce profiles are also called **spike dives.** Figure 6.4 graphically depicts these four profiles.

▶ Figure 6.3  Standard dive profile.

# Diagramming a Dive Profile

Diagram your dive profiles when planning and recording your dives. Include planned and actual depths, NDSLs, ABTs, repetitive group letter designations, and SITs. For repetitive dives, include RNTs and TBTs. A simple method for diagramming dive tables is to use a worksheet like the one shown in figure 6.5.

▶ Figure 6.4  Types of dive profiles.

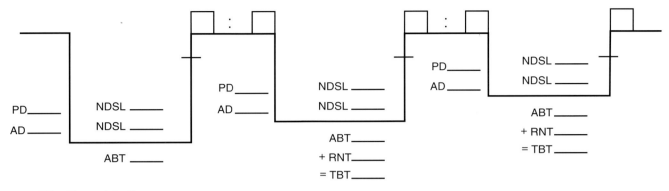

PD = Planned depth
AD = Actual depth

▶ Figure 6.5   Use this worksheet to plan your dives.

Try the following exercise, which combines diagramming with the dive table procedures you have learned. Use the blank diagramming worksheet in figure 6.5 as a template. If you have any difficulties, refer to the preceding section concerning use of each of the dive tables. Assume that all dive times include three-minute safety stops. Calculate and diagram the following series of dives (the answers to the diagramming problem are in the next paragraph and in figure 6.6):

- The first dive is to 78 feet (24 meters) with an ABT of 20 minutes, followed by a surface interval of 1.5 hours.
- The second dive is to 55 feet (16.8 meters) with an ABT of 25 minutes, followed by a surface interval of 2 hours.
- The third dive is to 40 feet (12 meters) with an ABT of 25 minutes.

Solution: The repetitive group following the first dive is E. Following the surface interval, the repetitive group changes to D. The RNT for a D diver at 60 feet (18 meters) is 24 minutes. The TBT (ABT + RNT) for the second dive is 49 minutes (25 + 24). The repetitive group following the second dive is H. Following the second surface interval, the group

PD = Planned depth
AD = Actual depth

▶ Figure 6.6   Completed diagramming worksheet.

changes to E. The RNT for an E diver at 40 feet (12 meters) is 49 minutes. The TBT for the third dive is 74 minutes (25 + 49). The repetitive group following the third dive is H.

The following tips help make dive profile diagramming easier:

- Begin by entering the NDSL for the planned depth. ABT or TBT must not exceed the maximum allowable time.
- Enter the repetitive group letter at every upper corner of a profile except the first corner.
- Add ABT and RNT to obtain TBT for every repetitive dive. Use the recall word "ART" to help remember that you add ABT and RNT to obtain TBT.

## Planning Time and Depth Limits

Now combine the dive table procedures to plan a series of dives. Use the blank diagram shown in figure 6.5. Assume the depth of the first dive—the deepest dive—is 60 feet (18 meters). The NDSL, according to table A, is 50 minutes. Plan an ABT of 22 minutes (including safety stop) for the dive. Your repetitive group designation following the first dive is E. Now plan a repetitive dive to the same depth. Refer to table C to plan the dive because table C provides the maximum allowable times for various letter group designations. If your surface interval is less than 55 minutes, you remain in the E group, your RNT is 30 minutes, and your ABT must not exceed 20 minutes. Your surface interval should be at least one hour, as recommended. If you wait an hour between the first and second dive, your repetitive group changes to D, your RNT is 24 minutes, and your ABT cannot exceed 26 minutes. If you want to dive for more than 26 minutes, you need to extend your surface interval to at least 3 hours and 25 minutes.

Assume that you repeat the first dive. Your RNT is 24 minutes and your ABT is 22 minutes, so your TBT is 46 minutes. Your repetitive group following the second dive is H.

Assume that the dive site is so good that you wish to make a third dive to 60 feet (18 meters). There is no allowable time at 60 feet (18 meters) for a diver with a group H designation. Only 6 minutes are allowed for a diver with a group G designation. Proceed up the column. If you want to dive to 60 feet (18 meters) again for more than 20 minutes, you need to attain repetitive group D, which allows 26 minutes of diving without required decompression. When you know the group that you need to attain and your starting group, you can plan your surface interval. Table B tells you that you must wait at least 2 hours and 24 minutes to move from group H to group D.

Use the tables to plan dives that avoid emergency decompression. There are three options for planning repetitive dives that do not require mandatory decompression. If your RNT prevents you from making a desired dive, you can (1) reduce the duration of the dive, (2) reduce the depth of the dive, or (3) increase the surface interval preceding the dive.

Test what you have learned by answering the following questions. Diagram the problems. Include a three-minute safety stop in all dive times. Compare your answers with the solutions provided.

## Special Procedures

Unusual circumstances may arise that require special procedures. When you have finished studying this section, you should be able to describe the procedures for dive profile planning for each of these situations when using the YMCA dive tables.

## Dive Planning Problems

1. After a dive to 71 feet (21.6 meters) for 27 minutes and a surface interval of 60 minutes, what is the maximum depth to which you can dive for at least 15 minutes without mandatory decompression?
2. Following a dive to 77 feet (23.5 meters) for 24 minutes and a surface interval of one hour and 45 minutes, what is the NDSL for a dive to a depth of 50 feet (15 meters)?
3. Following a dive to 60 feet (18 meters) for 21 minutes, what is the minimum surface interval that will allow a dive of the same duration to the same depth without mandatory decompression?

## Solutions to Dive-Planning Problems

1. The repetitive group following the first dive is G. The group changes to F after the surface interval. Refer to table C. Group F allows 9 minutes for 70 feet (21 meters), 14 minutes for 60 feet (18 meters), and 33 minutes for 50 feet (15 meters). The maximum depth to which you may dive for at least 15 minutes without emergency decompression is 50 feet (15 meters).
2. The repetitive group following the first dive is F. The group changes to D after the surface interval. The maximum allowable time without mandatory decompression for a group D diver at 50 feet (15 meters) is 51 minutes.
3. The repetitive group following the first dive is E. You must have a letter group designation of D for a repetitive dive of 21 minutes at 60 feet (18 meters) without mandatory decompression (refer to table C). Changing from group E to group D requires a minimum surface interval of 55 minutes.

• A cold or strenuous dive—When a dive is particularly cold or strenuous, use the next greater time for the dive. If the dive is both cold and strenuous, use the next greater time and depth.

• Variations in the rate of ascent—If you ascend faster than 30 feet (9 meters) per minute, extend your safety stop by at least two minutes. The faster you ascend, the more you should increase the stop time.

• Multilevel dives—Treat dives to multiple levels as square-profile dives, as if all the time of the dive was at the deepest depth of the dive. Do not attempt to extrapolate the dive tables.

• Omitted decompression—If you need to decompress but fail to do so, use the following procedure for omitted decompression. If you have no symptoms of DCS following the dive, remain out of the water, breathe oxygen in the highest concentration possible, rest, drink water, and be alert for symptoms of DCS. Wait 24 hours before diving again. If you suspect DCS, proceed at once to a hyperbaric facility for a medical examination. The USN has a procedure for in-water decompression, but diving medical experts agree that this procedure is inappropriate.

- A safety stop that causes your ABT or TBT to exceed NDSL—If a safety stop causes ABT or TBT to exceed the maximum time limits, determine your repetitive group letter designation using the NDSL for the profile.

- Diving after mandatory decompression—After a dive that requires decompression, wait at least 24 hours before diving again.

- The RNT for a repetitive dive exceeds the ABT of the previous dive—If the RNT for a repetitive dive exceeds the ABT of the previous dive, use the RNT for planning the repetitive dive.

- Altitude after diving—Ascending to altitude after diving increases the likelihood of decompression sickness because of further reduction in pressure. Driving in the mountains or flying after diving can cause DCS that would not occur if you remained at sea level until you eliminated the excess nitrogen.

The International Divers Alert Network (IDAN) recommends a minimum of 12 hours before ascent to altitude in a commercial jet airliner (higher than 8,000 feet, or 2,438 meters). If you make multiple dives for several days or dives that require decompression stops, wait for even longer than 12 hours before flight. The greater the interval before the flight, the less likely is DCS.

IDAN does not have a recommendation for flying or driving at lower altitudes. The most extensively tested tables for altitudes are the Swiss dive tables. The Swiss tables use a compartment with a much longer half-time than the USN tables. A reasonable approach to altitude delays after diving makes the USN dive table surface intervals equivalent to those of the Swiss tables. Converted USN minimum surface intervals in table 6.1 specify the minimum time to attain permissible nitrogen levels for various altitudes.

## Table 6.1 Altitude Delay Timetable

| Altitude (ft/m) | Starting repetitive group | | | | | | | | | | |
|---|---|---|---|---|---|---|---|---|---|---|---|
| | ABC | D | E | F | G | H | I | J | K | L | Group* |
| 2,000/610 | 0:00 | 0:00 | 0:00 | 0:00 | 0:00 | 0:00 | 0:00 | 0:00 | 0:00 | 2:26 | K |
| 3,000/914 | 0:00 | 0:00 | 0:00 | 0:00 | 0:00 | 0:00 | 0:00 | 0:00 | 2:37 | 4:08 | J |
| 4,000/1,219 | 0:00 | 0:00 | 0:00 | 0:00 | 0:00 | 0:00 | 0:00 | 2:53 | 4:30 | 5:51 | I |
| 5,000/1,524 | 0:00 | 0:00 | 0:00 | 0:00 | 0:00 | 0:00 | 3:04 | 4:57 | 6:29 | 7:44 | H |
| 6,000/1,829 | 0:00 | 0:00 | 0:00 | 0:00 | 0:00 | 3:20 | 5:24 | 7:12 | 8:38 | 9:54 | G |
| 7,000/2,134 | 0:00 | 0:00 | 0:00 | 0:00 | 3:41 | 6:02 | 8:06 | 9:43 | 11:10 | 12:36 | F |
| 8,000/2,438 | 0:00 | 0:00 | 0:00 | 4:08 | 6:50 | 9:11 | 11:04 | 12:41 | 14:19 | 15:40 | E |
| 9,000/2,743 | 0:00 | 0:00 | 4:57 | 8:06 | 10:48 | 12:58 | 14:51 | 16:39 | 18:11 | 23:09 | D |
| 10,000/3,048 | 0:00 | 6:18 | 10:37 | 13:25 | 15:56 | 18:05 | 20:10 | 21:18 | 23:24 | 24:50 | C |

*Note.* Times represent the minimum recommended time delay before ascending to listed altitude and are USN surface interval times with a delay factor of 5.4. Times are in hours:minutes; for example, 5:24 is 5 hours 24 minutes.

*Recommended minimum repetitive groups for indicated elevations.

Altitude is any elevation above 1,000 feet (305 meters). The altitude delay timetable provides recommended time delays for altitudes up to 10,000 feet (3,048 meters). To use the altitude delay timetable, enter the table horizontally on the top line and find your starting repetitive group. Next, find the altitude to which you wish to ascend. If you exceed a number, use the next greater one. The time at the coordinates of the desired altitude and your starting repetitive group indicate the minimum time delay recommended before ascending to the altitude selected.

## Profile Contingency Planning

When you plan a dive profile, you should also plan for contingencies. You should know what to do in case you unintentionally exceed your planned depth or time or both. A simple matrix, such as that depicted in figure 6.7, is helpful. Prepare a contingency matrix in advance of your dives and carry it with you while diving.

▶ Figure 6.7 A contingency matrix helps you plan ahead for unexpected events.

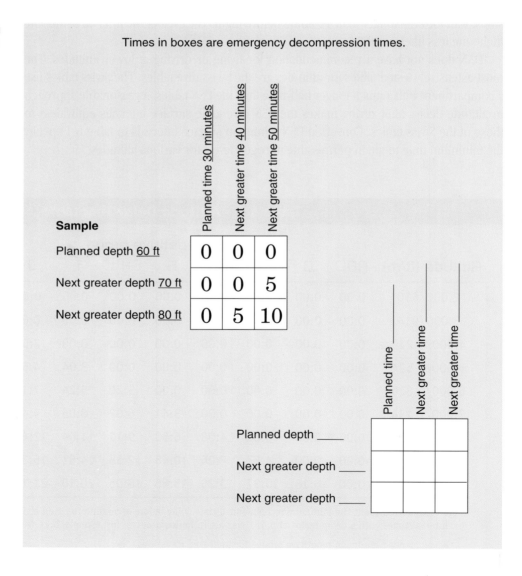

156

After you complete your plans, you need to implement them. The first rule of dive planning is to plan your dive, then dive your plan. You and your buddy should make every effort to do as you agreed to do before the dive. When circumstances force changes in your plans, it helps to have **contingency plans.** Here are some examples of possible contingencies for a dive. You should know what to do if you

- surface downcurrent from a boat when you had planned to surface in front of it,
- are unable to reach or use the exit point you had selected on shore,
- end the dive a long distance from your exit location,
- exceed the maximum allowable bottom time (ABT or TBT) for a dive,
- experience a failure of your dive computer while diving, or
- ascend directly to the surface without precautionary decompression.

# DIVE CALCULATORS AND DIVE COMPUTERS

The benefits of a dive computer (figure 6.8) outweigh the potential problems associated with its use. Learn how to use dive tables and dive calculators so that you will know how to plan a dive if you do not have a dive computer or if your dive computer fails to work. Because a dive computer simplifies dive planning, obtain a dive computer as soon as you can.

Dive calculators are circular planning devices that eliminate the mathematics required with the dive tables. Dive calculators provide precalculated numbers and eliminate the need to add and subtract times. Guides on the calculators help eliminate line-jumping errors frequently made when using dive tables.

Dive tables have 5- or 10-foot (1.5- or 3-meter) increments and require all the time of a dive to be counted at maximum depth of the dive. If the first part of your dive is deeper than the remainder of the dive, you suffer a penalty because the tables treat the entire dive as if it took place at the deepest depth (see figure 6.9). At the end of the dive you receive a repetitive group designation that is higher than you deserve. Dive tables are advance planning devices, while dive computers provide constant decompression status information.

Dive computers use one-foot (0.3-meter) increments for profile planning and calculate nitrogen absorption continuously. As you vary depth during a multilevel dive, you are "charged" only for the nitrogen you absorb. You do not incur the maximum-depth penalty (see figure 6.9) of the dive tables, so the result is less residual nitrogen time following a multilevel dive than calculated using dive tables. The penalty avoidance is the primary advantage of a dive computer as a planning device. Dive computers also provide advance planning information by **scrolling,** a sequential display of time limits for various depths. You must carry your dive computer with you when you dive because it provides information about your decompression status continuously and keeps track of your residual nitrogen.

▶ Figure 6.8  Dive computers make time and depth determinations easy.

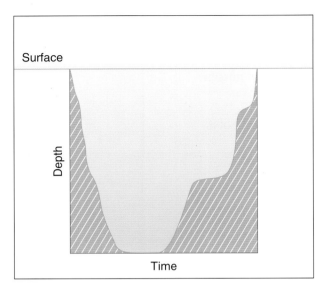

▶ Figure 6.9 The striped area represents penalty time imposed by dive table procedures.

## Dive Computers

### Advantages

- The maximum-depth penalty of the dive tables is avoided.
- Dive profile information is accurate.
- Dive computers store a record of the dive profile.
- You can eliminate common errors made when using manual dive planners.
- Dive computers offer additional features, such as an ascent rate indicator.

### Disadvantages

- Dive computers are electronic instruments that can fail.
- Dive computers are expensive to purchase and service.
- Each diver must have a separate computer.
- The mathematical model varies from one type of computer to another, so some confusion results when each diver of a buddy team uses a different type of computer.
- Not all dive-planning information displayed by a computer can be accepted at face value. You must learn and apply the dive computer guidelines included in this section.

Regardless of the type of dive computer that you choose, you need to understand some basic principles. First, be sure to read the instruction manual that comes with your computer. Wait 24 hours after diving with dive tables before using a dive computer. Do not exceed the ascent rate specified by the manufacturer, and do a five-minute safety stop at a depth of 15 to 20 feet (4.6 to 6.1 meters) at the end of every dive. If you exceed the rate of ascent specified for your computer, extend the duration of your precautionary stop by at least the amount of time it should have taken you to ascend to the stop depth. Do not make repetitive dives deeper than 80 feet (24 meters). Keep your dive computer activated until its outgassing is complete. If your computer fails at any time while diving at a depth in excess of 30 feet (9 meters), terminate the dive immediately with a safety stop. If your computer fails or if you switch it off accidentally, discontinue diving for 24 hours.

If you exceed the maximum time limit for a dive, decompression is mandatory. The computer displays a ceiling—the minimum depth to which you may ascend. As you decompress, the ceiling becomes shallower until it indicates that you may surface. After a minimum interval at the surface, the computer begins scrolling—displaying the time limits for various depths sequentially. Wait 24 hours before diving again after any dive for which a ceiling was displayed.

The concept of backup planning with dive tables is good for square profiles, but dive table planning for multilevel computer-planned dives is not feasible.

## POSTDIVE REVIEW

After a dive, you and your buddy should reflect upon your experience. How closely did the actual dive match the dive that you planned? If there were deviations from the plan, what caused them? Could you have prevented the deviations with a different plan or approach? What changes can you make to improve the next dive? Some problems require research, or you may need to ask the advice of a diving professional. The experience of each dive should affect your plans for future dives. Your dives with your buddy should progress more smoothly each time you dive together. Each time you visit a dive site, your dive procedures should improve. A review of each dive with your buddy and a discussion about future diving is a valuable part of dive planning. Even if you have a new dive buddy for a dive, you should plan your dives together and discuss the experience afterward.

## SUMMARY

The saying "If you fail to plan, you plan to fail" is true for scuba divers. All phases of dive planning are important and help ensure enjoyable and successful underwater experiences. Follow the recommended steps for planning, get area orientations when appropriate, have contingency plans, and discuss your dives with your buddy.

Dive profiles are a large portion of dive planning. Whether you use dive tables, a calculator, or a computer when you dive, plan conservatively. No dive-planning device can guarantee that you will not develop DCS after diving. The deeper, longer, and more frequently you dive, the greater your risk of DCS. Limit multiple-day, multilevel dives because repetitive multiple-depth profiles make you more susceptible to DCS. Make a safety stop at the end of every dive, avoid improper profiles, and have surface intervals of an hour or more. After three consecutive days of repetitive diving, wait a full day before diving again. Exercise good judgement and common sense.

## Scuba Wise

*Having reviewed dive accident reports for decades, I have found that failure to adequately plan or to carry out the plan for a dive is a common cause of accidents and injuries. I have been able to avoid serious injury during 37 years of diving. I have had some bad experiences, however, and they occurred when I failed to plan adequately, when I attempted activities without first completing training for the activity, or when I did not have adequate knowledge of a new dive site.*

*A favorite dive buddy and I were on a photo assignment in the Cayman Islands. At the end of the day, we went snorkeling in front of the dive resort. We swam through a break in an offshore coral barrier reef and enjoyed an hour of viewing the beautiful and colorful animals of the area. We had not*

*planned our exit. I suggested that we return to shore by swimming directly over the barrier reef, and my buddy agreed. Waves were breaking over the reef, but I was familiar with wave action, so the waves were not a concern to me. The wave action was stronger than expected, but I managed to avoid injury by holding on to dead coral between the waves. My buddy, who did not know how to manage the situation, was lacerated severely by the coral. Our failure to plan the dive was the cause of his injury. If we had discussed the exit procedures before the dive, his pain and suffering could have been avoided. Even a simple snorkel dive requires planning. One of the best rules of diving is to always plan your dive, and then dive your plan.*

# Diving Environment 7

## Dive In and Discover

By the end of this chapter, you will be able to do the following:

- Describe the aquatic food cycle and explain how the process contributes to red tide.

- List five types of aquatic life injuries and three ways to avoid such injuries.

- List four types of pollutants and describe the effects they have on the underwater environment.

- List three actions that divers can take to help preserve aquatic life.

- List five ways to keep from damaging the environment while you are underwater.

- Contrast the general diving conditions for freshwater diving and saltwater diving.

- Describe the hazards of cavern diving, cave diving, and ice diving.

- Explain the cause of tides and their effects on diving activities.

- Explain the cause of waves and surf and their effects on diving activities.

- Explain the causes of currents and their effects on diving activities.

- Describe a rip current and explain how to escape from one.

- Define the terms *plankton, bloom, red tide, kelp, stipes, fronds, ciguatera, scombroid, tetrodotoxin, thermocline, overturn, reverse thermocline, upwelling, eddies, cavern, cave, sink, siphon, turbid, continental shelf, tsunami, stand, spring tide, neap tide, flood, ebb, slack water, fetch, swell, crest, trough, wave height, wavelength, wave period, wave train, surge, surf, gyres, downwelling, rip current, drift, set, drift dive,* and *trail line.*

Learning to dive gives you an opportunity to become more familiar with the aquatic environment, which covers over 70 percent of the surface of the earth. The underwater world is fascinating. This chapter introduces you to biological and physical conditions of the diving environment. You will learn the effect of people upon the environment and the effect of the environment upon people. You affect the underwater world more than you might imagine.

# AQUATIC BIOLOGY

The plants and animals of the underwater world are wondrous and diverse. The millions of animals in the aquatic realm range from those that are microscopic to those weighing tons. To appreciate, respect, and enjoy aquatic life, you need to learn a bit about biology. This section familiarizes you with the flora and fauna of the aquatic realm. Aquatic life fits into three categories: life-forms that drift with the currents, those that swim freely and are able to move against the currents, and those that dwell on the bottom.

## Drifters

The drifters are called **plankton.** Animals that drift are called zooplankton. Drifting plants are called phytoplankton. Plankton begins the food cycle in the waters (see figure 7.1). Small animals eat plankton, and larger animals eat the smaller animals. When the large animals die, their remains sink to the bottom and decompose. The decomposed material rises to the surface where it becomes food for the plankton. Warm water and nutrients cause some plankton to multiply. Overpopulations of plankton, called **blooms,** can color the water, destroy underwater visibility, and form toxins in animals that feed by filtering water. Toxin from blooms makes clams and mussels unsafe for consumption during summer months in some areas. One type of red phytoplankton often creates blooms, known as **red tide,** in the seas. Diving conditions are poor in areas affected by plankton blooms.

▶ Figure 7.1 The underwater food cycle.

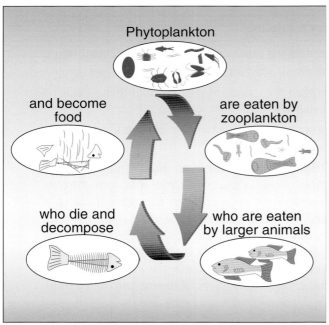

Phytoplankton

are eaten by zooplankton

who are eaten by larger animals

who die and decompose

and become food

Another type of aquatic plant, called algae, is an important part of the aquatic world. Plants use light to produce their own food and become food for animals. They convert water and carbon dioxide to oxygen and carbohydrates through the process of photosynthesis. Various types of algae are found in underwater areas where light is available. Most algae grows in shallow water where light is most abundant. Thick moss drapes objects in some freshwater areas. Turtle grass is a grasslike, green, tropical saltwater algae that provides a habitat for many forms of life. Some types of long, flowing algae in cold and shallow water, such as surf grass or eel grass, can cause you to trip if you try to walk in them. Slippery plants cover rocks and can cause you to slip and fall unless you move cautiously.

Giant algae, called **kelp,** produce long strands, called **stipes,** in which you can become entangled. You can learn how to avoid and how to deal with this problem. A rootlike structure, called a holdfast, anchors kelp to the bottom;

numerous gas bladders, called floats, lift the top parts toward the surface. What appear to be the leaves of kelp are **fronds.** Large areas of kelp are known as kelp beds, which have thick canopies that blanket the surface of the water (see figure 7.2). It is difficult to swim through a kelp canopy at the surface, but it is easy to swim between the clumps of stipes beneath the surface. Underwater navigational skills are important when diving in areas where kelp is dense. Kelp forests are popular diving areas because they contain great quantities of life.

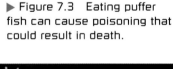

▶ Figure 7.2  A typical kelp bed.

## Swimmers

One of the rewards of diving is seeing fish. There are fish in nearly all the waters of the world. You cannot outswim even the slowest fish, so do not chase them. If you want to observe fish closely, blend into the environment. Fish will get closer to you than you could ever get to them.

Collecting for aquariums requires specialized knowledge and procedures. Most fish have an internal air bladder for buoyancy control. If taken to the surface too quickly, the air bladder expands and kills the animal. Avoid handling fish because the experience can be traumatic as well as physically damaging to the animal.

Eating some types of fish can harm you. Some fish are poisonous. Types of fish poisoning include **ciguatera, scombroid,** and **tetrodotoxin.** Ciguatera results from eating fish that consume a certain species of algae. Ciguatera poisoning causes gastrointestinal problems within 6 to 12 hours. Scombroid poisoning, which produces nausea and vomiting within an hour, can result if you eat fish that have not been kept chilled. Tetrodotoxin, the most serious fish poisoning, results from eating exotic fish such as puffer fish or blowfish (figure 7.3 shows an example of a puffer). Tetrodotoxin poisoning can cause death within minutes. Avoid eating large and unusual-looking fish. Check with local fishermen to determine which fish are safe for consumption.

▶ Figure 7.3  Eating puffer fish can cause poisoning that could result in death.

Many large mammals—sea lions, seals, dolphins, whales, and manatees—inhabit the water. They are graceful, beautiful, and sometimes awesome in appearance. Viewing is an exciting experience. Some are curious and may approach you. Aquatic mammals usually will not harm you in the water if you leave them alone. But sea lions and seals are defensive on land and might bite if you get too close.

## Bottom Dwellers

Bottom dwellers include animals that are stationary, such as coral and sea fans, as well as animals that move about, such as crabs and lobsters. Generally speaking, living, stationary bottom dwellers are not included in fish and

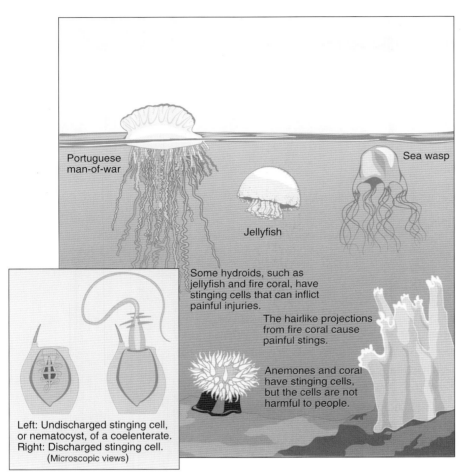

Left: Undischarged stinging cell, or nematocyst, of a coelenterate. Right: Discharged stinging cell. (Microscopic views)

▶ Figure 7.4  Several types of hydroids have stinging cells.

game regulations, and you should not take them. Do not take coral, sea fans, and animals that appear stationary, such as starfish. If you hunt crabs and lobsters for food, know how to determine the sex of the animals, how to catch them without harming them, and how to measure them for minimum size. Do not take females, particularly those bearing eggs. Some divers take only one claw from a crab to conserve the species. A crab can feed and defend itself with one claw and can regenerate a new claw to replace the one taken.

## Hydroids

If you dive in salt water, you should know about hydroids, a category of animals that includes bottom dwellers, such as coral, and swimmers, such as jellyfish (see figure 7.4). Some hydroids, like the beautiful sea anemone, have a round, column-like body with a mouth surrounded by tentacles. This is a polyp form of hydroid. Another type, called the colonial form, can assume many different shapes. Colonies of hydroids can encrust a surface, and groups of colonies form jellyfish. Learn to recognize and avoid hydroids that can injure you.

# POTENTIALLY DANGEROUS AQUATIC ANIMALS

Aquatic animals use a variety of mechanisms to obtain food and to defend themselves from attack. You can minimize your chances of injury by being familiar with the ways in which animals can inflict injury. Aquatic animals rarely are aggressive toward humans; they flee, hide, or stand still as you approach. If you do not touch, threaten, or provoke an animal, it is unlikely to injure you intentionally. But remember, aquatic animals are wild animals. If you feed them, and they bite you in the process, you should not blame the animals. Figure 7.5 lists types of injuries that you could sustain from aquatic animals and recommended first aid.

## Animals That Cause Abrasions or Cuts

Many animals, such as some types of coral and barnacles, have sharp, hard structures that easily cut flesh. Such cuts can be painful, are slow to heal, and can get infected. Avoid contact with reefs and rocks covered with sharp animals. Some fish have knifelike

Moray eel

Coral

## Potentially Dangerous Aquatic Animals

| Injury | First Aid |
|---|---|
| **Abrasions or cuts** Barnacle Coral | Scrub and disinfect the wound. |
| **Bites** Barracuda Moray eel Sea snake Shark Turtle, muskrat, alligator | Stop the bleeding, clean and disinfect the wound. For a sea snake bite, apply pressure, immobilize the area, and get prompt medical attention. |
| **Stings** Fire coral Jellyfish | Soak the injured area in vinegar. For a cone shell sting, apply pressure and immobilize the injured area. |
| **Puncture** Bristle worm Cone shell Sea urchin Venomous fish | Soak the injured area in hot water. |
| **Laceration** Stingray | Soak the injured area in hot water. |

Get medical attention as needed for all injuries.

Sea urchin

Stingray

Fire coral

▶ Figure 7.5   Potential injuries and recommended first aid.

protrusions on their gill plates or at the base of their tails. They defend themselves by flailing rapidly back and forth and slashing anything near them.

## Animals That Puncture

Sea urchins are the porcupines of the seas. Cold-water urchins have short, thick spines, while warm-water urchins have spines that are long and thin. The spines of all urchins can penetrate an exposure suit if you bump into them. The spines break off in your flesh and produce a painful, red, swollen wound. The spines can be difficult to remove, so if you are unable to avoid a sea urchin injury, see a physician to have the spines removed.

Some fish have a row of long, sharp spines along their back. The scorpion fish has hollow dorsal spines at the base, which are sacs filled with venom. If you are punctured by the spines and compress the venom sacs, you inject yourself with a toxin. The toxin of some species, such as the stone fish, can cause serious symptoms. Some fish, such as the lion fish (also called the turkey fish or zebra fish), have spines in other fins. The toxin of a lion fish produces serious symptoms in humans. Freshwater catfish also have venomous spines.

A tropical marine worm, called a bristle worm, has tufted, silky bristles along the sides of its body. The bristles, which are fine and brittle, penetrate the skin easily, are difficult to remove, and cause a burning sensation. Do not touch or handle these worms.

A shellfish called the cone shell uses venom to kill animals for food. The venom is highly toxic, and these animals can inject their venom into humans. Do not handle conical shells in tropical waters.

## Animals That Bite

Use discretion to avoid being bitten by aquatic animals. One large freshwater fish that can bite is the gar. Turtles can inflict serious wounds. Muskrats may attack in defense, and moray eels in the ocean can deliver a serious bite. Alligators also have the potential to inflict an injury but have not been known to hurt divers.

Sharks can bite, but attacks on scuba divers are nearly nonexistent. Hollywood has exaggerated the danger of sharks; only a few species of sharks are aggressive, and it is rare to encounter these types in the waters visited by divers. Most divers would be delighted to see a shark because the animals usually retreat from an area frequented by scuba divers.

Retreat from snakes if you encounter them. Do not handle snakes, which can be extremely venomous. A sea snake bite can produce a life-threatening emergency. Some freshwater snakes, such as the cottonmouth, also are venomous.

## Animals That Cause Lacerations

Rays are round, flat, bottom dwellers. Some rays have a sharp, serrated barb at the base of the tail. The rays blend into the bottom. When someone disturbs a ray, it defends itself by arching its back and thrusting its barb into the attacker. A sheath, which often remains in the laceration wound, covers the barb and contains a toxin. Stingray wounds in the ankles of divers, waders, and swimmers are common in some areas. Avoid stingray wounds by shuffling your feet along the bottom as you walk. The torpedo ray, an animal found on the west coast of the United States, can generate electricity. This ray can stun a diver, so be able to recognize it and avoid contact if you encounter one.

## Animals That Sting

Many aquatic animals can sting. Learn to identify and avoid contact with jellyfish, featherlike or whiplike hydroids, and even some sponges. Hydroids have tiny stinging cells, called nematocysts, that they use to kill food. The sting of some animals, such as encrusting fire coral, is merely annoying; but the sting of others, such as the Portuguese man-of-war or the box jellyfish, can cause a medical emergency. You should wear an exposure suit at all times while diving in the ocean. The suit provides protection from stings, but be careful when you remove it. The stinging cells of marine animals remain active even if they are not on the animal. Parts of jellyfish and other animals that are on your equipment can sting if they come into contact with your skin when you remove the equipment. Some jellyfish come to the surface at night in tropical waters. Dangerous stinging animals are seasonal in some regions. Check with local divers to find out what to avoid and when to be on the alert.

## Avoiding Danger

Many aquatic animals are potentially dangerous. Tropical waters have the most dangerous animals. Serious injuries to divers are not common because divers avoid animals that can hurt them. You should respect animals, but do not be overly concerned about them. Do not panic or flee just because you see a potentially dangerous animal; just avoid contact with it. Learn to recognize the dangerous animals in an area, know where to look for them, be alert for them, and keep clear of them. Move slowly and look carefully. Shuffle your feet when wading. Don't touch anything unless you know it is safe to touch it. Neutral buoyancy—the ability to hover—is an excellent defense against aquatic injuries.

The biology of the underwater world is so interesting that many divers study it as a hobby. It is fun to learn about animals and plants and then observe them in their natural habitats. Some divers, fascinated with aquatic life, pursue biology as a career.

# CONSERVATION AND PRESERVATION

Life in the waters is beautiful and precious, but pollution from people jeopardizes life in the lakes and seas. Divers are physically ruining beautiful reefs. Unless we take action immediately, there is a real danger that many areas of the underwater world will become barren and lifeless. We must preserve and conserve the resources of our waters.

Because the waters are so vast, people often take them for granted. Lakes and seas seem too big to be harmed, but that is not the case. The underwater environment is fragile; the balance of nature can be upset more easily than many people realize. We think of the seas as being great and powerful because we see big waves and pounding surf. People who do not see beneath the surface may not realize the delicate nature of the animals that inhabit the waters. Some living things in the seas grow slowly, only a fraction of an inch (or centimeter) per year.

As a diver, you can help reduce damage to the underwater world. It is essential for every diver to take two actions: (1) Do everything possible personally to preserve the diving environment, and (2) do everything possible to educate others and help them learn to preserve the aquatic environment. You will get closer to the aquatic environment than most of your friends. You will see firsthand the effects of pollution, litter, and

## Character Development

The ability to enter into the underwater realm also brings with it the responsibility to take care of that environment. The character development values of caring, respect, and responsibility are directly applicable to your actions when diving. What you do when diving can affect aquatic creatures and their world long after you have returned to the surface. Follow the suggestions made in this section to express your values and preserve the aquatic environment for everyone.

exploitation. You also will see the beauty and abundance that are possible when the environment is clean and unmolested. Your influence in society can make a difference. If you do not become part of the solution to problems in the aquatic environment, you are part of the problem.

## Pollution

Stemming pollution is one of the greatest challenges facing the world. Humans are incredible polluters of the environment; we have polluted the air, the land, and the waters. People dump billions of gallons and pounds of waste into water every day. People seem to think that when something is out of sight, it no longer is a problem. This is not true of pollutants. Sewage, industrial waste, garbage, and sediment have killed and are continuing to kill many underwater environments. If we stopped all pollution today, the aquatic environment would continue to suffer for decades from the waste materials that are already in the water.

Runoff from land that enters rivers and streams and flows into the ocean also causes pollution. Chemicals used in agriculture, on lawns, and in gardens cause death and destruction in the aquatic environment. Sediment from construction and drilling that finds its way into water blocks out life-giving sunlight and smothers bottom-dwelling creatures.

Lakes and oceans have been viewed as bottomless toilets for waste disposal. There are two problems with this narrow view: (1) Animals and plants live in the water and are killed by the pollution; (2) the water cannot be replaced because large bodies of water cannot be flushed.

## Diver Impact

As a diver, you can harm the environment in several ways. You can remove living things from the environment, you can smash and kill living things while moving about underwater, or you can stir up clouds of silt on the bottom. The silt can choke and kill some organisms. Good intentions also can cause problems; handling and feeding animals can kill them.

You can be an effective predator underwater. There are many animals you can hunt and take. A few callous individuals kill things for sport, but responsible people take only what they will eat. While the impact of divers is of little significance compared with commercial fishing, keep in mind that you do have an effect. If you spearfish on a reef, it will not be long before the fish in the area will be unapproachable by divers. If you want to be a predator, you must do so in a responsible manner. Conservation and preservation of aquatic resources are important topics that are discussed later in this section.

It is difficult to resist touching animals underwater, but you should refrain until you know what animals may be touched and how to touch them without harming them. Many animals are delicate; rough handling will kill them. Predators will eat animals removed from a protected area for viewing. Some animals, including fish, have a protective coating of mucus. If the coating is removed by handling, the animal can develop an infection and die. The stress of being handled by a gigantic, bubble-blowing monster may be more than some aquatic animals can take. Sea turtles may abort their eggs after being harassed by a playful diver. Do not be guilty of killing things for your amusement. After you learn how, you can get extremely close to animals underwater. You can interact with them and enjoy them without handling them.

Feeding animals underwater was a popular activity until environmentalists showed that this is harmful (not to mention dangerous). There are several potential problems. Unnatural food given to animals can interfere with their digestion. The animals may become dependent on the food fed to them by divers and may not be able to forage if the food supply is discontinued. Food can make animals overcome their natural fear of divers. When an animal that would normally take cover at the sight of a diver becomes accustomed to divers providing food, the animal will readily approach a diver who is a hunter.

A diver underwater has the potential to be a bull in a china shop. Overweighted divers plow along the bottom with their fins pointed downward, stirring up great clouds of silt. Buoyancy difficulties cause divers to hold on to and crash into reefs and other living things. Divers who rest on the bottom crush plants and animals without realizing the damage. Divers who swim too close to a reef often kick animals to death.

## Diver Impact Prevention

One of the most important reasons for good buoyancy control skills is to prevent damage to the underwater environment. An environmentally responsible diver is properly weighted and in control of buoyancy at all times. Make your diving no-contact diving. You should be able to hover above a reef, move your mask within inches of an animal, and view it without touching anything but water and without stirring up silt. Learn to use your hands to scull into position while your fins remain still. Sculling is positioning achieved with short movements of the hands (not the arms). Buoyancy control and sculling are excellent skills for reducing diver impact. Figure 7.6 shows a diver sculling.

Another way to protect the environment is to keep your equipment secured close to you so that it does not dangle and drag. Equipment that drags along the bottom for an entire dive can

▶ Figure 7.6 Sculling helps reduce diver impact.

do a lot of damage. Streamline your equipment. Moving slowly underwater conserves energy and air and makes you less likely to come into contact with animals. This helps you avoid injuring both yourself and animals.

If you must hold on to something underwater or push yourself away from something, look before you touch, and avoid touching anything that is living. If you must settle onto the bottom for some reason, select an area where there is no visible life. If you are weightless, keep in mind that one finger may be all you need to provide the leverage to move. Leave no evidence that you ever visited an underwater area.

## Conservation

Many animals that once were plentiful are nearly extinct because of a lack of conservation. Buffalo and passenger pigeons are good examples of this happening on land. In some areas, this is happening to aquatic animals. Bait fish that once swarmed in enormous schools in some areas no longer exist. With no food to eat, larger predatory fish no longer frequent the areas.

Fish and game regulations are designed to conserve natural resources. Rules regarding sizes, seasons, limits, and the means by which game may be taken have been established to help ensure an ongoing supply of a resource. Obey fish and game regulations, and encourage others to abide by them as well. The rules can benefit everyone in the long run.

If you take living things from the water, do it in a responsible manner. Avoid taking animals from areas that are popular dive sites. Limit hunting and collecting to remote areas where the impact of divers is much less. Take only what you need, not what you can get or what you are allowed. The two types of hunters most harmful to the environment are the quantity hunter and the trophy hunter. The quantity hunter seeks to take as much and as many of everything as possible to build an image as a mighty hunter. The trophy hunter seeks the largest animals, which destroys the fittest of the breeding stock. If you kill an animal, you have a duty to know how large one must be to breed and what the maximum size of the animal is. You should take animals that have had the opportunity to reproduce, but do not take the largest ones. It is difficult at times to be selective, but you should attempt to conserve life.

Nature left undisturbed maintains a balance of life. Animals are both predator and prey. An animal eats another animal and is in turn eaten by others. If there are too many predators, their population diminishes due to an inadequate food supply. If there is a temporary overpopulation of prey, the number of predators increases. People upset nature's balance. We are the most efficient predators of all. We disturb the food cycle with pollution, hunting, fishing, boating, and every way in which we affect the aquatic environment. It takes nature longer to recover from our impact than from any natural disaster. It is important today to lessen the effect of people on the environment to reduce interference with the natural management of the life within the waters.

## Preservation

Preservation is everyone's business, but it is more your business now than it was before you became a diver. You probably know more than your friends and neighbors about the aquatic environment. You must be an ambassador for preservation. You must educate and motivate people to help preserve the diving environment.

What people do above water affects life beneath the surface. What people put down their drains and toilets winds up in the aquatic environment. So do the chemicals they use on their lawns and gardens. Litter in and around the water kills animals, birds, and fish (see figure 7.7). Think twice about the products you buy, how you use what you purchase, and how you dispose of your wastes. Where will the toxic chemicals and waste you use end up? Be environmentally conscientious; then teach others to be so, too. A simple act, such as the use of detergents without phosphates, can make a difference. Phosphates are powerful nutrients that upset the balance of nature when dumped into the aquatic environment.

▶ Figure 7.7   Litter is ugly, and it kills sea life.

Be involved in your community. Be concerned about issues such as sewage treatment, toxic wastes, and construction, which can be extremely harmful, as are waste products from manufacturing. Help others understand the seriousness of pollution.

Become more informed and keep informed. Join groups that are working to preserve the environment. Organizations such as the Center for Marine Conservation, Reef Environmental Education Foundation (REEF), Project Reefkeeper, and the Oceanic Society merit your membership. These groups provide up-to-date information and details on how you can help. Various organizations sponsor underwater clean-ups from time to time; these are enjoyable and worthwhile. (For a list of environmental organizations you can join, see the appendix.)

There are actions you can and should take when you go diving. Dispose of trash properly, and encourage others to do the same. If you have a boat for diving, anchor it away from reefs to avoid reef damage caused by the anchor and chain. Retrieve trash you find in the environment, especially plastic. Collect plastic, monofilament, lead, and stainless steel leaders. Not all trash is bad. Bottles and cans provide homes for animals. Report unlawful dumping and lost or discarded fishing nets and traps, which continue to catch and kill after abandonment.

# AQUATIC CONDITIONS

The particular state of the environment or the physical situations in which divers find themselves that are of concern include the temperature, visibility, and degree of movement of the water. You need to be familiar with aquatic conditions in general and local aquatic conditions specifically.

## The Big Picture

Many factors affect the seas. The sun bears down on the Earth at the equator more directly than on other parts of the Earth. The climate and waters near the equator are warm; the greater the distance from the equator, the colder the water. The difference in water temperatures in different parts of the world causes the movement of air and water by convection currents. Winds move from areas of high pressure to areas of low pressure. Winds and the turning of the Earth move water. On a global scale, water currents move in a clockwise direction in the northern hemisphere of the Earth and in a counterclockwise direction in the southern hemisphere. Weather moves from west to east. The gravitational attraction between the Earth and other planetary bodies produces changes in the water level called tides. Storms at sea produce energy in the form of waves that travel thousands of miles before giving up their energy in the form of surf.

Seasonal changes, winds, and storms affect inland bodies of water. Water from snow and rain in the mountains and hills flows into streams, rivers, and lakes. Water seeping into the ground resurfaces in quarries and springs.

Weather, seasons, geography, and other factors affect both surface and underwater diving conditions. The water can be rough at the surface but calm at depth. There may be a current at the surface but none on the bottom. The visibility may be good at the surface but poor on the bottom. The temperature usually is warmer at the surface than it is at depth. You should become familiar with both surface and underwater conditions and their effect on your diving.

Perhaps the most important fact to remember about diving conditions is that they vary. Thus, an environmental orientation is important when you dive in a new region. The diving conditions usually dictate the way you dive. What works well in one area may be totally ineffective for another. An understanding of the effects of diving conditions in an area is important. You should know the conditions to expect, how the conditions affect your approach to diving, and how to manage the effects of the conditions. For example, it's safe to wade into the water and put on your fins in one area, but in another area you need to put your fins on before you wade in.

## General Freshwater Diving Conditions

Fresh water is 2.5 percent less dense than salt water, so you are less buoyant in fresh water than in salt water. The density of water varies with temperature. Fresh water is most dense at a temperature of 39.2 °F (4 °C), the usual temperature and density of the water at depths greater than 60 feet (18 meters) in freshwater lakes and quarries. The water becomes lighter when it is either warmer or cooler than this. Fresh water often forms layers: a layer of warmer, lighter water on top of a layer of colder, denser water. The change from the warm water to the colder water, called a **thermocline**, is abrupt. When the water is calm, the thermocline appears to have wisps of smoke on top of it when viewed from above. The refraction of light is different when the density of the water is different, so there is a slight visual blurring at the interface of a thermocline. When you dive in fresh water, you must insulate yourself for the water temperature below the thermocline. While the surface of a lake may be warm and sunny, the water at the bottom may be close to freezing.

**thermocline**—An abrupt transition from a warmer layer of water to a colder layer of water.

The best season for diving in a freshwater lake or quarry depends on the body of water. Spring and fall are often good times because the water temperature is the same from surface to bottom, there is oxygen for fish at all depths, populations of plankton are low, and visibility usually is good.

In later spring, the sun warms the surface water, and the lack of wind keeps it from mixing with the colder water at depth. The water stratifies, and a thermocline forms that remains until fall. The layer of water below the thermocline stagnates in most lakes during the summer. Decaying matter depletes oxygen and creates toxins. Fish seek refuge above the thermocline. Sunlight and warm water often lead to plankton blooms, which are aggravated by pollution.

In the fall, surface waters in lakes and quarries cool until they equal the temperature of the water at depth. Colder water and reduced sunlight stifle plankton growth and visibility improves. Winds cause water circulation. The movement of water from the top to a depth of about 60 feet (18 meters), called an **overturn,** carries oxygenated water to the bottom and leads to what is called spring diving conditions. Visibility tends to be poor during an overturn.

In the winter, the surface water in a lake or quarry is colder than the water at the bottom. A **reverse thermocline** exists and remains until the surface water temperature warms to that of the water at the bottom. This allows the spring overturn to begin.

# Freshwater conditions

Water becomes 10 percent lighter when it freezes. If ice sank when it froze, bodies of water could become solid ice from top to bottom. Ice that forms over water insulates the water beneath it. Figure 7.8 shows the annual cycle of freshwater lakes and the concept of thermoclines.

When a strong wind blows along a shore for a sustained period over a body of water, the surface water is pushed away from shore. This water is replaced by colder water flowing up from the depths. This is called an **upwelling,** which also can occur in the ocean. If the wind conditions persist, the water temperature can become constant throughout the water column, even in the summer. An upwelling carries nutrients from the depths into shallow water and brings animals into the area. Following an upwelling, a bloom can occur because of the increase in nutrients in warm, shallow water.

## Specific Freshwater Diving Conditions

There are good diving experiences in many kinds of freshwater environments. Springs, low-altitude lakes, and quarries are good sites for divers who do not live near a coast. Other freshwater environments, such as rivers, caverns and caves, high-altitude and frozen lakes, and areas with submerged wreckage, can be dangerous (see figure 7.9). Complete specialty training courses before diving in any hazardous area.

You may encounter strong currents in rivers. The currents are strongest at the surface and on the outside of bends. Countercurrents and swirling currents, called **eddies,** are

▶ Figure 7.8
*(a)* Thermocline, *(b)* reverse thermocline, and *(c)* the annual cycle of overturn in lakes.

**upwelling**—The replacement of warm water at the surface with colder water flowing up from the depths as a result of a strong wind blowing along the shore for a sustained time.

▶ Figure 7.9 River diving provides unique experiences but shouldn't be attempted without specific training.

**Caution:**

*Diving in caves without proper training and equipment is a leading cause of dive fatalities.*

common, and entanglements are likely in many rivers. Currents can undercut the bank of a river, so direct access to the surface can be impossible at times. Rivers are especially prone to seasonal changes and are often unpredictable.

Freshwater springs can provide beautiful diving environments. The flow of clean, calm water, which usually is at a moderate temperature (65 to 78 °F, or 18 to 26 °C), provides excellent visibility. The water often flows through underground limestone cave systems that extend for thousands of feet. Diving in open-water basins in a spring is appropriate for certified divers, but entering any overhead area where a direct, vertical ascent to the surface is not possible is not appropriate. A large, roomlike opening where light from the surface can be seen is called a **cavern.** Areas that extend further than a cavern where no surface light can be seen are called **caves** (see figure 7.10). Divers must complete specialty courses and must meet several requirements to dive in caverns and caves. Entering such an environment—even for a short distance—without the required training and equipment can be fatal. No amount of diving experience without cave-diving training qualifies a diver to enter a cave. It is easy to become disoriented, to stir up thick clouds of silt that instantly reduce visibility to nothing, and to panic and drown. You may dive in spring basins, but stay out of caverns and caves unless you meet the requirements to dive in them. The appendix contains contact information for organizations that offer cavern- and cave-diving training.

Sometimes the earth collapses into an underground cave system and forms a **sink.** The water flowing into the sink forms a basin. An opening called a **siphon** channels water from a sink back into the system. Diving in siphons can be dangerous. The amount of water moving through a system depends on the amount of rainfall in the area. Under extreme conditions the normal flow of water can reverse.

People dig pits to excavate sand, gravel, and stone. At some depth they encounter the water table, and the pit floods, forming a quarry or sand pit. At some of these sites you can see submerged construction equipment that was abandoned when the pit flooded.

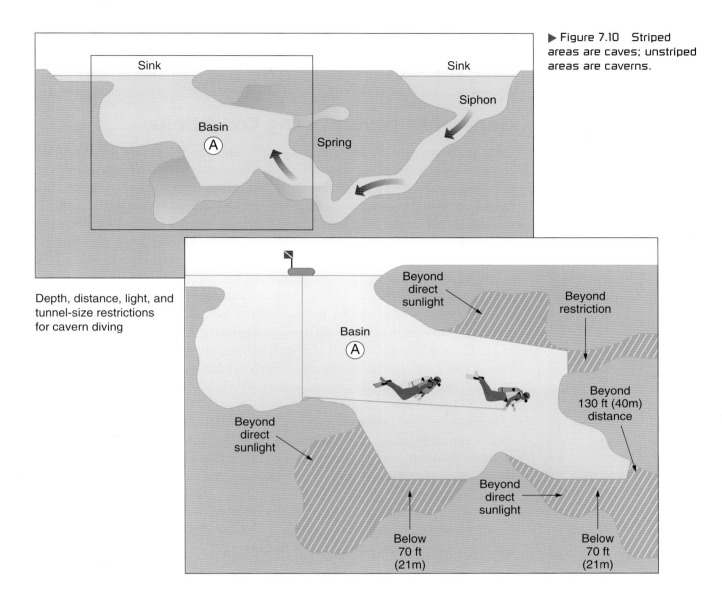

Depth, distance, light, and tunnel-size restrictions for cavern diving

Sand pits and quarries tend to have fair to good visibility, although the disturbance of silt that has settled to the bottom can ruin the visibility quickly. Gravel quarries usually have more silt than other types of quarries, so the water may be **turbid.**

Lakes can be excellent dive sites. There are freshwater lakes at altitudes above 10,000 feet (3,048 meters). Diving at altitudes above 1,000 feet (305 meters), a specialty called altitude diving, presents many hazards because the rate of pressure change is greater when you descend into water at an atmospheric pressure that is less than the pressure at sea level. You must follow special procedures to avoid decompression sickness. Problems also can result from the thinner air, which provides less oxygen with each breath taken above water.

When ice forms over water in the winter, diving becomes hazardous. Perils of ice diving include hypothermia, the freezing of regulator and buoyancy control valves, and getting lost beneath the ice. Ice diving can be beautiful and adventurous, but it is dangerous when attempted without the proper training, equipment, and procedures.

Potential hazards when diving in fresh water include body heat loss, submerged trees, wire, fishing line, hooks and lures, log jams, debris, currents, rapids, whirlpools, poor visibility, silt, and overhead restrictions. You can minimize these hazards with training, experience, equipment, correct diving techniques, area orientations, and good judgment.

## General Saltwater Diving Conditions

There are five oceans on the earth; seas, gulfs, and bays are smaller sections of the oceans. The land beneath the oceans is not flat. The **continental shelf** is an underwater area that extends from land and slopes gradually to a depth of about 600 feet (183 meters). Beyond the continental shelf are great underwater canyons and mountains, as well as hills, valleys, and great plains. In some areas, the tips of mountains and volcanoes extend above the surface of the ocean from great depths. In other areas, deep canyons sever the continental slope, creating deep-water conditions close to shore.

The saltwater environment varies greatly from one part of the Earth to another. The clear waters of the Caribbean, with temperatures that can exceed 85 °F (29 °C) feature coral reefs covered with beautiful, lush animals that look like plants. Schools of colorful tropical fish abound. Temperate waters, with temperatures ranging from 55 to 70 °F (13 to 21 °C), may have great forests of kelp, which contain more life per volume than a tropical rain forest. Cold ocean waters in northern latitudes are nutrient rich and team with life. There are beautiful sights and wonders to behold in all the oceans of our planet. Figure 7.11 shows one example.

Oceans always are in motion. Tides, winds, and currents cause water movement. An underwater earthquake can move water by creating gigantic seismic waves known as **tsunami.** Although these giant waves also are called tidal waves, the tide has nothing to do with them. Tsunamis can cause great destruction, but they are rare and can be forecasted.

The energy source for movement of ocean water may be local or may originate thousands of miles away. You need to understand what causes water to move, how it moves, and how to dive in ocean water that is in motion.

▶ Figure 7.11 Sights like this are common in the temperate waters of the Caribbean.

# Tides

The gravitational attraction between the moon and the Earth pulls water toward the moon. The resulting increase in water depth is a high tide. Water pulled away from the sides of the earth in the process produces a decrease in water depth called low tide. A high tide forms on the side of the earth opposite the moon because the attraction of the moon is least at that point and because of the centrifugal effect created by the rotation of the earth. At any given time, two areas on the Earth are experiencing high tides and two areas are experiencing low tides. There is a brief period of time, called a **stand,** when the tide neither rises nor falls; there can be four tidal stands per day—two high and two low. Geographical formations interfere with or enhance the rising and falling of the water in some areas.

The sun also affects the tides, but only about half as much as the moon because the moon is much closer to the Earth. When the moon and the sun are aligned with the Earth, which occurs twice monthly (during the new and full moons), tides are highest and are called **spring tides** (see figure 7.12). When the moon and sun are at right angles to each other in relation to the Earth, tides are lowest and are called **neap tides.**

The moon rotates around the Earth in the same direction that the Earth spins, and so the duration of a lunar day (moonrise to moonrise) is nearly 25 hours. This causes tides to occur at different times each day and explains why the heights of subsequent tides vary.

During a tidal change, water flows from one area to another. The water movements caused by the tides are called tidal currents, and they vary in velocity between tides. The flow of water into an area due to high tide is called a **flood.** The flow of water away from an area due to low tide is called an **ebb.** There is a period of time between flood and ebb when the water has minimal movement. The term for this period is **slack water.** Because of geographical features of the earth, water cannot move instantly in many areas. There usually is a delay between the predicted time of a tide and the time when the water is slack.

Tidal changes affect diving activities and operations. Large differences in the water level between tides affect visibility and other conditions. Water height also affects entries and exits, shoal areas when boating, the mooring of boats, and the loading and unloading of vessels. It is a good idea to know how high the tide will be. Tidal changes are small (less than two feet, or 0.6 meters) in some areas or on some days but large (more than six feet, or 1.8 meters) in other areas or on other days. The greater the difference between high and low tide, the greater the effect of the tides.

Because the Earth, moon, and sun follow set courses, the tides are predictable. Tides vary because the distance between planetary bodies and their positions relative to one another change constantly. Despite all the variables, scientists can predict with accuracy when the tides will occur and the heights of the tides. The government publishes tide tables, and national weather channels broadcast tidal information continuously. Local correction tables and current tables can provide more precise information. Tide tables

**spring tides**—The twice-monthly period of highest tides, which occurs when the moon and sun are aligned with the Earth.

**neap tide**—The twice-monthly period of lowest tides, which occurs when the moon and sun are at right angles to each other in relation to the Earth.

▶ Figure 7.12  The effect of the sun and moon on tidal patterns.

**November 1986**

| | Low tide | | | | High tide | | | |
|---|---|---|---|---|---|---|---|---|
| | a.m. | ht. | p.m. | ht. | a.m. | ht. | p.m. | ht. |
| | Sunrise 6:19 | | -PST- | | Sunset 5:08 | | | |
| 1 Sa | 1:35 | 1.0 | 2:35 | 0.5 | 7:49 | 6.4 | 8:46 | 4.7 |
| 2 Su | 2:06 | 1.3 | 3:17 | 0.9 | 8:21 | 6.7 | 9:36 | 4.4 |
| 3 M | 2:38 | 1.7 | 4:06 | 1.0 | 8:56 | 8.8 | 10:35 | 4.0 |
| 4 Tu | 3:14 | 2.1 | 5:02 | 0.9 | 9:33 | 6.7 | 11:44 | 3.7 |
| 5 W | 3:50 | 2.6 | 6:03 | 0.7 | 10:19 | 6.5 | — | — |
| | Sunrise 6:24 | | -PST- | | Sunset 5:03 | | | |
| 6 Th | 4:42 | 3.0 | 7:17 | 0.4 | 1:14 | 3.5 | (11:15 | 6.0) |
| 7 F | 6:00 | 3.3 | 8:36 | 0.2 | 2:57 | 3.8 | 12:28 | 5.4 |
| 8 Sa | 8:23 | 3.3 | 9:43 | 0.1 | 4:15 | 4.0 | 2:03 | |
| 9 Su | 10:12 | 2.8 | 10:42 | 0.1 | 5:01 | 4.4 | 3:39 | |
| 10 M | 11:22 | 2.1 | 11:27 | 0.3 | 5:37 | 4.9 | 4:55 | |
| | Sunrise 6:28 | | -PST- | | Sunset 5:00 | | | |
| 11 Tu | — | — | 12:14 | 1.4 | 6:09 | 5.3 | 5: | |
| 12 W | 12:06 | 0.6 | 12:59 | 0.8 | 6:34 | 5.6 | 6 | |
| 13 Th | 12:38 | 0.9 | 1:38 | 0.3 | 6:59 | 5.9 | | |
| 14 F | 1:07 | 1.3 | 2:13 | 0.1 | 7:24 | 8.1 | | |
| 15 Sa | 1:31 | 1.6 | 2:45 | 0.3 | 7:47 | 6.2 | | |
| | Sunrise 6:33 | | -PST- | | Sunset | | | |
| 16 Su | 1:56 | 2.0 | 3:21 | 0.4 | 8:1 | | | |
| 17 M | 2:21 | 2.2 | 3:53 | 0.3 | | | | |
| 18 Tu | 2:40 | 2.5 | 4:33 | 0 | | | | |
| 19 W | 3:03 | 2.7 | 5:1 | | | | | |
| 20 Th | 3:21 | 3.0 | | | | | | |

▶ Figure 7.13  Tide table.

**wave height**—The distance from a wave crest to the trough.

**wavelength**—The distance between waves.

**wave period**—The time it takes two waves to pass a given point.

refer to the height of the tide in relation to an average of the low tides in an area (see figure 7.13). Wind and barometric pressure affect the height of tides, aiding or opposing the movement of tidal waters.

Generally, it is best to dive at high tide, but you may need to time your diving to coincide with slack water in areas with strong tidal currents. The timing may not be important in areas where tidal changes are small. Consider local knowledge about the effects of tides when planning dives.

## Waves and Surf

Ripples form when wind blows across water. You can see this in a puddle on a windy day. When ripples form on a large body of water and the wind continues to blow, the sides of the ripples form a surface against which the wind can push to set the water in motion. The longer and harder the wind blows in a constant direction, the larger the waves that form. As waves move away from the area in which they were created—an area called the **fetch**—the tops of the waves become rounded, undulating forms called **swells.** The water within a swell moves in a circular motion but has little forward motion. The effect is similar to the transmission of a waveform along a rope that is tossed up and down at one end. Waves of energy travel along the rope, but the rope itself does not move forward.

Swells are energy forms that can travel thousands of miles through water and still contain a great deal of energy. The top of a wave is called its **crest.** The bottom is called the **trough.** The distance from the crest to the trough is the **wave height.** The distance between waves is a **wavelength.** The time it takes two waves to pass a given point is a **wave period.** A long series of waves is a **wave train.** The greater the height of a wave and the greater the wavelength of a train of waves, the greater the energy contained in the waves. Two trains of waves can have phases during which the waves of each train reinforce one another and produce larger waves, called wave sets. The formation of larger and smaller waves can occur in phases. By timing the rhythm of the surf, you can make entries and exits easier by moving through the surf zone when the wave sets are small. Figure 7.14 illustrates fundamental concepts of waves and surf.

The water within a passing wave moves in a circular motion, called an orb. The diameter of the motion equals the height of the wave at the surface and diminishes with depth. Motion from a passing wave can be felt to a depth equal to half the wavelength for a series of waves. If there is 100 feet (30 meters) between waves, you can feel the effect of a passing wave to a depth of 50 feet (15 meters).

When waves enter shallow water, contact with the bottom interrupts the circular motion of the water within the waves. The circular movements flatten and eventually become a back-and-forth subsurface motion called **surge.** Wave contact with the bottom causes waves to slow and to become steeper. The wave height increases as the depth of the water decreases. When the depth of the water is about the same as the wave height, the wave becomes unstable and tumbles forward. At this point the water within the wave moves forward and gives up its energy in breaking waves known as **surf.** In areas with offshore reefs, sand bars, and underwater obstructions, waves can break in shallow water, pass over the obstruction, reform, and break again in shallow water near the shore. Waves that break offshore indicate the presence of shallow water in the area where the waves are breaking.

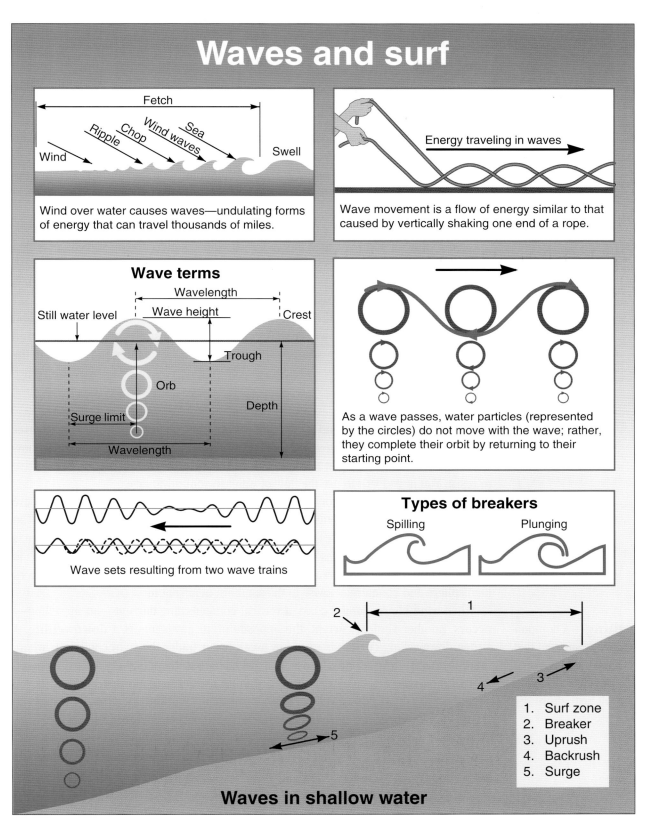

# Waves and surf

### Fetch

Wind · Ripple · Chop · Wind waves · Sea · Swell

Wind over water causes waves—undulating forms of energy that can travel thousands of miles.

Energy traveling in waves

Wave movement is a flow of energy similar to that caused by vertically shaking one end of a rope.

### Wave terms

Wavelength · Still water level · Wave height · Crest · Trough · Orb · Depth · Surge limit · Wavelength

As a wave passes, water particles (represented by the circles) do not move with the wave; rather, they complete their orbit by returning to their starting point.

Wave sets resulting from two wave trains

### Types of breakers

Spilling · Plunging

1. Surf zone
2. Breaker
3. Uprush
4. Backrush
5. Surge

## Waves in shallow water

▶ Figure 7.14   Wind speed, the absence or presence of obstacles, and the shape and depth of the ocean floor influence the formation of waves and surf.

Waves can break and release their energy all at once, or they can spill forward and expend their energy over a wide area. Waves that build quickly and break suddenly form plunging breakers. Waves that spill forward over some distance to shore are spilling breakers. Plunging breakers occur on steeply sloping shores, while spilling breakers occur on bottoms with shallow slopes. Spilling breakers tend to reduce visibility more than plunging breakers.

The crashing water of surf contains air. The white water and foam in the surf zone do not provide as much buoyancy as water that does not contain air. It can be difficult to remain above water in the foam of surf, but you should not attempt to rise above the breakers because you can be picked up and tossed forward by the moving water. It is best to remain low in the wave and breathe from your scuba regulator.

Surf rushes up the face of a beach and then flows back again to the still water level. The return flow of water is called the backrush. This countercurrent, sometimes called an undertow, does not extend beyond a depth of three feet (about a meter). While backrush can be strong when surf is large on a steep beach, it is a misconception that an undertow can carry a swimsmer out to sea.

The surf's crashing onto the shore moves sand. Gentle summer waves carry sand onto the beach; large, rough, winter waves carry the sand offshore, where it forms sand bars. This action explains why some beaches are rocky in the winter and smooth in the summer.

## Currents

Currents are to water what wind is to air: fluid in motion. Since water is 800 times denser than air, water poses much more resistance to movement than air. You need to know how and why water moves and how to move with it. The force of water in motion is too great to resist. You must learn to use the flow of water to your advantage.

Wind, gravity, tides, and convection cause currents; the most common currents are wind-generated surface currents. Because of the rotation of the earth, currents flow at an angle to the wind that generates them. When the wind pushes water away from an area, a compensating current replaces the water displaced. Overall, the effect on the earth is to produce large circulating currents, called **gyres,** that move clockwise in the northern hemisphere and counterclockwise in the southern hemisphere.

**downwelling**—A compensating downward current that occurs when wind blows along a coast where there is a steep drop-off near shore.

When wind blows along a coast, a vertical compensating current—an upwelling—occurs. Another vertical current, the opposite of an upwelling, is a **downwelling.** A strong downwelling current is rare, but it can occur under the right conditions where there is a steep drop-off near shore. It is frightening to be pulled downward in water. Learn if and where a downwelling occurs in an area, and avoid that location. If you should get caught in a downwelling, swim horizontally until you are clear of the current. Trying to swim up against the current can lead to exhaustion and panic.

Water flows in layers (see figure 7.15). The water at the surface moves quickly with the wind, whereas the water a few feet beneath the surface moves slower. The greater the depth, the less the effect of a surface current. After 12 hours of a sustained wind in a given direction, the speed of a surface current is approximately 2 percent of the wind that drives it. Because water flows in layers, it is possible for a surface current to flow in one direction and for a subsurface current to flow in the opposite direction only a few feet beneath the surface.

Surface water at the equator expands as it is warmed and flows slowly toward the poles of the Earth. At the same time, water cooled near the poles increases in density and sinks. Slow-moving convection currents result. These currents do not affect diving procedures, but they greatly affect the oceans by moving nutrients and pollution.

Water can move swiftly, and water movement intensifies whenever an amount of water passes through a restriction. When water moves past irregular formations, turbulence produces dangerous eddies and whirlpools. Swift-water diving is a specialty that is considered hazardous even with experience and training.

Incoming waves can pass over an underwater obstruction, such as a sand bar, and trap water on a shore. If the backrush of water flows back to sea through a narrow opening in the obstruction, a **rip current** exists. The current is narrow and strong and moves away from shore. The current dissipates shortly after passing through the restricted area. You can identify rips by a fan-shaped area of water on the shore, by muddy and foamy water in the rip area, and by a section of waves that breaks before the other waves (see figure 7.16). Rip currents can be stationary or moving. Recognize and avoid rip currents. If you are unable to swim toward shore, you probably are in a rip current. Swim parallel to the shore for about 60 feet (18 meters) to get clear of the rip; then turn and proceed toward shore.

Waves breaking on a shore at a slight angle move water along the shore. The current, called a longshore current, affects diving. On steep beaches, the current can cut a shallow trough in the bottom close to shore. The trough, called a longshore trench, is a sudden

**rip current**—The narrow, strong current that moves away from shore as a result of water flowing back to sea through a narrow opening in an underwater obstruction.

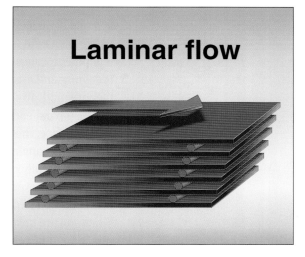

▶ Figure 7.15 The laminar flow of water is similar to a stack of boards with rollers between them. When the stack is tipped, the top board moves much farther than the bottom board. Surface water moves more than water at depth.

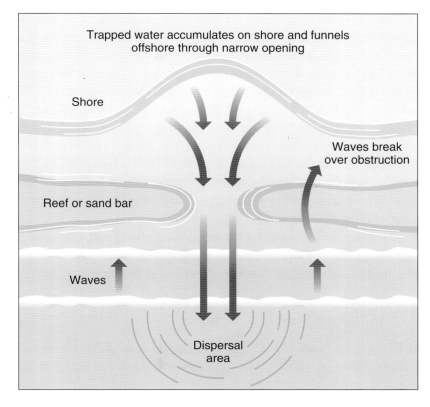

▶ Figure 7.16 A classic rip current.

drop-off and can cause an unsuspecting wading diver to fall. Items dropped into the surf zone move along the shoreline in the direction of the longshore current. The movement of sand on beaches occurs because of wave action combined with longshore currents.

Two types of currents result from all the forces of nature: standing currents, which are constant, and transitory currents, which occur briefly. The Gulf Stream that flows around Florida and up the eastern coast of the United States and the Antilles Current that flows through the Caribbean are examples of standing currents. A longshore current is a transitory current. A rip current can be either type. Be familiar with the currents you will encounter or may encounter in an area.

Currents can flow at a rate of hundreds of feet per minute. The speed of a current is its **drift,** and the direction assumed by a current is its **set.** A fully equipped diver can swim at a rate of 60 to 100 feet (18 to 30 meters) per minute (0.6 to 1.0 knots). Attempting to fight even a mild current is a futile waste of energy. Strong water movement can dislodge equipment, cause regulators to free-flow, and cause rapid heat loss. You must learn to recognize and estimate currents. If the currents are strong, you must avoid them. Even if they are mild, avoid struggling against them. The primary rule for diving in currents when you begin and end your dive at the same point is to dive in a direction opposite the flow at the surface; then use the surface current to aid you when you return at the end of the dive. (See chapter 6 for techniques to estimate currents.)

There are other general rules for diving in currents. Water movement is minimal at the bottom. Whenever possible, descend along a line from the surface to the bottom. If the current is still strong when you reach the bottom, ascend on the line and abort the dive. When you are unsure of your location during a dive, it may help to surface, determine the direction to the exit point, redescend, and move along the bottom toward your destination.

When there is a surface current, minimize the time spent at the surface. Whenever possible, hold on to a fixed object at the surface to keep from drifting downcurrent at a dive site. When a surface current is mild, swim against it to maintain your position at the surface. Develop the habit of noting your surface position in relation to a fixed reference. If you are caught in a sudden, strong current, swim across it to escape from it.

**drift dive**—A dive in which the divers move with the flow of current.

A dive that moves with the flow of a current is a **drift dive.** Simple drift dives along a coast are acceptable when planned. You enter the water at one point, move along the shore with the current, and exit at another point downstream. Another type of drift diving, which is a specialty activity, involves diving in currents from a boat. This type of diving is hazardous because the boat must be operated while divers are in the water. Do not attempt drift diving from boats unless you have completed specialty training and have a trained, experienced captain for the vessel.

Potential saltwater diving hazards include body heat loss, currents, surf, marine life, poor visibility, and fishing nets and equipment. You can minimize the hazards of ocean diving by following the recommendations that were described in this section.

## BOAT DIVING

All divers eventually dive from boats, either small private boats or large charter vessels. Space is limited aboard boats, so organize your equipment compactly and pack it in the order in which you will need it. You frequently must carry equipment for some distance to a boat, so plan to wear your scuba tank and weight belt and carry a bag in each hand. One bag should contain your dive gear and the other bag should hold your lunch, camera, and any items that you want to keep dry.

## Charter Boat Diving

Be well rested and avoid partying the night before boat diving. Eat a meal that is free of acid and fat before you depart. Arrive at least 30 minutes before the scheduled departure time. Check in with a crew member. Usually you must sign a roster and complete some forms. Ask where to stow your gear, and pick out a suitable space to store your dry items. If you are prone to seasickness, take preventive medication before the boat gets underway.

Tour the vessel. Locate the head (bathroom) and the emergency equipment. Stay out of the engine room and the wheelhouse (see example in figure 7.17). If you did not come with a buddy, find one before reaching the dive site. Listen carefully to the orientation provided by the captain or crewmember.

If you begin to feel queasy after the boat gets underway, go outside to the center of the boat and concentrate on the horizon. Sleep may help you acclimate to the boat's motion. If you are nauseated or vomiting when it is time to dive, avoid scuba diving. Vomiting underwater is hazardous. Mildly seasick divers may recover by snorkeling or by swimming to a nearby shore and waiting until they feel better.

Diving operations begin only when indicated by the captain. When you are ready to enter the water, check out with the divemaster. Usually you enter the water by stepping off the side of the boat and exit the water by boarding a swim step at the stern (rear) of the vessel. It is a good practice to use the anchor line for your descent.

Begin your dive against any current so that the water movement can assist you back to the boat at the end of the dive. Crew members often deploy a **trail line**—a long line with a float attached—to the stern for you to use in pulling yourself to the boat against the current (see figure 7.18). Dive upcurrent, but if you end up downcurrent from the boat and are unable to reach the trail line, make yourself buoyant, signal the boat, remain calm, and wait to be picked up after all the other divers have boarded the vessel.

If you hear a yelping, sirenlike sound while underwater, surface. The sound is from an electronic diver recall system. Remain where you are, and look to the boat for instructions. Learn the vessel's recall procedures in advance.

▶ Figure 7.17  Typical charter boat configuration.

▶ Figure 7.18 Divers can use a trail line to pull themselves to the boat if they surface downcurrent.

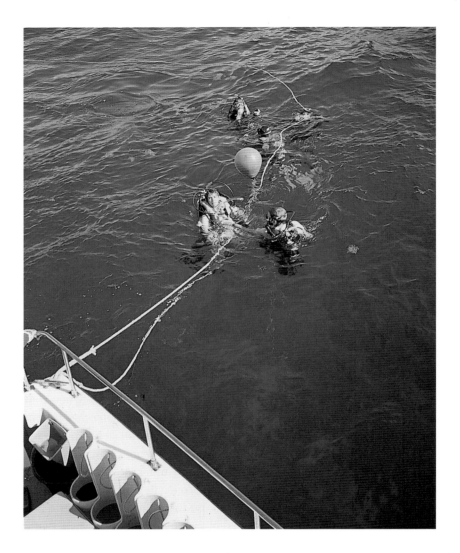

At the end of the dive, return to the boat on the bottom or at the surface. Avoid skimming (swimming just beneath the surface), because you cannot be seen and could be struck by a passing boat. Avoid crowding the exit area. Divers should exit one or two at a time and remain clear of divers climbing the boarding ladder. Retain your equipment until immediately before exiting the water. If you do not know what equipment to remove, ask or follow instructions. Immediately upon exiting, pick up any equipment that you handed to someone during your exit and clear the exit area to make room for others.

Following your last dive, pack your equipment before the boat gets underway and be available for a visual roll call, which is required. Watch and learn from experienced divers.

Charter boat dives provide memorable diving experiences. Learn the proper techniques for diving from charter boats and then do what you have learned.

## Small-Boat Diving

Be sure a small boat is equipped for safety and has all Coast Guard–required equipment and a first aid kit. Leave a float plan—information about where you are going and when

# Scuba Wise

*There are similarities between the environments above and below water. Temperature, weather, plants, and animals change when you travel from region to region on land. We enjoy the variety of mountain, plain, forest, and desert regions. The world beneath the water similarly varies from region to region. The enjoyment that the various underwater environments provide is a major reason why dive travel is so popular.*

*When you go to places on land that are rugged, remote, and hazardous, you need special training and equipment. Careful planning and preparation are essential. A guide makes exploration safer and more enjoyable. When you go diving in places that are rugged, remote, and hazardous, the same requirements apply. Enjoy the wonderful differences beneath the waters—coral reefs, vertical walls, wrecks, and so forth—but always be properly prepared and equipped and always obtain an orientation to a new area.*

you plan to return—with someone who can summon assistance if you are delayed. Have a radio or cell phone aboard for emergency communications. Check the weather and water conditions in advance, and reschedule the dive if conditions will be unfavorable or are marginal on the planned dive day. Diving is not good when the weather is bad.

Small boats pitch, roll, and pound, so stow your equipment securely and expect it to get wet. If the trip to the dive site is short, it is easier and safer to suit up on shore. If you must suit up in a small boat, remain seated and help one another. Make sure that there is a means to get back into the boat before you enter the water. More than one diver has been stranded alongside a boat, unable to exit the water. Display the dive flag, but only while diving. Deploy a trail line and float.

The usual entry from a small boat is a seated back-roll made by two divers at the same time to avoid rocking the boat and causing one diver to lose balance and fall in when unprepared. The descent should be down the anchor line to ensure that the anchor is set and clear. It is desirable to leave an operator in the boat. A sudden weather change, a slipping anchor, or a change of water movement could pose serious problems at the end of a dive if the boat is unattended.

At the end of the dive, remove your weights and scuba unit before exiting. If you cannot hand them to someone in the boat, clip them to gear lines that have been hung over the side. Exit the water and pull in your equipment.

Boat diving is good diving. Be prepared, conserve space, plan ahead, learn the rules, and follow them. Learn more about boating to make boat diving more enjoyable. Complete a course in seamanship and small-boat handling

# SUMMARY

The aquatic environment is vast and wonderful. We depend on it for our existence. We need to learn about it, care for it, and respect it. We must protect the environment and encourage everyone we know to assist in that effort. Because the environment varies greatly from place to place, you need an area orientation. There are hazards in the underwater world, just as there are hazards on land. You can minimize aquatic hazards with training, experience, planning, proper procedures, and common sense.

# Diving

# Opportunities

# 8

## Dive In and Discover

By the end of this chapter, you will be able to do the following:

- List 11 special-interest areas for novice divers and 6 special-interest areas for advanced divers.

- List at least five ways to continue your scuba diving education.

- List at least three ways to get involved with the local diving community.

- List several actions to take when preparing for a dive travel trip.

As a qualified scuba diver, you can do many things. You can learn more, dive in different areas, be recognized for expertise, help others, or earn money, just to name a few. Opportunities abound.

# CONTINUING EDUCATION

A good diver never stops learning. You cannot learn everything you need to know about diving during a single course of instruction. After you complete your entry-level course, you can enroll in an intermediate or advanced scuba course immediately. These courses allow you to gain additional experience under supervision, help you develop important skills (such as navigation), and introduce you to special interest areas of diving. When you have identified a diving specialty you would like to pursue, complete a specialty course for that topic. A specialty course helps you begin enjoying the special area from the outset and helps you avoid mistakes and injury. Specialty areas that are of interest to new divers include the following:

- Underwater photography
- Underwater hunting and collecting
- Underwater environment
- Scuba lifesaving and rescue
- Night diving
- Boat diving
- Dry-suit diving
- Drift diving
- Cavern diving
- Altitude diving
- Nitrox diving

The following specialty courses may be of interest to experienced scuba divers with advanced training:

- Wreck diving
- Ice diving
- Cave diving
- Deep diving
- River diving
- Search and recovery

▶ Underwater photography is an enjoyable diving activity.

Courses are only one way to learn about diving. Many diving seminars, workshops, and conferences also are available. Check the calendar section of diving publications to learn of events scheduled in your area. Diving changes constantly, so you need to keep updating your knowledge of diving medicine, diving equipment, and diving procedures. Continuing education programs give you the opportunity to learn from professionals who are involved in diving continually.

You can learn more about scuba diving by reading books, magazines, and newspapers. Subscribe to a scuba periodical and read all you can about diving. The appendix contains a list of scuba periodicals. If you have Internet access, you can visit Web sites by and for scuba divers. The scuba sites feature libraries, conferences, and topic discussions.

Another good way to continue your diving education is to join a dive club. Dive clubs offer many benefits to divers, including education. A talk on an interesting subject by a good speaker usually is part of the monthly meeting of a local club.

Continuing your education is important for your safety and enjoyment. When you have increased your knowledge about diving, you may become interested in helping others to learn.

# LOCAL OPPORTUNITIES

You do not need to live in a coastal area to dive regularly or to get involved in diving. You can dive nearly anywhere you can find water, and there are dive stores, dive clubs, and diving events in noncoastal areas. Get involved in diving in your area right away. Find all the diving-related businesses and groups in your area: dive clubs, dive stores, dive boats, diving events, and diving publications. Join a dive club, attend the meetings, and participate in club dives. Find a local diving Web site to make contact with other divers in the area. Complete continuing education courses. Attend local diving seminars, workshops, conferences, and shows, and talk to other divers when you attend diving events. Seize every opportunity to learn and every opportunity to dive with those who are more experienced than you.

## Scuba Wise

*Scuba equipment is a means to an end—a mechanism that enables you to go to areas that are otherwise unreachable by the average person. I think of scuba diving as a means of transporting myself to a destination where I can explore or participate in a special activity. Scuba diving without an objective loses its thrill after only a few dives. You need to develop an interest area, which can be anything from bottle collecting to wreck diving. When you have an objective for your dives, diving can be extremely rewarding. Over the years, I have participated in many different diving activities. My favorite underwater pursuit is photography. I can collect priceless memories without removing anything from the environment. In my opinion, underwater photography is the most challenging and the most satisfying dive activity. Select a diving activity that appeals to you, complete training for the activity, and then pursue it. You may choose several different activities. No matter what you choose to do while diving, I hope that your experiences will be as wonderful as mine have been.*

# DIVE TRAVEL

Many divers enjoy taking dive trips to exotic destinations, and there are thousands of beautiful and exciting diving locations to choose from around the world. If you plan to travel somewhere to dive, you need to know how to arrange dive travel, how to prepare to travel, and how to enjoy your trip.

Travel agencies that specialize in dive trips provide valuable information, so it is a good idea to book your trip through one of them. You might want to consider a dive package that includes accommodations and diving. Dive resorts advertise these packages in diving publications and often offer packages for bargain prices at dive shows. There are many toll-free numbers you can call to obtain information about dive packages. To ensure the best value for your money, compare several packages before you book a trip. If a brochure from a dive resort is out of date, check with the resort for current offers.

When planning a dive travel trip, you need to decide whether you want to dive from a live-aboard dive boat or from a shore-based dive resort. A live-aboard trip allows you to dive in a variety of locations. The vessel moves from place to place throughout the day. You dive in remote areas that only a few divers visit. You may find a live-aboard dive trip to be a wonderful experience if diving is the only objective of your trip and you are not affected by motion sickness.

▶ You can travel to exotic destinations on dive trips.

Consider a shore-based dive trip if you do not care for confinement and if you want to participate in activities other than diving. Many beautiful islands and resorts offer a great deal to do in addition to diving. Nondiving members of your travel party usually can find many sources of enjoyment at a land-based diving destination.

Many magazine articles and diving publications are available to help you decide where to dive, although making a choice from all the fantastic destinations available can be difficult. Recommendations from other divers, trips sponsored by your dive club or dive store, and travel presentations can help you decide.

When you have decided on the region for your dive trip, get as much information as possible about diving in the area. Obtain and review brochures, books, articles, videotapes, and any other materials you can get on the region. The Internet is another excellent resource for dive location information. Talk to divers who have been to the location where you plan to go. The more you know in advance, the more enjoyable you can make your experience.

After you select your diving destination, you should make your reservations well in advance, confirm all arrangements in writing, and get clarification concerning cancellations, refunds, and so forth.

Research and plan your dive trip by learning about the water temperature for the time of year when you will be diving, and obtain appropriate exposure protection. Remember that too much insulation is better than too little. Also make sure that all your equipment is in good working order.

Plan to avoid sunburn. Sunlight in tropical areas is more intense than in other climates. Use a sunscreen, and unless you are well tanned, keep yourself covered at all

▶ A live-aboard boat trip immerses you in scuba diving.

times, even while in the water. Use lip balm with a sunscreen ingredient. You cannot develop a tan in a few days, so it is silly to try if you do not already have one. Sunburn can ruin an expensive vacation, and it is painful to don an exposure suit when you are burned. It takes only a few minutes for an untanned person to get burned in the tropics, so be careful!

Obtain all required documentation well in advance. Obtaining passports and visas can take months. Be sure to find out whether the country to which you are traveling requires immunizations.

Learn what to expect when you arrive at your destination. Know the frequency and voltage of the electricity; take converters if you are taking electrical appliances that operate on a different voltage. Know the monetary exchange rate. Consider taking a small pocket calculator to help compute the conversion of money.

If you have an expensive camera, video equipment, or jewelry, take your property to a customs office before you leave the country and have it documented to avoid being charged duty on the items when you return home.

Do not procrastinate in making your preparations. Procrastination can cause a cancellation of your trip, a forfeiture of your deposit, and a great deal of frustration.

Limit what you pack for your trip. You do not need much clothing for a dive trip unless you plan to attend formal events. A few pairs of shorts and T-shirts, some swimsuits, and a couple of sets of nice clothes for dinner should suffice. Experienced dive travelers travel light when it comes to clothing and personal effects.

Diving destinations provide tanks and weights, so you do not need to take those items with you. When you pack for your trip, keep in mind that there may be weight limitations for your baggage. Excess baggage costs can be very high. To guard against theft, avoid flaunting expensive diving, photography, and video equipment. Use inconspicuous containers to ship your equipment and it will be less likely to disappear. Insure luggage that contains expensive equipment.

▶ Dive resorts accommodate any need a vacationing diver may have.

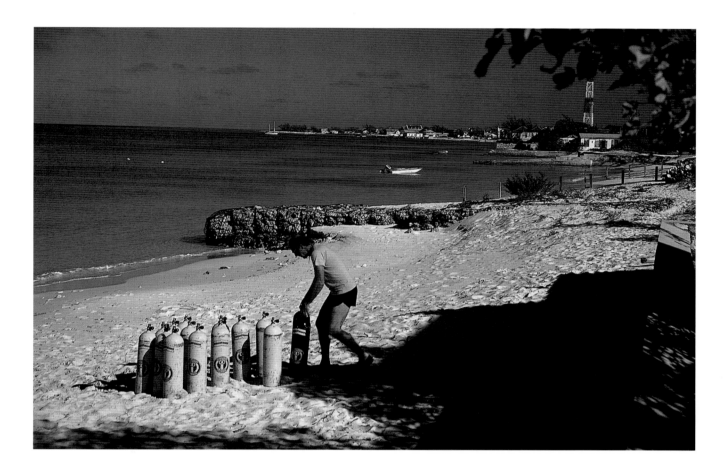

Be prepared for travel illnesses. It is easier to obtain medications for nausea, diarrhea, and colds before a trip than it is if you become ill in a foreign land.

Flying is the most common method of transportation for dive travel. Air travel usually produces jet lag and dehydration. A viral illness a couple of days after reaching your destination is common because many virus germs are concentrated inside the cabins of airliners. Following are some tips and suggestions concerning air travel:

▶ It is not necessary to transport tanks because most destinations provide them.

- Schedule your flight to arrive the day before you start diving. It is unwise to plan to dive the same day you arrive.

- Drink a full glass of water or apple juice every hour during your flight to avoid dehydration. Avoid alcohol, milk, and drinks containing sugar. The humidity in an aircraft is about 8 percent, so you will become dehydrated unless you drink plenty of fluids.

- Avoid eating heavy meals and salty foods when flying. Light foods cause less dehydration than fatty foods. Consider ordering a special meal of salad and fruit.

- Wash your hands frequently when traveling. Germs from your hands can get into your eyes and nose and lead to viral infections.

- Baggage compartments on airliners are unpressurized, and the reduced atmospheric pressure can damage your gauges. Either bring your gauges inside the cabin in your carry-on luggage or store them in airtight containers.

- As soon as possible after reaching your destination, get some exercise and drink plenty of liquids. Limit your consumption of alcohol, which causes dehydration. Getting intoxicated at the outset of a diving vacation is one of the worst things you can do because you increase your chances of getting DCS.
- Confirm your return air reservations as soon as you arrive, especially if you travel to another country. If you fail to do this, you are likely to lose the reservations. It is frustrating to arrive at the airport to go home and discover that your tickets are not valid.

Your first dive at your destination should be an orientation dive. In addition to learning about diving in the area, use the dive to check your buoyancy and make any needed adjustments. Work out any equipment problems during a dive in shallow, still, calm water. Avoid deep dives or moving water until you have acclimated to the area.

After three days of repetitive diving, refrain from diving for a day so that your body can outgas. Go shopping or take a land tour for a refreshing change of pace. Allow one day between your final scuba dive and your scheduled flight home. The nondiving day before flying helps prevent DCS caused by altitude and gives you the opportunity to rinse, dry, and pack your diving equipment. Snorkeling is a good last-day activity, and your mask, snorkel, and fins dry quickly for last-minute packing.

Dive travel can be fun, exciting, and memorable when you plan it well. You can avoid unpleasant, frustrating, and disappointing experiences by researching your destination and preparing properly. Good diving to you!

## CAREER OPPORTUNITIES

Some people love diving so much that they want it to be their vocation. Career opportunities exist for those who are willing to put forth the effort to achieve their desires. Jobs within the recreational dive industry include resort dive guide, instructor, journalist, dive travel coordinator, retail salesperson, and sales representative for equipment manufacturers. There are also nonrecreational scuba jobs, such as scientific research, archaeology, engineering studies, hull cleaning, salvage, and underwater repairs. Two of the same rules that apply to recreational pleasure diving also apply to underwater work: (1) Complete training for an activity before you attempt it, and (2) use complete, proper equipment for the activity. Career training opportunities abound. If you are interested in diving as a vocation, you can find information about training in dive periodicals.

## Character Development

Taking advantage of leadership opportunities allows you to demonstrate character development values in many different ways. In every class you can try to be a caring instructor or assistant, one who is always honest with participants. You can offer instruction and help in ways that are respectful of students, and you can take responsibility for seeing that all students learn what they need to skin or scuba dive safely.

# LEADERSHIP OPPORTUNITIES

After you have become an experienced diver, you may desire to help others learn and enjoy scuba diving. There are courses you can take to qualify as a divemaster, assistant instructor, and instructor. Many people who love diving work part-time in the industry in a leadership position. When you are ready for leadership training, contact your scuba training agency for information.

# SUMMARY

Always remember that a good diver never stops learning. Complete additional training, be trained for any special activity before you attempt the specialty, read as much as possible, join a dive club, attend educational events, and take advantage of every opportunity to learn more about diving.

Increase your diving abilities and experience by applying what you learn. Participate in dive trips and charters. Research and plan your excursions thoroughly to maximize your enjoyment and minimize your disappointment. There are many opportunities for diving adventures throughout the world.

Another opportunity for you as a diver is to make a positive contribution to the diving community. You can do this by conducting yourself in a responsible manner at all times and encouraging other divers to act responsibly. Help establish a good image of diving, get involved in issues that pertain to the diving environment, and help educate people who do not dive. Whether your contribution is small and personal or vast and international, you can make a difference. Decide now that your involvement in the wonderful pursuit of scuba diving will be a positive one.

# Lists and Checklists

## DIVER TRAINING ORGANIZATIONS

**International Diving Educators Association (IDEA)**
Box 8427
Jacksonville, FL 32239-8427

**Multinational Diving Educators Association (MDEA)**
Box 523433
Marathon Shores, FL 33052

**National Association for Cave Diving**
Box 14492
Gainesville, FL 32604

**National Association of Underwater Instructors (NAUI)**
Box 89789
Tampa, FL 33689-0413

**National Speleological Society Cave Diving Section**
Box 38057
Tallahassee, FL 32315-8057

**National YMCA Scuba Program**
101 N. Wacker Dr.
Chicago, IL 60606
www.ymcascuba.org

**Professional Association of Diving Instructors (PADI)**
30151 Tomas Street
Rancho Santa Margarita, CA 92688-2125

**Professional Diving Instructors Corporation (PDIC)**
Box 3633
Scranton, PA 18505

**Scuba Schools International (SSI)**
2619 Canton Court
Fort Collins, CO 80525-4498

## ENVIRONMENTAL ORGANIZATIONS

**Cousteau Society**
870 Greenbrier Circle
Suite 402
Chesapeake, VA 23320

**CEDAM**
One Fox Road
Croton-on-Hudson, NY 10520

**Greenpeace**
702 H Street Northwest
Suite 300
Washington, DC 20001

**NOAA Sanctuary and Reserves Ocean and Coastal Resource Management**
Universal Building Room 714
1825 Connecticut Avenue Northwest
Washington, DC 20235

**The Ocean Conservancy**
1725 DeSales Street
Suite 600
Washington, DC 20036

**Oceanic Society**
Fort Mason Center
San Francisco, CA 94123

**Project Reefkeeper**
16345 West Dixie Highway
Suite 1121
Miami, FL 33160

**Reef Environmental Education Foundation (REEF)**
Box 246
Key Largo, FL 33037

**Sea Shepard**
22774 Pacific Coast Highway
Malibu, CA 90265

**Wildlife Conservation International**
Bronx Zoo
New York, NY 10460

# SCUBA PERIODICALS

**DAN Alert Diver (out of print)**
Box 3832
Duke University Medical Center
Durham, NC 27710

**Discover Diving Magazine**
Box 83727
San Diego, CA 92138

**Dive Training Magazine**
5215 Crooked Road
Parkville, MO 64152

**Rodale's Scuba Diving Magazine**
6600 Abercorn Street #208
Savannah, GA 31405

**Scuba Times**
Box 6268
Pensacola, FL 32503

**Skin Diver Magazine**
6420 Wilshire Boulevard
Los Angeles, CA 90048-5515

**Sources (the Journal of Underwater Education)**
NAUI
9942 Currie Davis Drive #11
Tampa, FL 33619-2667

# DIVING EQUIPMENT CHECKLIST

- ☐ Mask, snorkel, and snorkel keeper
- ☐ Fins and boots
- ☐ Scuba tank (filled)
- ☐ Buoyancy compensator
- ☐ Exposure suit, hood, and gloves
- ☐ Weight system
- ☐ Regulator with pressure gauge
- ☐ Alternate air source
- ☐ Instruments to monitor depth, time, and direction
- ☐ Signaling devices (whistle, mirror, safety tube)
- ☐ Dive knife
- ☐ Float, dive flag, and anchor
- ☐ Dive tables
- ☐ Dive light
- ☐ Slate and pencil
- ☐ Marker buoy
- ☐ Collecting bag
- ☐ Gear bag

- ☐ Spare equipment
  - ☐ Scuba tank(s)
  - ☐ Weights
  - ☐ Straps
  - ☐ O-rings
  - ☐ Snorkel keeper
- ☐ Secondary equipment
  - ☐ First aid kit
  - ☐ Emergency phone numbers and radio frequencies
  - ☐ Logbook
  - ☐ Swimsuit
  - ☐ Towel
  - ☐ Jacket
  - ☐ Hat or visor
  - ☐ Sunglasses
  - ☐ Dive kit
  - ☐ Save-a-dive kit
  - ☐ Drinking water

# Glossary of Scuba Diving Terms

**AAS**—See alternate air source.

**absolute pressure**—The combined force of atmospheric pressure and gauge pressure.

**ABT**—See actual bottom time.

**actual bottom time**—The elapsed time in minutes (rounded up to the next whole minute) from the time a diver leaves the surface in descent until the diver begins a safety stop or surfaces.

**AGE**—See arterial gas embolism.

**alternate air source**—An additional second-stage regulator for emergency use by a buddy diver (also called an octopus) or a completely independent scuba unit for emergency use.

**ambient pressure**—The surrounding pressure.

**Archimedes' principle**—A body immersed in a fluid is buoyed up by a force equal to the weight of the displaced fluid.

**arterial gas embolism**—The blockage of blood flow to the brain caused by air bubbles escaping into the blood from the lungs.

**atmospheric pressure**—The pressure exerted by the atmosphere.

**backpack**—An item of dive equipment that holds a scuba tank on a diver's back.

**barotrauma**—A pressure-related injury.

**BC**—See buoyancy compensator.

**bezel**—A movable reference ring on a dive instrument.

**bloom**—A plankton overpopulation that can color the water, destroy underwater visibility, and form toxins in animals that feed by filtering water.

**blowout plug**—A rubber plug on the back of a submersible pressure gauge to prevent the face of the gauge from exploding if the high-pressure tube inside ruptures.

**Bourdon tube**—A curved or spiral tube that tries to straighten under pressure; the movement is mechanically coupled to a needle to indicate pressure.

**Boyle's law**—The inverse relationship between pressure and volume.

**buddy breathing**—Two divers' sharing a single air source.

**buddy line**—A short line extended between two divers to help the divers maintain contact in limited visibility.

**buddy system**—A standard practice for people to dive in teams of two.

**buoyancy**—An upward force on an object placed in water; equal to the weight of the water displaced.

**buoyancy compensator**—An item of dive equipment that a diver can inflate to increase buoyancy and deflate to decrease buoyancy.

**burst disk**—A thin, metal disk in a scuba valve, designed to rupture and relieve pressure when the tank pressure exceeds a safe limit.

**capillary gauge**—A gauge made with a hollow tube that is open on one end and closed on the other. The gauge indicates pressure on a dial when the air inside the tube is compressed.

**cave**—A naturally occurring room or passage in bedrock or coral, large enough for a human to enter. Extends farther than a cavern and beyond the point where surface light can be seen.

**cavern**—A large, roomlike natural formation where light from the surface can be seen.

**C-card**—A card that documents successful completion of scuba diving training.

**ceiling**—A minimum depth to which a diver can ascend with minimal risk of decompression sickness.

**Charles' law**—The volume of a given mass of gas at a constant pressure varies directly as the absolute temerature varies.

**ciguatera**—A type of fish poisoning that results from eating fish that consume a certain species of algae.

**compartment**—A decompression mathematical model that represents a body tissue half-time.

**compass course**—A course determined by compass headings.

**compass heading**—A direction relative to magnetic north.

**console**—A device that combines several instruments into a display unit.

**continental shelf**—A region of relatively shallow water surrounding each continent.

**contingency plan**—A backup plan for unexpected developments.

**controlling compartment**—The area of the body that determines how long a diver can remain at a given depth. The determination is made by how quickly a gas diffuses from that compartment.

**crest**—The highest part of a wave.

**Dalton's law**—The partial pressure of a given quantity of gas is the pressure it would exert if it alone occupied the same volume. Also the total pressure of a mixture of gases is the sum of the partial pressures of the components of the mixture.

**DCS**—See decompression sickness.

**decompression illness**—A condition in which a diver has minor symptoms of AGE upon surfacing, recovers, and then develops a severe case of DCS.

**decompression sickness**—Identifiable signs and symptoms caused by the formation of inert gas bubbles within a diver's body.

**decompression stops**—Delays in ascent at specified depths to allow the elimination of excess nitrogen before surfacing.

**defogging**—Applying a substance to a mask lens to prevent condensation.

**dehydration**—A lack of adequate body fluids.

**density**—Weight per unit volume, for example, pounds per cubic foot.

**DIN valve**—A new type of outlet for a scuba tank valve that is threaded and has a recessed O-ring seal. It was designed for pressures greater than 3,000 psi.

**dive profile**—A graphic representation of a diver's times at various depths.

**diver's push-ups**—The use of buoyancy to raise and lower the body by breath control.

**dolphin kick**—An undulating kick that uses the entire body for propulsion.

**downwelling**—A compensating current that occurs when wind blows along a coast where there is a steep drop-off near shore and that pulls the water downward.

**drag**—Resistance to movement through a fluid.

**drift**—The speed of water current.

**drift dive**—A dive in which divers use water current as the primary propulsion means.

**eardrum**—The membrane separating the middle and outer ears.

**ebb**—An outgoing tide.

**eddies**—Circulating currents caused by turbulent flow.

**emergency decompression**—A required delay in ascent to eliminate excess nitrogen and help avoid decompression sickness; must be taken if actual bottom time or total bottom time exceeds the no-decompression-stop limit for a dive.

**equalization**—Techniques used to prevent squeezes.

**eustachian tubes**—The tubes that connect the middle ears to the throat; allow divers to equalize pressure in the middle ears.

**Farmer Johns**—An over-the-shoulders wet-suit design.

**fetch**—The distance over which wind blows to create waves.

**flaring**—A technique of maximizing a diver's cross-sectional area to slow the speed of an ascent.

**flood**—An incoming tide.

**flutter kick**—A means of propulsion in which the legs move upward and downward in opposite directions.

**fronds**—Kelp leaves.

**gauge pressure**—Absolute pressure minus atmospheric pressure; the pressure indicated by a gauge that reads zero at sea level.

**Gay-Lussac's law**—For any gas at a constant volume, the pressure of the gas will vary directly with the absolute temperature.

**gyre**—Large circulating currents.

**half-time**—The exponential rate of absorption or elimination of gas in tissues.

**heat exhaustion**—An illness caused by overheating and characterized by fatigue, weakness, and collapse.

**heatstroke**—A life-threatening illness caused by overheating and characterized by hot, dry, flushed skin.

**Henry's law**—At a constant temperature, the amount of a gas that dissolves in a liquid with which it is in contact is proportional to the partial pressure of that gas.

**hyperthermia**—Higher-than-normal body core temperature.

**hyperventilation**—Rapid, deep breathing in excess of the body's needs.

**hypothermia**—Excessive loss of heat from the core of the body.

**hypoventilation**—Shallow breathing that doesn't allow carbon dioxide to be flushed out of the lungs.

**ingassing**—The absorption of gas by tissues.

**J-valve**—A spring-loaded scuba cylinder reserve valve; also known as a constant reserve valve.

**jumpsuit**—A one-piece wet suit that covers nearly all of the body.

**kelp**—A collective term for large, brown seaweed.

**K-valve**—A nonreserve scuba cylinder valve; a simple on-off valve.

**lubber line**—A reference line on a compass.

**mediastinal emphysema**—A lung injury caused by overexpansion and characterized by air in the middle of the chest.

**middle ear**—The air-filled space between the outer ear and the inner ear.

**modified frog kick**—A kick with the ankles rotated so the tips of the fins are pointed outward, the feet are moved apart, and then the bottoms of the fins are pulled together quickly in an arcing motion.

**multilevel dive profile**—A dive to multiple depth levels, from the deepest depth to shallower depths.

**NDSL**—See no-decompression-stop limit.

**neap tide**—Tides with the minimum range between high water and low water.

**nitrogen narcosis**—A dangerous state of stupor caused by the narcotic effect of nitrogen in the body under pressure.

**no-decompression-stop limit**—The maximum time that a diver may stay at a specified depth indicated by dive table A (see chapter 6). For repetitive dives, the residual nitrogen time (RNT) from table C must be added to the actual bottom time (ABT) to obtain the total bottom time (TBT), which must not exceed the NDSL specified in table A. Table C also indicates the maximum ABT for various depth and repetitive group designation combinations that will prevent the TBT from exceeding the NDSL.

**nonreference descent**—A descent controlled by buoyancy and swimming motions and without maintaining contact with something such as a line or a slope.

**octopus**—A common term for an alternate air source.

**open-valve ascent**—A method for maintaining neutral buoyancy during an ascent by keeping the BC inflator-deflator valve open while holding the valve in a special way.

**O-ring**—A circular sealing ring for underwater equipment.

**outgassing**—The elimination of gas from tissues; occurs when gas dissolved in a liquid comes out of solution.

**overturn**—The process of surface water in lakes moving to deep water (up to 60 feet or 18 meters) as a result of temperature differences and wind movement.

**partial pressure**—The pressure exerted by individual gases in a mixture of gases.

**perfusion**—The delivery of oxygen and other nutrients to body cells and the elimination of waste products; results from the constant, adequate circulation of blood through body capillaries.

**plankton**—Minute aquatic animals and plants and their eggs, spores, larvae, and so forth that drift in the water that are generally found near the surface in the sea.

**pneumothorax**—A lung injury caused by overexpansion and characterized by air in the pleural cavity.

**pony tank**—A small, redundant scuba system attached to the primary scuba system.

**port**—A threaded opening in the first stage of a scuba regulator. Also the left-hand side of a vessel when facing the bow with your back to the stern.

**pressure**—Force per unit area.

**pulmonary barotrauma**—A pressure-related injury to the lungs.

**reciprocal compass course**—A course in which a diver moves in a given heading for a given distance and returns to the origination point by reversing the direction of travel.

**red tide**—An extremely heavy bloom of plankton or algae.

**reference descent**—A descent controlled by maintaining contact with something such as a line or a slope.

**repetitive dive**—Any dive made within 6 to 24 hours (depending on dive table used) of a previous dive.

**repetitive group**—Letters that indicate the amount of residual nitrogen in a diver's tissues for 12 hours after diving.

**residual nitrogen**—Nitrogen remaining within a diver following a dive.

**residual nitrogen time**—The time in minutes, converted from a letter group designation, that is equivalent to the nitrogen remaining in the body from a previous dive.

**reverse block**—A situation in which some form of blockage prevents compressed air from escaping along the route by which it entered a body air space.

**reverse thermocline**—A horizontal, abrupt transition from a colder layer of water to a warmer layer of water where the colder layer is shallower than the warmer layer.

**RG**—See repetitive group.

**rip current**—A strong, narrow current that moves away from shore and forms when water in a surf zone accumulates on shore and funnels out through a narrow gap.

**RNT**—See residual nitrogen time.

**safety stop**—A precautionary decompression stop during ascent.

**sawtooth dive profile**—A dive that progresses repeatedly from deep to shallow during a given time.

**scissors kick**—A resting fin kick done by extending one leg backward and the other forward while lying on the side, then pulling the legs together quickly.

**scombroid**—A type of fish poisoning that can result from eating fish that has not been kept chilled.

**scrolling**—A function of a dive computer to display the time limits for various depths sequentially.

**set**—The direction of a current; also a group of larger-than-average waves.

**shorty**—A one-piece wet suit with short legs and sleeves.

**sink**—An area where the ground collapses into an underground cave system.

**siphon**—An area where water in an underground cave system is channeled from a sink back into the system.

**SIT**—See surface interval time.

**skip breathing**—A dangerous attempt by a scuba diver to extend an air supply by holding each breath for several seconds.

**slack water**—The time during high tide when water movement is minimal.

**Spare Air unit**—A small backup scuba unit designed for use during an emergency ascent.

**SPG**—See submersible pressure gauge.

**spike dive**—A dive in which a diver descends to a depth and ascends again quickly.

**spring tide**—Tides with the greatest range between high water and low water.

**square compass course**—A series of headings that allows the diver to travel in a square pattern so that the dive ends where it began.

**squeeze**—An injury that results when the pressure inside a body air space or an air space that is attached to the body is less than the surrounding pressure.

**stage**—A pressure-reduction step in a regulator or compressor.

**stand**—Time during which the tide neither rises nor falls.

**step dive**—A dive that progresses from deep to shallow during a given time.

**stipes**—Strands of kelp.

**subcutaneous emphysema**—A lung injury caused by over-expansion and characterized by air around the base of the neck.

**submersible pressure gauge**—An instrument used to measure the pressure in a scuba cylinder while submerged.

**surf**—Breaking waves releasing their energy in shallow water.

**surface interval time**—The time spent at the surface between repetitive dives.

**surge**—The back-and-forth subsurface movement of water produced by passing waves in shallow water.

**swells**—Rounded, undulating waves moving through deep water.

**TBT**—See total bottom time.

**tetrodotoxin**—The most serious type of fish poisoning; results from eating exotic fish such as puffer.

**thermocline**—A horizontal, abrupt transition from a warmer layer of water to a colder layer of water.

**total bottom time**—The sum of ABT and RNT. For times not indicated at a particular depth, use the next longer time available for that depth.

**Toynbee maneuver**—A method of opening the eustachian tubes by blocking the nostrils, closing the mouth, and swallowing.

**trail line**—A line with a float extended behind a boat to assist divers in returning to the vessel if they surface downcurrent.

**trapdoor effect**—The situation that exists when a diver cannot equalize pressure in the middle ear because ambient pressure holds the opening of the eustachian tube closed.

**trough**—The lowest part of a wave.

**tsunami**—Giant waves caused by underwater geological disturbances; erroneously called tidal waves.

**turbidity**—Poor water visibility caused by suspended particles.

**upwelling**—The vertical, upward movement of water in a body of water and the subsequent replacement of that water from beneath.

**Valsalva maneuver**—A method of opening the eustachian tubes by blocking the nostrils, closing the mouth, and gently trying to exhale.

**valve seat**—The portion of the valve that closes and stops the flow of air.

**vasoconstriction**—Narrowing of the blood vessels.

**vertigo**—A feeling of dizziness or disorientation.

**wave height**—The vertical distance between the crest and trough of a wave.

**wavelength**—The horizontal distance between waves.

**wave period**—The time required for two consecutive waves to pass a given point.

**wave train**—A long series of waves.

# Bibliography

Auerbach, P. (1987). *A medical guide to hazardous marine life*. Jacksonville, FL: Progressive Printing.

Barnhart, R., & Steinmetz, S. (1986). *Dictionary of science*. Maplewood, NJ: Hammond.

Bascom, W. (1964). *Waves and beaches*. Garden City, NY: Anchor Books.

Bove, A., & Davis, J. (1990). *Diving medicine*. Philadelphia: W.B. Saunders.

Divers Alert Network. (1989). *Medical requirements for scuba divers*. Durham, NC: Author.

Edmonds, C., Lowry, C., & Pennefather, J. (1981). *Diving and subaquatic medicine*. Mosman, NSW, Australia: Diving Medical Centre.

Foley, B. (1989). *Physics made simple*. New York: Doubleday.

Lee, P., Lidov, M., & Tyberg, T. (1986). *The sourcebook of medical science*. New York: Torstar.

Lehrman, R. (1990). *Physics the easy way*. Hauppauge, NY: Barron's Educational Series.

Lippmann, J. (1992). *The essentials of deeper sport diving*. Locust Valley, NY: Aqua Quest.

Maloney, E. (1983). *Chapman piloting seamanship and small boat handling*. New York: Hearst Marine Books.

McGraw-Hill Professional Publishers (1998). Concise encyclopedia of science. Camden, Maine: McGraw-Hill.

Miller, J. (Ed.). (1979). *NOAA diving manual* (2nd ed.). Washington, DC: U.S. Government Printing Office, U.S. Department of Commerce.

National Association of Underwater Instructors (NAUI). (1991). *Advanced diving technology and techniques*. Montclair, CA: Author.

Professional Association of Diving Instructors (PADI). (1998). *The encyclopedia of recreational diving*. Santa Ana, CA: Author.

Sebel, P., Stoddart, D., Waldhorn, R., Waldmann, C., & Whitfield, P. (1985). *Respiration: The breath of life*. New York: Torstar.

*Skin Diver*. Various equipment articles from 1991 and 1992 issues. Los Angeles: Peterson.

Taylor, E. (Ed.). (1985). *Dorland's illustrated medical dictionary*. Philadelphia: W.B. Saunders.

Whitfield, P., & Stoddart, D. (1984). *Hearing, taste, and smell: Pathways of perception*. New York: Torstar.

# Index

*Note:* The italicized *f* and *t* following page numbers refer to figures and tables, respectively.

**A**

abbreviations, table of 96*t*
absolute pressure 106, 106*f*
actual bottom time (ABT) 146, 148-149
air
    composition 98-100, 99*f*, 109*t*
    consumption rate 110, 112-113
    contaminated 125-128
    density of 102-104, 103*f*, 104*t*
    gas laws 106-110, 107*f*
    humidity 111-113, 130
    partial pressures 109-110, 109*t*
    pressure 105-106, 106*f*
air consumption rate 110, 112-113
air-supply duration (ASD) 113
air-supply loss 86-88, 87*f*
air-supply volume 112-113
air travel tips 193-194
alcohol consumption 134, 194
Alpha flag 45*f*, 46
alternate air sources (AAS) 39-40, 39*f*, 87
alternobaric vertigo 129
altitude delay after diving 150, 155-156, 155*t*
altitude diving 175
aluminum cylinders 28-29, 28*f*, 30*t*
ambient pressure 130
anatomy 96-98, 97*f*
animals, dangerous 164-167, 165*f*
Archimedes' principle 104, 105*f*
arterial gas embolism (AGE) 127, 127*f*, 134
ascents
    buoyancy control in 72
    buoyant emergency 87*f*, 88
    emergency swimming 87-88, 87*f*
    lung overexpansion 125, 126*f*
    pressure equalization 124
    procedures 60, 61*f*, 77-79
Asken, Michael J. 83
asthma 7
ATA (atmospheres absolute) 106
atmospheric pressure 105, 106*f*

**B**

backpacks 24-27, 26*f*, 27*f*, 62-63
back-roll entries 68, 68*f*

backup scuba units 39-40
bands, tank 62-63
barotrauma 127
bends. *See* decompression sickness
biceps push 89, 89*f*
bites 165*f*, 166
biting on mouthpiece 98
blocks 108*f*
blooms 162
blowout plugs 43, 63
boat diving 182-185, 183*f*, 191*f*
boots 16, 19-20, 20*f*, 22, 22*f*, 28
bounce dive profiles 151, 151*f*
Bourdon tubes 40-41, 41*t*
Boyle's law 41, 57, 106-107, 107*f*, 110
breakers 179*f*, 180. *See also* surf
breathing
    adaptation to pressure changes 124-128, 126*f*
    buddy 39-40, 87-88, 87*f*
    contaminated air 125-128
    dehydration and 111, 134-135
    heat loss and 118
    hyperventilation/hypoventilation 100
    importance of continuing 125, 126*f*
    mechanics of 100-102, 101*f*
    overexertion and 125
    rescue 91
    shallow-water blackout 100, 102*f*
    skip 125
    water inspiration 128
breathing masks 91, 91*f*
breathing rate volume (BRV) 112-113
buddy breathing 39-40, 87-88, 87*f*
buddy system 74-75
    assisting your buddy 88-89, 89*f*
    buddy lines 75
    duties and responsibilities 54-55
    exits 80
    head-to-toe buddy check 65
    planning procedures 143
    sharing air 39-40, 87-88, 87*f*
buoyancy
    controlling 72, 122
    of equipment 13, 16, 18-19, 18*t*, 30, 30*t*
    factors affecting 120-121, 121*f*

loss of control 85-86, 86*f*
neutral 56, 105*f*
principles of 104, 105*f*
testing 56, 71-72, 72*f*
weighting systems and 24-25, 24*f*
buoyancy compensators (BC)
    as alternate air sources 39-40
    buoyancy testing 71-72
    drag from 135
    inflation and deflation 70-71
    inflator valves stuck open 86
    in silted areas 75, 75*f*
    types of 25-27, 26*f*, 26*t*, 27*f*
buoyant emergency ascents (BEA) 87*f*, 88
burst disks 32, 33*f*

**C**

calculators, dive 157-158, 157*f*
capillary depth gauges 40-41, 41*t*
carbon dioxide ($CO_2$)
    breathing mechanics 99-100, 102*f*
    $CO_2$ detonators 27, 56, 86
    in pressure reduction 131
    in skip breathing 125
    surface-equivalent effect 109, 109*t*
carbon monoxide (CO) 99-100, 125-128
cardiorespiratory system 100, 101*f*
career opportunities 194
CARE system 90-92
carotid sinuses 100, 102*f*
caves and caverns 174, 175*f*
C-cards 5
ceilings 44, 158
Charles, Jacques 107
checklist, equipment 198
ciguatera 163
circulation, blood 100-102, 101*f*, 118, 130
closed-circuit system 3
CMAS 4
$CO_2$ detonators 27, 56, 86
colds 122, 122*f*
cold water 113, 154
colors, at depth 114, 114*f*, 130
compartments, in models 131
compasses 42, 43*f*, 76-77, 76*f*

computers, dive 43-44, 43f, 157-158, 157f, 158f
conduction of heat 104t, 111
cone shells 165f, 166
congestion 122, 122f
conservation, environmental 167-171
consoles 43
contact lenses 13-14
contaminated air 125-128
continental shelf 176
contingency plans 156-157, 156f
continuing education courses 188-189
controlling compartment 131
convection 111, 111f
coral 164f, 165f
corrective lenses 13-14, 13f
corrosion 28, 31
cost of training courses 8-9
coughing 84, 96, 128
countercurrent 180
Cousteau, Jacques 4
CPR training 90-92, 127
cramps 84, 85f
crests 178, 179f
CTC/DOT markings 29
currents 173-174, 178, 180-182, 181f, 184f
current velocity estimation 142, 142f
cuts 164-166, 165f
cylinders 27-31, 28f, 30t, 39-40, 40f
cylinder valves 31-34, 32f, 33f

**D**

Dalton's law 108-110
Davis, Robert 3
decompression, in-water 154
decompression illness (DCI) 134
decompression sickness (DCS) 91-92, 99, 131f, 132-134, 144, 175
decompression stops tables 148, 149t
decongestants 122
dehydration 111, 134-135, 193
Denayrouze, Auguste 4
density 102-103, 103f, 104f, 106-107, 107f, 180
dental problems 98
depth air consumption rate (DACR) 112-113
depth gauges 40-41, 41t
descents 60, 73-74, 122-124
diabetes 7
diagramming worksheets 151-153, 152f
diaphragm depth gauges 40-41, 41t
diaphragm regulators 35, 35f, 38
DIN valves 32, 32f, 35, 37
disorientation 129-130
distress 82-84, 83f
dive boats 66, 80, 81f
dive computers 43-44, 43f, 157-158, 157f, 158f
dive flags and floats 45-46, 45f, 73
dive kits 46, 47f
dive lights 46, 46f
dive planning 140-159

advance 140-142
area orientation 143-144
current velocity estimation 142, 142f
dive computers 43-44, 43f, 157-158, 157f
dive profiles 144-145, 144f, 147f, 151-153, 151f, 152f
dive tables 145-156
equipment checklist 198
on-site 142-143, 142f
postdive reviews 158-159
profile contingency 156-157, 156f
sample problems 154
short-term 142
skin diving 52-55, 53f
special-equipment 150-151
special procedures 153-156
time and depth limits 153
dive profiles 144-145, 144f, 147f, 151-153, 151f, 152f
diver's push-ups 71-72, 72f
dive slates 47
dive tables 145-156
altitude delay timetables 154-155, 155t
decompression stops 148, 149t
dive computers and 157-158, 157f, 158f
example of 147f
modifications to 145-147
residual nitrogen time 148, 149t
surface interval times 146, 148, 148t
Swiss 155
terminology 146
total bottom time 148, 148t
use of 148-150, 148f, 149f
dive techniques 59, 60f
dive travel 190-194
diving conditions 171-176, 173f, 175f
diving opportunities 188-195
diving prerequisites 6-7, 115
diving skills 65-81
ascents 72, 77-79, 87-88, 124-125
assembling equipment 62-64, 63f
BC inflation and deflation 70-71
buddy diving 54-55, 74-75
buoyancy control 72, 85-86, 86f, 122
buoyancy testing 56, 71-72, 72f
descents 60, 73-74, 122-124
disassembling equipment 81
dive flag use 73, 73f
donning equipment 64-65
entry techniques 65-68, 66f, 67f, 68f
exit techniques 79-80, 80f, 81f
handling equipment 79
hand signals 77, 78f
lifesaving 90-92
mask clearing 74
monitoring instruments 77
most important rules 69
navigating 76-77, 76f
packing equipment 62, 62f

physiological problems 81-84
proficiency testing 81
regulator clearing 69-70
skin diving 55-62
snorkel-regulator exchanges 70
surface snorkeling with scuba equipment 68-69
underwater swimming 60, 75-76
dizziness 82, 129-130
dolphin kick 58-59, 60f
do-si-do push 89, 89f
DOT markings 29, 29f
downstream-valve regulators 36-37
downwelling 180
drag 103, 135, 136f
drift 182
drift dives 182
dry suits 21-22, 21t, 22f, 26, 26t

**E**

eardrums 98, 99f, 124, 129
earplugs, dangers of 124
ears 98, 99f, 122-124, 123f
ebbs 177
eddies 173, 181
elastic compensators 24, 25
electronic depth gauges 40-41, 41t
embolism 127, 127t, 134
emergencies
contingency planning 156-157, 156f
emergency decompression 149-150, 156f
injuries 124, 127, 129, 164-167, 165f
managing accidents 93
planning for 90, 143, 159
scuba lifesaving 90-92
emergency decompression 149-150, 156f
emergency swimming ascents (ESA) 87-88, 87f
entanglement 84-85
entry techniques 65-68, 66f, 67f, 68f
environmental impacts of diving 168-170
environmental organizations 171, 197
equipment 12-24, 12f
alternate air sources 39-40, 39f, 87
assembling 62-64, 63f
buoyancy compensators 25-27, 26f, 26t, 27f, 70-72
checklist 198
compasses 42, 43f, 76-77, 76f
cylinders 27-31, 28f, 29f, 30t, 39-40, 40f
depth gauges 40-41, 41t
disassembling 81
dive computers 43-44, 43f, 157-158, 157f, 158f
dive flags and floats 45-46, 45f
dive kits 46, 47f
dive knives 44-45, 44f
donning and inspecting 64-65
dry suits 21-22, 21t, 22f
emergency 90
fins 15-16, 16f, 54-55, 58-59, 61, 66

equipment *(continued)*
  first aid kits 47, 48*f*
  gear bags 45
  handling 79
  instrument consoles 43
  lights 46, 46*f*
  masks 12-14, 13*f,* 52-54
  packing 62, 62*f*
  regulators 34-39, 34*f,* 35*f,* 36*f,* 37*f,* 63-64
  signaling devices 47
  for skin diving 12, 16-17, 17*f*
  snorkels 12, 14, 14*f,* 15*f*
  specialized 48
  streamlining 135, 136*f*
  submersible pressure gauges 32, 35, 42-43, 43*f*
  for training courses 8*f,* 9
  underwater timers 42
  vests 16-17, 17*f,* 20, 20*f*
  weighting systems 24-25, 24*f*
  wet suits 17-20, 18*f,* 18*t,* 19*f*
eustachian tubes 98, 99*f,* 123
evaporation 111, 111*f*
exercise, postdive 132
exit techniques 79-80, 80*f,* 81*f*
exposure suits 17-24, 18*t,* 21*t,* 22*f,* 52, 53*f*

**F**

Farmer Johns 19, 19*f*
fear of water 6-7
feet-first dives 59, 60*f*
feet-first entries 66-67, 67*f*
feet-together entries 67, 67*f*
fetch 178, 179*f*
fin push 89, 89*f*
fins 15-16, 16*f,* 54-55, 58-59, 61, 66
first aid 91-93, 91*f,* 132, 165*f*
first aid kits 47, 48*f*
fish 163, 163*f,* 165*f,* 166
fitness 6-7, 115, 120
flags 45-46, 45*f,* 73
flaring 85, 86*f,* 88
Fleuss, Henry 3
float plans 184-185
floats 45-46, 45*f,* 73
floods, tidal 177
flutter kick 58, 59*f*
flying after diving 150, 155, 194
foam neoprene suits 18-19, 18*f,* 18*t,* 21, 21*t,* 22*f*
footwear 19-20, 20*f*
forces on a diver 135, 136*f*
freezing temperatures 113
Freminet, Sieur 3
fresh water diving 40-41, 121, 172-175, 173*f,* 175*f*
fronds 163, 163*f*

**G**

Gagnan, Emile 4
gars 166
gas diffusion 130-131

gas laws 106-110, 107*f*
gauge pressure 105, 106*f*
Gay-Lussac's law 107-108, 110
gear bags 45
giant-stride entries 67, 67*f*
gloves 20, 20*f,* 22, 22*f*
Griffiths, Tom 83
gyres 180

**H**

half-times 130, 145
hand signals 55, 56*f,* 77, 78*f*
head-to-toe buddy check 65
hearing 98, 99*f,* 114
heart effects 128-129
heat capacity 103, 104*t*
heat exhaustion 120, 120*f*
heat loss 111, 111*f,* 118-120, 119*f*
heat packs 19
heatstroke 120, 120*f*
hemoglobin 100, 128
Henry's law 108-110
history of diving 3-4
hoods 20, 20*f,* 22, 23-24
hose protector sleeves 37
humidity 111-113, 130
hydroids 164, 164*f,* 167
hyperbaric treatment 133, 133*f*
hyperthermia 118, 119-120, 120*f*
hyperventilation 100
hypothermia 118-119, 119*f*
hypoventilation 100

**I**

ICC markings 29
ice diving 175
ingassing 108
injuries 124, 127, 129, 164-167, 165*f*
instrumentation 32, 35, 40-44, 41*t,* 43*f,* 77
integrated weighting systems 24-25
International Divers Alert Network (IDAN) 154

**J**

James, William 4
jellyfish 164*f,* 165*f,* 167
jumpsuits 19
J-valves 32-33, 32*f,* 33*f*

**K**

keepers 14, 15*f*
kelp 162-163, 163*f*
knives 44-45, 44*f*
knots (units) 135
K-valves 32, 32*f,* 33*f*

**L**

lacerations 165*f,* 166
ladder exits 80, 80*f,* 81*f*
laminar flow 181, 181*f*

lead shot 24, 25
LePrieur, Yves 4
Lethbridge, John 3
lift forces 135, 136*f*
lifting techniques 135
light in water 113-114, 114*f*
longshore currents/trenches 181-182
loss of air supply 86-88, 87*f*
loss of buoyancy control 85-86, 86*f*
loss of consciousness 91, 100, 102*f,* 127
low-impact diving 169-170
lubber line 42, 76
lungs 96-98, 97*f,* 125, 126*f,* 127*t*

**M**

maintenance
  buoyancy compensators 27
  cylinders 30-31, 33-34, 40
  dive knives 45
  exposure suits 20-21, 22-23
  instrumentation 44
  regulators 38-39
  skin diving equipment 17
  weighting system 25
masks 12-14, 13*f*
  clearing 56-57, 57*f,* 74
  equalizing pressure in 124
  preparing to use 52-54
  removing in the water 61
  rescue-breathing 91, 91*f*
maximum-depth indicators 41
mediastinal emphysema 127, 127*f*
medications 122, 129
menstruation 7
mitts 20, 20*f*
mixed-gas equipment 48
mobility adaptations 135, 136*f*
modified frog kick 58, 59*f*
motion sickness 82, 129-130, 183
mouthpieces 98
multilevel dive profiles 151, 151*f,* 154
multiple dives 144, 144*f,* 146, 147*f,* 150, 194

**N**

narcosis, nitrogen 134
navigation 76-77, 76*f*
neap tide 177
neutral buoyancy 56, 105*f*
nitrogen narcosis 99, 134. *See also* decompression sickness
nitrox 48, 99, 150-151
no-decompression-stop limit (NDSL) 146, 147*f,* 148-150, 149*t*
nonreference descents 74
nylon suits 18*f,* 18*t,* 19, 21*t,* 22*f*

**O**

octopus 39
open-circuit system 4

open-valve ascent 72
open-water entries 65-66
orientation to area 143-144
O-rings 32, 33f, 34, 35f
outgassing 44, 109, 131
overexertion 84, 125
overheating 118, 119-120, 120f
over-the-shoulder reach method 69
overturn 173, 173f
overweighting 75, 75f
oxygen 99, 102f, 109t, 110

**P**

panic 82-84, 83f
partial pressure 108-110, 109t
perfusion 130
periodicals 198
perspiration 119
pharynx 97f
physical problems 84-89, 85f, 87f, 89f
physiological problems 81-84, 85f
Pia, Frank 83
pike dives 59, 60f
pilot-valve regulators 36-37, 38
piston regulators 35, 35f
pits 174-175
plankton 162, 162f, 172-173
planning. See dive planning
pneumothorax 127, 127f
pollution 168, 171
pony tanks 40, 40f
ports 35
Portuguese man-of-war 164f, 167
postdive activity 132
postdive reviews 158-159
pregnancy 7
preservation, environmental 167-171
pressure
    absolute 106, 106f
    air consumption and 110, 112-113
    altitude and 103-104, 103f
    ambient 130
    atmospheric 105, 106f
    in Boyle's law 106-107, 107f, 110
    decompression theory 130-132, 131f
    effects of changes in 107
    equalization 122-124, 122f, 123f
    gauge 105, 106f
    in Gay-Lussac's law 108, 110
    measurement of 105-106, 106f
    partial 108-110, 109t
    squeezes and blocks 107, 108f
    surface-equivalent effects 109t
    working 28, 30t
pressure-testing cylinders 29, 31
proficiency testing 81
psia (pounds per square inch, absolute) 106
puffer fish 163, 163f

**Q**

quick-release systems 24

**R**

radiation, of heat 111, 111f
Rankine temperature scale 107
rapture of the deep 134
rebreathers 48
recall systems 183
reciprocal compass course 76-77
recompression chambers 133, 133f
Recreational Scuba Training Council (RSTC) 4
red tide 162
reference descents 74
reflection 114, 114f
refraction 113, 114f, 172
regulator bags 37
regulators 34-39
    accessories 37-38
    assembling 63, 63f
    clearing 69-70
    environmental shielding 36, 38
    extra second stages 39-40, 39f
    first stages 34-36, 34f, 35f, 38
    loss of air supply 86-88, 87f
    maintenance 38-39
    overexertion and 125
    second stages 36-38, 36f
    selection 38
    testing 64
repetitive dives 144, 144f, 146, 147f, 150, 194
repetitive group designations (RGD) 145, 148-150, 155t
rescue techniques 90-92
reserve valves 32-33, 33f
residual nitrogen 144, 144f
residual nitrogen time (RNT) 146, 148-150, 149t, 157, 158f
respiration 98-102, 101f. See also breathing
Responsible Diver Code 9
reverse blocks 107, 108f
reverse thermocline 173, 173f
rip currents 181-182, 181f
risks 7-8
river diving 173-174, 174f
Rouquayrol, Benoit 4

**S**

safety stops 144, 155
safety tubes 47
saltwater, swallowing 128
save-a-dive kits 46, 47f
sawtooth dive profiles 151, 151f
scissors kick 58, 59f
scombroid poisoning 163

scrolling, computer 157, 158
sculling 169, 169f
sea anemones 164, 164f
seasickness 82, 129-130, 183
seated back-roll entries 68, 68f, 185
seated entries 66, 67f
sea urchins 165f, 166
seizure disorders 7
semi-closed circuit system 4
servicing. See maintenance
set 182
shallow-water blackout 100, 102f
sharing air 39-40, 87-88, 87f
sharks 165f, 166
shivering 119
Siebe, Augustus 3
signal mirrors 47
silting 75, 75f
sinks 174, 175f
sinuses 96, 97f, 100, 102f, 122, 122f
siphons 174, 175f
skimming 184
skin diving
    buoyancy compensators 26, 26t, 52-54
    buoyancy testing 56
    descents and ascents 60, 61f
    equipment 12, 52-55, 53f
    fin use 58-59, 59f
    handling equipment 60-61
    hand signals 55, 56f
    mask clearing 56-57, 57f
    removing equipment 61-62
    snorkel use 57, 58f
    surface dives 59, 60f
    underwater swimming 60
    vests 16-17, 17f, 52-56, 53f
    weight belts 52
skip breathing 125
slack water 177-178
slates 47
sleeves, tank 30
snakes 165f, 166
snorkeling 12, 68-69. See also skin diving
snorkel-regulator exchanges 70
snorkels 14, 14f, 15f, 57, 58f
sound travel 103, 104t, 114
Spandex suits 17-18, 18t
Spare Air units 40, 40f
spike dive profiles 151, 151f
springs, freshwater 174, 175f
spring tides 177
squatting back-roll entries 68, 68f
squeezes 107, 108f
stages 34-38, 34f, 35f, 36f, 37f
standing currents 182
stands 177
steel cylinders 28, 28f, 30, 30t
step dives 151, 151f

stings 92, 165*f,* 167

stipes 162-163, 163*f*

stress 82-84, 83*f*

subcutaneous emphysema 127, 127*f*

submersible pressure gauges (SPGs) 32, 35, 42-44, 43*f,* 63-64

sunscreen 191-192

surf 65-66, 80, 81*f,* 178-180, 179*f*

surface air consumption rate (SACR) 112-113

surface currents 180, 182

surface dives 59, 60*f*

surface-equivalent effect 109, 109*t*

surface interval times (SIT) 146, 148-150, 148*t*

surge 178

sweep method 69

swells 178, 179*f*

**T**

tangling problems 84-85

tank boots 28

tanks (cylinders) 27-31, 28*f,* 30*f,* 39-40, 40*f*

task-relevant instructional self-talk (TRIST) 83

teeth 98

temperature, body 118-119

temperature scales 107-108

tetrodotoxin 163

thermocline 172, 173*f*

thermoplastic suits 18, 18*t,* 23

throat 96, 97*f*

thrust 136*f*

tides 177-178, 177*f,* 178*f*

timers 42

total bottom time (TBT) 146, 148-150, 148*t*

touching animals 169-170

Toynbee maneuver 123

trail lines 183, 184*f*

training 6-9, 8*f,* 90, 115, 188, 197

trapdoor effect 123, 123*f*

troughs 178, 179*f*

tsunamis 176

tuck dives 59, 60*f*

turbid water 175

**U**

unconsciousness 91, 100, 102*f,* 127*t*

undertow 180

underwater swimming 60, 75-76

upwelling 173

urination 22

U.S. Navy (USN) dive tables 145, 155

**V**

Valsalva maneuver 123

valves 31-35, 32*f,* 33*f*

valve snorkels 32, 33*f*

vasoconstriction 118

venomous wounds 92

vertigo 82, 129-130

vests

    skin diving 16-17, 17*f,* 52-56, 53*f*

    using 55-56, 62

    with wet suits 20, 20*f*

visual distortions 113-114, 114*f,* 130

volume of air calculation 112

vomiting 82, 91, 183

**W**

wading entries 66

wading exits 80, 81*f*

watches, digital 42

water, inspiration of 128

water density 103-104, 104*t*

water vapor 111-113

waves and surf 65-66, 80, 81*f,* 178-180, 179*f*

weather 142, 172

weighting systems

    adjusting 54, 56, 61-62

    choosing 24-25, 24*f*

    loss of buoyancy control 85-86, 86*f*

    overweighting 75*f*

wet suits

    accessories 19-20

    overview 17-19, 18*f,* 18*t,* 19*f,* 23

    putting on 52, 53*f*

whistles 47

working pressure 28, 30*t*

World Underwater Federation 4

**Y**

YMCA character development 9, 55, 65, 143, 168, 194

YMCA diving tables 147*f,* 148-150

YMCA scuba program 4, 9

*YMCA Scuba Standards and Procedures Manual (2000)* 4

# About the Author

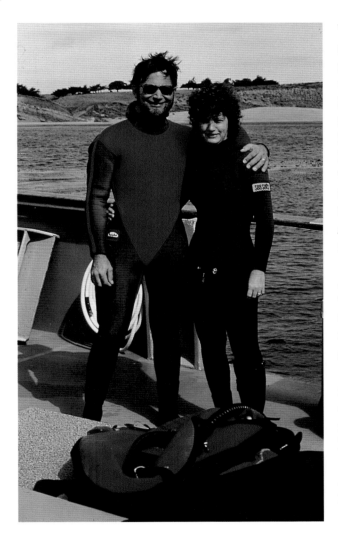

With over a quarter-century of experience as a scuba instructor and instructor trainer, Dennis Graver has authored 27 books and manuals on the subject of scuba diving. In his position as director of training for the Professional Association of Diving Instructors (PADI), he designed the PADI modular scuba course and wrote the *PADI Dive Manual*, which revolutionized scuba instruction. During his tenure as director of education for the National Association of Underwater Instructors (NAUI), Graver wrote the *NAUI Openwater I Scuba Diver Course Instructor Guide* as well as several other diving texts. He has also contributed hundreds of articles on diving to such magazines as *Skin Diver*, *Sources*, and *Undercurrents* as well as several NAUI technical publications.

From the Red Sea off the coast of Egypt to the barrier reefs of Australia, Graver has spent the past 32 years photographing the wonders under the water. He has won numerous awards from the Underwater Photographic Society, and his photos have graced the covers of many magazines and illustrated several diving texts and audiovisual educational programs.

Graver has greatly influenced scuba diving with his development of a dive table multilevel diving technique for recreational diving and a breathing mask technique for diving rescue. He also has designed the NAUI Dive Time Calculator and the first PADI dive tables.

Graver is currently a member of NAUI, the Handicapped Scuba Association, and the Divers Alert Network. Dennis and his wife, Barbara, reside in Camano Island, Washington.